Private Pilot

ORAL EXAM GUIDE

MICHAEL D. HAYES

THIRTEENTH EDITION

COMPREHENSIVE PREPARATION
FOR THE FAA CHECKRIDE

AVIATION SUPPLIES & ACADEMICS, INC.
NEWCASTLE, WASHINGTON

Private Pilot Oral Exam Guide
Thirteenth Edition
by Michael D. Hayes

Aviation Supplies & Academics, Inc.
7005 132nd Place SE
Newcastle, Washington 98059
asa@asa2fly.com | 425-235-1500 | asa2fly.com

ASA-OEG-P13
ISBN 978-1-64425-302-1

Additional formats available:
eBook EPUB   ISBN 978-1-64425-303-8
eBook PDF   ISBN 978-1-64425-304-5

Printed in the United States of America
2027   2026   2025   2024   2023   9   8   7   6   5   4   3   2   1

Library of Congress Cataloging-in-Publication Data
Names: Hayes, Michael D., author.
Title: Private pilot oral exam guide : comprehensive preparation for the FAA
   checkride / Michael D. Hayes.
Other titles: Private oral exam guide
Description: Thirteenth edition. | Newcastle, Washington : Aviation Supplies &
   Academics, Inc., 2023. | Original edition entitled: Private oral exam guide.
Identifiers: LCCN 2023006158 (print) | LCCN 2023006159 (ebook) | ISBN
   9781644253021 (trade paperback) | ISBN 9781644253038 (epub) | ISBN
   9781644253045 (pdf)
Subjects: LCSH: United States. Federal Aviation Administration—Examinations—
   Study guides. | Aeronautics—Examinations, questions, etc. | Private flying—
   Examinations, questions, etc. | Private flying—Examinations—Study guides. |
   Airplanes—Piloting—Examinations, questions, etc. | Oral examinations. | LCGFT:
   Examinations. | Study guides.
Classification: LCC TL546.5 .H33 2023 (print) | LCC TL546.5 (ebook) | DDC
   629.132/5217076—dc23/eng/20230302
LC record available at https://lccn.loc.gov/2023006158
LC ebook record available at https://lccn.loc.gov/2023006159

This guide is dedicated to the many talented students, pilots, and flight instructors I have had the opportunity to work with over the years. Also special thanks to Mark Hayes, David Sickler, the staff at Howell Aircraft Service, and the many others who supplied the patience, encouragement, and understanding necessary to complete the project.

—M.D.H.

Contents

Introduction

The *Private Pilot Oral Exam Guide* is a comprehensive guide designed for student pilots who are involved in training for the Private Pilot Certificate.

This guide was originally designed for use in a Part 141 flight school but has quickly become popular with those training under Part 61 and not affiliated with an FAA-approved school. The guide will also prove beneficial to private pilots who wish to refresh their knowledge or who are preparing for a flight review.

The *Private Pilot—Airplane Airman Certification Standards* (FAA-S-ACS-6) specifies the areas in which knowledge must be demonstrated by the applicant before a pilot certificate or rating can be issued. The *Private Pilot Oral Exam Guide* has been designed to evaluate a pilot's knowledge of those areas. This guide contains questions and answers organized into thirteen chapters representing those areas of knowledge required for the practical test. Check the ASA website (**asa2fly.com** and dedicated Reader Resource page for this book **asa2fly.com/OEGP**) periodically for downloadable Updates, which are created whenever changes occur in FAA regulations and procedures affecting this book; future Updates may also contain additional study material and new FAA information regarding the Private Pilot checkride.

At any time during the practical test, an FAA examiner may ask questions pertaining to any of the subject areas within these divisions. In addition, Chapter 13 provides scenario-based questions that often test multiple subjects or areas. Using intensive post–private pilot checkride debriefings, we provide you with the most consistent questions asked along with the information necessary for a knowledgeable response.

This guide may be supplemented with other comprehensive study materials as noted in parentheses after each question. For example: (FAA-H-8083-3). The abbreviations for these materials and their titles are listed below. Be sure to use the latest revision of these references when reviewing for the test.

AC 90-114	*Automatic Dependent Surveillance–Broadcast Operations*
AC 91-63	*Temporary Flight Restrictions*
AC 91-73	*Part 91 & Part 135 Single-Pilot Procedures during Taxi Operations*
AC 91-78	*Use of Class 1 or 2 Electronic Flight Bag (EFB)*
AC 91-92	*Pilot's Guide to a Preflight Briefing*
AC 107-2	*Small Unmanned Aircraft Systems (sUAS)*
AC 117-3	*Fitness for Duty*
AC 120-71B	*Standard Operating Procedures and Pilot Monitoring Duties for Flight Deck Crewmembers*
AERONAV FAQ	*FAA Aeronautical Information Systems FAQ*
AFM	*FAA-Approved Airplane Flight Manual*
AIM	*Aeronautical Information Manual*
AWC	*Aviation Weather Center (aviationweather.gov)*
CAMI OK-06-033	*Basic Survival Skills for Aviation*
CSUS	*Chart Supplement U.S.*
DAT	*Dictionary of Aeronautical Terms*
FAA-H-8083-1	*Aircraft Weight & Balance Handbook*
FAA-H-8083-2	*Risk Management Handbook*
FAA-H-8083-3	*Airplane Flying Handbook*
FAA-H-8083-9	*Aviation Instructor's Handbook*
FAA-H-8083-15	*Instrument Flying Handbook*
FAA-H-8083-16	*Instrument Procedures Handbook*
FAA-H-8083-19	*Plane Sense: General Aviation Information*
FAA-H-8083-25	*Pilot's Handbook of Aeronautical Knowledge*
FAA-H-8083-28	*Aviation Weather Handbook*
FAA-H-8083-30	*Aviation Maintenance Technician Handbook—General*
FAA-H-8083-31	*Aviation Maintenance Technician Handbook—Airframe*
FAA InFO 07015	*Flight Risk Assessment Tool*

FAA-P-8740-35	*All About Fuel*
FAA-P-8740-36	*Proficiency and the Private Pilot*
FAA-P-8740-41	*Medical Facts for Pilots*
FAA-P-8740-24	*Winter Flying Tips*
FAA-P-8740-47	*Radio Communications Phraseology and Techniques*
FAA-S-ACS-6	*Private Pilot Airplane Airman Certification Standards*
FAA Safety	*General Aviation Pilot's Guide to Preflight Weather Planning, Weather Self-Briefings, and Weather Decision Making*
FAA Safety ALC-25	*Flight Review Prep Guide*
FAA Sustainability	*Working to Build a Net-Zero Sustainable Aviation System by 2050 (www.faa.gov/sustainability)*
FSSAT	*Flight School Security Awareness Training*
NTSB Part 830	*Notification and Reporting of Aircraft Accidents and Incidents*
P/CG	*FAA Pilot/Controller Glossary*
POH	*Pilot Operating Handbook*
SAIB CE-11-17	*Instruments (Maneuvering Speed)*
SAFO	*FAA Safety Alert for Operators*
SAFO 11004	*Runway Incursion Prevention Actions*
TCDS	*Type Certificate Data Sheet*
TSA	*Transportation Security Administration*
USRGD	*FAA Aeronautical Chart User's Guide*

These documents are available from www.faa.gov. Many of the publications are also reprinted by ASA and are available from aviation retailers nationwide. A review of the *Private Pilot—Airplane Airman Certification Standards* and the information in this guide should provide the necessary preparation for the FAA Private Pilot Certification Practical Test.

Pilot Qualifications 1

A. Certification and Currency

1. What are the eligibility requirements for a Private Pilot (Airplane) Certificate? (14 CFR 61.103)

a. Be at least 17 years of age.

b. Be able to read, speak, write, and understand the English language.

c. Hold at least a current third-class medical certificate.

d. Received the required ground and flight training endorsements.

e. Meet the applicable aeronautical experience requirements.

f. Pass the required knowledge and practical tests.

Exam Tip: The evaluator may ask you to demonstrate that you're current and eligible to take the practical test. When preparing for your practical test, verify that you have the required hours, that you're current, and don't forget to double-check all of your endorsements (especially the 90-day solo flight endorsement). Make sure you have totaled all the logbook columns and that the entries make sense.

2. What are the requirements to remain current as a private pilot? (14 CFR 61.56, 61.57)

a. Within the preceding 24 months, a pilot must have accomplished a flight review given in an aircraft for which that pilot is rated by an authorized instructor and received a logbook endorsement certifying that the person has satisfactorily completed the review.

b. To carry passengers, a pilot must have made, within the preceding 90 days:

- Three takeoffs and landings as the sole manipulator of flight controls of an aircraft of the same category, class, and, if a type rating is required, type.

- If the aircraft is a tailwheel airplane, the landings must have been made to a full stop in an airplane with a tailwheel.

- If operations are to be conducted during the period beginning 1 hour after sunset and 1 hour before sunrise, with passengers on board, the pilot-in-command (PIC) must have, within the preceding 90 days, made at least three takeoffs and three landings to a full stop during that period in an aircraft of the same category, class, and type (if a type is required) of aircraft to be used.

Note: Takeoffs and landings required by this regulation may be accomplished in a flight simulator or flight training device that is approved by the administrator and used in accordance with an approved course conducted by a certificated training center.

3. You have not kept up with logging each of your recent flights. Are you in violation of any regulation? (14 CFR 61.51)

No. You're only required to document and record the training and aeronautical experience used to meet the requirements for a certificate, rating, or flight review and the aeronautical experience required for meeting the recent flight experience requirements.

4. You're flying in a single-engine, high-performance, complex airplane. You hold a Private Pilot Certificate with an airplane single-engine land rating, but you don't have a high-performance or complex airplane endorsement. Your friend, who has those endorsements, is acting as PIC for the flight. Can you log PIC time for the time you act as sole manipulator of the controls? Explain. (14 CFR 61.31, 61.51)

Yes, 14 CFR §61.51 governs the logging of PIC time and states that a sport, recreational, private, commercial, or airline transport pilot may log PIC time for the time during which that pilot is "sole manipulator of the controls of an aircraft for which the pilot is rated or has privileges."

Note: This means you can log PIC time, but you cannot act as PIC. For pilots to act as PIC, they must be properly rated in the aircraft and authorized to conduct the flight, which would include having the required endorsements for complex and high-performance airplanes as required by 14 CFR §61.31.

5. Explain the difference between being current and being proficient. (FAA-H-8083-2, FAA-P-8740-36)

Being current means that a pilot has accomplished the minimum FAA regulatory requirements within a specific time period and can exercise the privileges of their certificate. It means that you're legal to make a flight, but it does not necessarily mean that you're proficient or competent to make that flight.

Being proficient means that a pilot is capable of conducting a flight with a high degree of competence; it requires that the pilot have a wide range of knowledge and skills. Being proficient is not about just being legal in terms of the regulations but about being smart and safe in terms of pilot experience and proficiency.

6. How will establishing a personal minimums checklist reduce risk? (FAA-H-8083-25)

Professional pilots live by the numbers, and so should you. Pre-established numbers can make it a lot easier to come to a smart go/no-go or diversion decision, than would the vague sense that you probably can deal with the conditions you face at any given time. A written set of personal minimums also makes it easier to explain tough cancelation or diversion decisions to passengers who are, after all, trusting their lives to your aeronautical skill and judgment.

7. The airplane you normally rent has been grounded due to an intermittent electrical problem. You ask to be scheduled in another airplane. During preflight of the new airplane, you discover that it has avionics you're unfamiliar with. Should you go ahead and depart on your VFR flight? (FAA-H-8083-2)

Pilot familiarity with all equipment is critical in optimizing both safety and efficiency. If a pilot is unfamiliar with any aircraft system, this will add to workload and can contribute to a loss of situational awareness. This level of proficiency is critical and should be looked upon as a requirement, not unlike carrying an adequate supply of fuel. As a result, pilots should not look upon unfamiliarity with the aircraft and its systems as a risk control measure, but instead as a hazard with high-risk potential. Discipline is the key to success.

8. If a pilot's permanent mailing address changes, and the pilot fails to notify the FAA Airmen Certification branch of the new address, how long may the pilot continue to exercise the privileges of a pilot certificate? (14 CFR 61.60)

30 days after the date of the move.

9. **What flight time can a pilot log as second-in-command time?** (14 CFR 61.51)

A person may log second-in-command (SIC) time only for flight time during which that person:

a. Is qualified in accordance with the SIC requirements of 14 CFR §61.55 and occupies a crewmember station in an aircraft that requires more than one pilot by the aircraft's type certificate; or

b. Holds the appropriate category, class, and instrument rating (if an instrument rating is required) for the aircraft being flown, and the type certification of the aircraft or the regulations under which the flight is being conducted requires more than one pilot.

B. Privileges and Limitations

1. **What privileges and limitations apply to a private pilot?** (14 CFR 61.113)

No person who holds a private pilot certificate may act as PIC of an aircraft that is carrying passengers or property for compensation or hire; nor may that person, for compensation or hire, act as PIC of an aircraft. A private pilot:

a. May act as PIC of an aircraft in connection with any business or employment if it is only incidental to that business or employment and does not carry passengers or property for compensation or hire.

b. May not pay less than the pro rata share of the operating expenses of a flight with passengers, provided the expenses involve only fuel, oil, airport expenditures, or rental fees.

c. May act as PIC of a charitable, nonprofit, or community event flight described in 14 CFR §91.146, if the sponsor and pilot comply with the requirements of that regulation.

d. May be reimbursed for aircraft operating expenses that are directly related to search and location operations, provided the expenses involve only fuel, oil, airport expenditures, or rental fees, and the operation is sanctioned and under the direction and control of local, state, or federal agencies or organizations that conduct search and location operations.

(continued)

e. May demonstrate an aircraft in flight to a prospective buyer if the private pilot is an aircraft salesperson and has at least 200 hours of logged flight time.

f. May act as PIC of an aircraft towing a glider or unpowered ultralight vehicle, provided they meet the requirements of 14 CFR §61.69.

g. May act as PIC for the purpose of conducting a production flight test in a light-sport aircraft intended for certification in the light-sport category under 14 CFR §21.190, provided they meet the requirements of §61.113.

2. **Explain the statement: "A private pilot may not pay less than pro rata share of the operating expenses of a flight." (14 CFR 61.113)**

Pro rata means proportional. The pilot may not pay less than a proportional share of the operating expenses of a flight with passengers, provided the expenses involve only fuel, oil, airport expenditures or rental fees.

3. **The annual inspection for your aircraft is now due, and you ask several friends that fly with you regularly to contribute money to help you pay for the inspection. Do the regulations allow for these contributions? (14 CFR 61.113)**

No. A private pilot may not pay less than the pro rata (proportional) share of the operating expenses of a flight with passengers, provided the expenses involve only fuel, oil, airport expenditures or rental fees.

Note: The regulation applies to the operating expenses of a flight, and does not allow for the sharing of fixed or long-term operating costs of the airplane with passengers.

4. **To act as a required pilot flight crewmember of a civil aircraft, what must a pilot have in physical possession or readily accessible in the aircraft? (14 CFR 61.3)**

a. A pilot certificate (or special purpose pilot authorization)

b. A photo identification

c. A medical certificate (with certain exceptions as provided in 14 CFR §61.3)

5. **While you are performing a preflight inspection on your aircraft, an inspector from the FAA introduces herself and says she wants to conduct a ramp inspection. What documents are you required to show the inspector?** (14 CFR 61.3)

Each person who holds a pilot certificate, medical certificate, authorization, or license required by Part 61 must present it and their photo identification for inspection upon a request from the administrator, an authorized NTSB representative, any federal, state, or local law enforcement officer, or an authorized representative of the TSA.

6. **What is the definition of a *high-performance airplane*, and what must you do to act as pilot-in-command of such an airplane?** (14 CFR 61.31)

A high-performance airplane is one with an engine of more than 200 horsepower. To act as PIC of a high-performance airplane you must have:

a. Received and logged ground and flight training from an authorized instructor in a high-performance airplane or in a flight simulator or flight training device that is representative of a high-performance airplane and been found proficient in the operation and systems of that airplane.

b. Received and logged a one-time endorsement in your logbook from an authorized instructor who certifies you are proficient to operate a high-performance airplane.

Note: The training and endorsement required by this regulation is not required if the person has logged flight time as PIC of a high-performance airplane or in a flight simulator or flight training device that is representative of a high-performance airplane prior to August 4, 1997.

7. **Other than high-performance and complex aircraft, what other types of aircraft (airplane single engine land [ASEL]) require specific training and logbook endorsements from an appropriately rated flight instructor?** (14 CFR 61.31)

High-altitude airplane—No person may act as pilot-in-command of a pressurized airplane that has a service ceiling or maximum operating altitude (whichever is lower) above 25,000 feet MSL unless that person has completed the ground and flight training specified and has received a logbook or training record endorsement from an authorized instructor certifying satisfactory completion of the training.

Tailwheel airplane—No person may act as pilot-in-command of a tailwheel airplane unless that person has received and logged flight training from an authorized instructor in a tailwheel airplane and received a logbook endorsement from an authorized instructor who found the person proficient in the operation of a tailwheel airplane. This training and endorsement are not required if the person logged pilot-in-command time in a tailwheel airplane before April 15, 1991.

8. **What is the definition of a *complex airplane*, and what must you do to act as pilot-of-command of such an airplane?** (14 CFR 61.1, 61.31)

A *complex airplane* is defined as an airplane that has retractable landing gear, flaps, and a controllable pitch propeller; including airplanes equipped with a full-authority digital engine control (FADEC). To act as PIC of such an airplane, you must have:

a. Received and logged ground and flight training from an authorized instructor in a complex airplane or in a flight simulator or flight training device that is representative of a complex airplane and been found proficient in the operation and systems of the airplane.

b. Received a one-time endorsement in your logbook from an authorized instructor who certifies you are proficient to operate a complex airplane.

Note: The training and endorsement required by this regulation is not required if the person has logged flight time as PIC of a complex airplane or in a flight simulator or flight training device that is representative of a complex airplane prior to August 4, 1997.

9. With respect to certification, privileges, and limitations of pilots, define the terms: *category*, *class*, and *type*. (14 CFR Part 1)

Category—a broad classification of aircraft, e.g., airplane, rotorcraft, glider.

Class—a classification of aircraft within a category having similar operating characteristics, e.g., single-engine land, multi-engine land.

Type—a specific make and basic model of aircraft including modifications that do not change its handling or flight characteristics, e.g., Boing 737, Cessna 150, Cirrus SR22.

C. Medical Certificates

1. To exercise the privileges of a private pilot certificate, what medical certificate is required, and how long is it valid? (14 CFR 61.23)

You must hold at least a third-class medical certificate. The medical certificate expires at the end of the last day of:

a. The 60th month after the month of the examination shown on the certificate, if on the date of your most recent medical examination you were under the age of 40.

b. The 24th month after the month of the examination shown on the certificate, if on the date of your most recent medical examination you were over the age of 40.

Note: This does not include a pilot who meets the regulatory requirements under BasicMed.

2. What can a pilot do if they develop a condition that prevents them from obtaining a medical certificate? (14 CFR 67.401)

At the discretion of the Federal Air Surgeon, a Statement of Demonstrated Ability (SODA) may be granted, instead of an authorization, to a person whose disqualifying condition is static or nonprogressive and who has been found capable of performing pilot duties without endangering public safety. A SODA does not expire and authorizes a designated aviation medical examiner to issue a medical certificate of a specified class if the examiner finds that the condition described on its face has not adversely changed.

3. Spring has finally arrived, and the weather looks great, so you decide to rent an airplane and go fly. The problem is, your allergies are giving you a problem, and you have just taken your medication. Can you still go fly? Explain. (14 CFR 61.53, 91.17, FAA-H-8083-25)

The safest rule is not to fly while taking any medication, unless approved to do so by the FAA. Some of the most commonly used over-the-counter (OTC) drugs, antihistamines and decongestants, have the potential to cause noticeable adverse side effects, including drowsiness and cognitive deficits. 14 CFR prohibits pilots from performing crewmember duties while using any medication that affects the body in any way contrary to safety. If there is any doubt regarding the effects of any medication, consult an Aviation Medical Examiner (AME) before flying.

Note: Information on the FAA's "Do Not Issue/Do Not Fly" medications can be found at: www.faa.gov/ame_guide/pharm/dni_dnf

4. Where can you find a list of the medical conditions that may disqualify you from obtaining a medical certificate? (14 CFR Part 67, FAA-H-8083-25)

The standards for medical certification are contained in Part 67 and the requirements for obtaining medical certificates can be found in Part 61.

5. What requirements must be met to fly under BasicMed? (AC 68-1)

a. Hold a current and valid U.S. driver's license.

b. Hold or have held a medical certificate issued by the FAA at any point after July 14, 2006.

c. Answer the health questions on the Comprehensive Medical Examination Checklist (CMEC).

d. Get your physical examination by any state-licensed physician, and have that physician complete the CMEC (be sure to keep your copy of the CMEC).

e. Take a BasicMed online medical education course. Keep the course completion document issued to you by the course provider.

6. **What privileges and limitations apply when flying under BasicMed?** (14 CFR 61.113, AC 68-1)

You can conduct any operation that you would otherwise be able to conduct using your pilot certificate and a third-class medical certificate, except you are limited to:

a. Fly with no more than five passengers.

b. Fly an aircraft that has a maximum takeoff weight of not more than 6,000 pounds.

c. Fly an aircraft that is authorized to carry no more than six occupants (i.e., five passengers plus the pilot).

d. Flights within the United States at an indicated airspeed of 250 knots or less and at an altitude at or below 18,000 feet MSL.

e. You may not fly for compensation or hire.

7. **What is required to maintain BasicMed privileges?** (AC 68-1)

a. Be sure you have a CMEC that shows that your most recent physical examination was within the past 48 months. Keep the completed, signed CMEC in a safe place.

b. Be sure you are being treated by a physician for medical conditions that may affect the safety of flight.

c. Be sure you have a course completion certificate that was issued by a BasicMed medical training course provider within the past 24 calendar months.

Additional Study Questions

1. **One way a pilot can limit exposure to risks is to set personal minimums for items in each risk category (PAVE). Describe the individual minimums you will establish for yourself.** (FAA-H-8083-2)

2. **As a newly certificated private pilot, you are ready to utilize your certificate. I'm a friend and need you to fly a package to a distant destination. I will pay for the airplane if you accept. Do the regulations allow you to accept the offer?** (14 CFR 61.113)

3. **For a person under the age of 40, when will a third-class medical certificate issued on March 15, 2016, expire?** (14 CFR 61.60)

4. **What are some examples of general medical conditions that are temporarily disqualifying?** (AIM 8-1-1, 14 CFR 61.53)

5. **If your driver's license was recently suspended for driving under the influence of alcohol (DUI) but you have not been actually convicted of the crime, must you report this to the FAA?** (14 CFR 61.15)

6. **You have allowed over 24 months to lapse since your last flight review. Is your Private Pilot Certificate now invalid? What do you have to do to be legal to fly again?** (14 CFR 61.19, 14 CFR 61.56)

7. **Are there any other activities a pilot can accomplish that can be substituted for a flight review?** (14 CFR 61.56)

8. **What regulatory requirements must be met prior to a pilot acting as PIC of an aircraft towing a glider?** (14 CFR 61.69)

Airworthiness
Requirements

2

A. Aircraft Certificates and Documents

1. **What documents are required on board an aircraft prior to flight?** (14 CFR 91.203, 91.9)

   Remember: ARROW+CE

   Airworthiness Certificate (14 CFR §91.203)

   Registration Certificate (14 CFR §91.203)

   Radio Station License (if operating outside of U.S. (FCC 47 CFR §87.18)

   Operating Limitations—Airplane flight manual (AFM)/pilot's operating handbook (POH) and supplements, placards, markings (14 CFR §91.9)

   Weight and balance data (current)

   Compass Deviation Card (14 CFR §23.1547)

   External Data Plate/Serial Number (14 CFR §45.11)

   Exam Tip: During the practical test, your evaluator may wish to examine the various required aircraft documents (ARROW) in the preflight inspection, as well as the currency of any aeronautical charts, EFB data, etc., on board the aircraft. Prior to the test, verify that all the necessary aircraft documentation, on-board databases, and charts are current and available.

2. **What is an airworthiness certificate?** (FAA-H-8083-25)

   An airworthiness certificate is issued by the FAA to an aircraft that has been proven to meet the minimum design and manufacturing requirements and is in condition for safe operation. Under all circumstances, the aircraft must meet the requirements of the original type certificate, or it is no longer airworthy. These certificates come in two different classifications: standard airworthiness and special airworthiness.

3. **What is the difference between standard and special airworthiness certificates?** (FAA-H-8083-25)

   Standard airworthiness certificates (white paper) are issued for normal, utility, acrobatic, commuter, or transport category aircraft. Special airworthiness certificates (pink paper) are issued for primary, restricted, or limited category aircraft and light sport aircraft.

4. What is an experimental airworthiness certificate? (FAA-H-8083-25)

A special airworthiness certificate in the experimental category is issued to operate an aircraft that does not have a type certificate or does not conform to its type certificate yet is in a condition for safe operation. Additionally, this certificate is issued to operate a primary category kit-built aircraft that was assembled without the supervision and quality control of the production certificate holder.

5. Does an airworthiness certificate have an expiration date? (FAA-H-8083-25)

No. A standard airworthiness certificate remains valid for as long as the aircraft meets its approved type design, is in a condition for safe operation, and the maintenance, preventative maintenance, and alterations are performed in accordance with Parts 21, 43, and 91.

6. Where must the airworthiness certificate be located? (14 CFR 91.203, FAA-H-8083-19)

The certificate must be displayed at the cabin or cockpit entrance so that it is legible to passengers or crew.

7. For an aircraft to be considered airworthy, what two conditions must be met? (FAA-H-8083-19)

a. The aircraft must conform to its type design (type certificate). This is attained when the required and proper components are installed consistent with the drawings, specifications, and other data that are part of the type certificate. Conformity includes applicable supplemental type certificate(s) (STC) and field-approval alterations.

b. The aircraft must be in a condition for safe operation, referring to the condition of the aircraft in relation to wear and deterioration.

8. Explain how a pilot determines if an aircraft conforms to its approved type design and is in a condition for safe operation. (14 CFR Part 21)

a. For type design, a pilot must determine that the maintenance, preventive maintenance, and alterations have been performed in accordance Parts 21, 43, and 91 and that the aircraft is registered in the U.S. The pilot does this by ensuring that all required inspections, maintenance, preventive maintenance, repairs, and alterations have been appropriately documented in the aircraft's maintenance records.

b. For safe operation, the pilot conducts a thorough preflight inspection of the aircraft for wear and deterioration, structural damage, fluid leaks, tire wear, inoperative instruments and equipment, etc. If an unsafe condition exists or inoperative instruments or equipment are found, the pilot uses the guidance in 14 CFR §91.213 for handling the inoperative equipment.

9. What records or documents should be checked to determine that the owner or operator of an aircraft has complied with all required inspections and airworthiness directives? (14 CFR 91.405)

The maintenance records (aircraft and engine logbooks). Each owner or operator of an aircraft shall ensure that maintenance personnel make appropriate entries in the aircraft maintenance records indicating the aircraft has been approved for return to service.

10. Who is responsible for ensuring that an aircraft is maintained in an airworthy condition? (14 CFR 91.403)

The owner or operator of an aircraft is primarily responsible for maintaining an aircraft in an airworthy condition.

11. Describe some of the responsibilities an aircraft owner has pertaining to aircraft documents, maintenance, and inspections of their aircraft? (FAA-H-8083-25)

Aircraft owners must:

a. Have a current airworthiness certificate and aircraft registration in the aircraft.

b. Maintain the aircraft in an airworthy condition including compliance with all applicable Airworthiness Directives.

c. Ensure maintenance is properly recorded.

d. Keep abreast of current regulations concerning the operation of that aircraft.

e. Notify the FAA Civil Aviation Registry immediately of any change of permanent mailing address, the sale or export of the aircraft, or the loss of citizenship.

f. Have a current FCC radio station license if equipped with radios, including an emergency locator transmitter (ELT) if operated outside of the United States.

12. What are airworthiness directives (AD)? (FAA-H-8083-25)

An AD is the medium by which the FAA notifies aircraft owners and other potentially interested persons of unsafe conditions that may exist because of design defects, maintenance, or other causes, and specifies the conditions under which the product may continue to be operated. ADs are regulatory in nature, and compliance is mandatory. It is the aircraft owner's or operator's responsibility to ensure compliance with all pertinent ADs.

13. What are the two types of ADs? (FAA-H-8083-19)

ADs are divided into two categories: Those of an emergency nature requiring immediate compliance prior to further flight, and those of a less urgent nature requiring compliance within a specified period of time.

14. When are emergency ADs issued? (FAA-H-8083-19)

An emergency AD is issued when an unsafe condition exists that requires immediate action by an owner/operator. The intent of an emergency AD is to rapidly correct an urgent safety-of-flight situation. All known owners and operators of affected U.S.-registered aircraft or those aircraft that have an affected product installed will be sent a copy of an emergency AD.

Exam Tip: Be capable of finding and explaining the status of all ADs and recurring ADs that exist for your aircraft. Locate and tab prior to the practical test.

15. **While reviewing the aircraft logbooks, you discover that your aircraft is not in compliance with an AD's specified time or date. Are you allowed to continue to operate that aircraft until the next required maintenance inspection? Do the regulations allow any kind of buffer?** (AC 39-7)

    The assumption that AD compliance is only required at the time of a required inspection (e.g., at a 100-hour or annual inspection) is not correct. The required compliance time/date is specified in each AD, and no person may operate the affected product after expiration of that stated compliance time without an Alternative Method of Compliance (AMOC) approval for a change in compliance time.

16. **You determine that you need to fly your aircraft with an expired AD to another airport where a repair facility can do the work required by the AD. How can you accomplish this?** (AC 39-7, 14 CFR 21.199)

    Unless the AD states otherwise, you may apply to the FAA for a special flight permit following the procedures in 14 CFR §21.199.

17. **What is a type certificate data sheet?** (FAA-H-8083-30)

    The FAA issues a type certificate when a new aircraft, engine, propeller, etc., is found to meet safety standards set forth by the FAA. The type certificate data sheet (TCDS) lists the specifications, conditions, and limitations under which airworthiness requirements were met for the specified product, such as engine make and model, fuel type, engine limits, airspeed limits, maximum weight, minimum crew.

18. **What is a supplemental type certificate?** (FAA-H-8083-3, FAA-H-8083-30, AC 21-40)

    A supplemental type certificate (STC) is the FAA's approval of a major change in the type design of a previously approved type certificated product. The certificate authorizes an alteration to an airframe, engine, or component that has been granted an approved type certificate. Sometimes alterations are made that are not specified or authorized in the TCDS. When that condition exists, an STC will be issued. STCs are considered a part of the permanent records of an aircraft and should be maintained as part of that aircraft's logs.

19. What is an aircraft registration certificate?
(FAA-H-8083-25)

Before an aircraft can be flown legally, it must be registered with the FAA Aircraft Registry. The Certificate of Aircraft Registration, which is issued to the owner as evidence of the registration, must be carried in the aircraft at all times.

20. Does an aircraft's registration certificate have an expiration date? (14 CFR 47.31, 47.40)

Yes. A Certificate of Aircraft Registration that is in effect on January 23, 2023, expires seven years after the last day of the month in which it is issued, notwithstanding the expiration date on the valid Certificate of Aircraft Registration. The Aircraft Registration Application (pink copy) is valid until the applicant receives the aircraft registration certificate, the application is denied by the FAA, or 12 months have elapsed during which the registration is pending on the aircraft.

21. Where can you find information on the placards and marking information required to be in the airplane?
(FAA-H-8083-25, AC 60-6, 14 CFR 91.9, 14 CFR 23.1541)

The principal source of information for identifying the required airplane flight manuals (AFM), approved manual materials, markings, and placards is the FAA type certificate data sheet or aircraft specification issued for each airplane eligible for an airworthiness certificate. The required placards are also reproduced in the "Limitations" section of the AFM or as directed by an AD.

22. What are several examples of placards and markings required in the airplane? (14 CFR 23.1545 through 23.1567)

Placards—Day-Night-VFR-IFR placard, "Flight Maneuvers Permitted" placard, "Caution Control Lock Remove before Starting," "Maneuvering Speed," "Compass Calibration Card," etc.

Markings—Airspeed indicator markings; cockpit control markings; fuel, oil, and coolant filler openings; etc.

B. Aircraft Maintenance Requirements

1. What are the required tests and inspections to be performed on an aircraft? Include inspections for instrument flight rules (IFR). (14 CFR 91.409, 91.171, 91.411, 91.413, 91.207)

Remember: AAV1ATE

Annual inspection within the preceding 12 calendar months (14 CFR §91.409)

Airworthiness directives and life-limited parts compliance, as required (14 CFR §91.403, §91.417)

VOR equipment check every 30 days (for IFR ops) (14 CFR §91.171)

100-hour inspection, if used for hire or flight instruction in aircraft a CFI provides (14 CFR §91.409)

Altimeter, altitude reporting equipment, and static pressure systems tested and inspected (for IFR ops) every 24 calendar months (14 CFR §91.411)

Transponder tests and inspections, every 24 calendar months (14 CFR §91.413)

Emergency locator transmitter, operation, and battery condition inspected every 12 calendar months (14 CFR §91.207)

Exam Tip: Be prepared to locate all the required inspections, ADs, life-limited parts, etc., in the aircraft and engine logbooks, and be able to determine when the next inspections are due. Create an aircraft status sheet that indicates the status of all required inspections, ADs, life-limited parts, etc., and/or use post-it notes to tab the specific pages in the aircraft and engine logbooks. Write the due date of the next inspection on the post-it note.

2. What is an annual inspection, and which aircraft are required to have annual inspections? (FAA-H-8083-25)

An annual inspection is a complete inspection of an aircraft and engine as required by the regulations that is required to be accomplished every 12 calendar months on all certificated aircraft. Only an A&P (airframe and powerplant rated) technician holding an inspection authorization (IA) can conduct an annual inspection.

3. Which aircraft are required to have 100-hour inspections? (FAA-H-8083-25, 14 CFR 91.409)

a. All aircraft under 12,500 pounds (except turbojet/turbopropeller-powered multiengine airplanes and turbine powered rotorcraft) used to carry passengers for hire.

b. Aircraft used for flight instruction for hire, when provided by the person giving the flight instruction.

4. If an aircraft is operated for hire, is it required to have a 100-hour inspection as well as an annual inspection? (14 CFR 91.409)

Yes, if an aircraft is operated for hire it must have a 100-hour inspection as well as an annual inspection when due. If not operated for hire, only an annual inspection is required.

5. What is the difference between an annual inspection and a 100-hour inspection? (14 CFR Part 43)

The main difference is who is allowed to perform these inspections. Only an A&P mechanic with an IA can perform an annual inspection. 100-hour inspections may be performed by any A&P mechanic (no IA required). Part 43, Appendix D ("Scope and Detail of Items to be Included in Annual and 100-Hour Inspections") contains a list of items to be checked during inspections.

6. If an aircraft has been on a schedule of inspection every 100 hours, under what condition may it continue to operate beyond the 100 hours without a new inspection? (14 CFR 91.409)

The 100-hour limitation may be exceeded by not more than 10 hours while en route to a place where the inspection can be done. The excess time used to reach a place where the inspection can be done must be included in computing the next 100 hours of time in service.

7. **If the annual inspection date has passed, can an aircraft be operated in flight to a location where the inspection can be performed?** (FAA-H-8083-25)

   An aircraft overdue for an annual inspection may be operated under a Special Flight Permit issued by the FAA for the purpose of flying the aircraft to a location where the annual inspection can be performed. However, all applicable ADs that are due must be complied with before the flight.

8. **What are special flight permits, and when are they necessary?** (14 CFR 91.213, 14 CFR 21.197)

   A special flight permit may be issued for an aircraft that may not currently meet applicable airworthiness requirements but is capable of safe flight. These permits are typically issued for the following purposes:

   a. Flying an aircraft to a base where repairs, alterations, or maintenance are to be performed or to a point of storage.

   b. Delivering or exporting an aircraft.

   c. Production flight testing new-production aircraft.

   d. Evacuating aircraft from areas of impending danger.

   e. Conducting customer demonstration flights in new-production aircraft that have satisfactorily completed production flight tests.

9. **How are special flight permits obtained?** (FAA-H-8083-25)

   If a special flight permit is needed, assistance and the necessary forms may be obtained from the local FSDO (Flight Standards District Office) or Designated Airworthiness Representative (DAR).

10. **After aircraft inspections have been made and defects have been repaired, who is responsible for determining that the aircraft is in an airworthy condition?** (14 CFR 91.7)

    The pilot-in-command of a civil aircraft is responsible for determining whether that aircraft is in a condition for safe flight. The pilot-in-command shall discontinue the flight when unairworthy, mechanical, electrical, or structural conditions occur.

11. What regulations apply concerning the operation of an aircraft that has had alterations or repairs that may have substantially affected its operation in flight? (14 CFR 91.407)

No person may operate or carry passengers in any aircraft that has undergone maintenance, preventative maintenance, rebuilding, or alteration that may have appreciably changed its flight characteristics or substantially affected its operation in flight until an appropriately rated pilot with at least a private pilot certificate:

a. Flies the aircraft;

b. Makes an operational check of the maintenance performed or alteration made; and

c. Logs the flight in the aircraft records.

12. Can a pilot legally conduct flight operations with known inoperative equipment onboard? (14 CFR 91.213)

Yes, under specific conditions. Part 91 describes acceptable methods for the operation of an aircraft with certain inoperative instruments and equipment that are not essential for safe flight. They are:

a. Operation of an aircraft with a minimum equipment list (MEL), as authorized by 14 CFR §91.213(a); or

b. Operation of an aircraft without a MEL under 14 CFR §91.213(d)

Exam Tip: Know this regulation well. Unfamiliarity with 14 CFR §91.213 is a common weakness of applicants at all levels. You must demonstrate that you know this regulation and how to apply it.

13. What limitations apply to aircraft operations conducted using the deferral provision of 14 CFR §91.213(d)? (FAA-H-8083-25)

When inoperative equipment is found during preflight or prior to departure, the decision should be to cancel the flight, obtain maintenance prior to flight, or to defer the item or equipment. Maintenance deferrals are not used for inflight discrepancies. The manufacturer's POH/AFM procedures are to be used in those situations.

14. During the preflight inspection in an aircraft that doesn't have a MEL, you notice that an instrument or equipment item is inoperative. Describe how you will determine if the aircraft is still airworthy for flight. (14 CFR 91.213(d), FAA-H-8083-25)

I will ask myself the following questions to determine if I can legally fly the airplane with the inoperative equipment item:

a. Are the inoperative instruments or equipment part of the VFR-day type certification?

b. Are the inoperative instruments or equipment listed as required on the aircraft's equipment list or Kinds of Operations Equipment List (KOEL) for the type of flight operation being conducted?

c. Are the inoperative instruments or equipment required by 14 CFR §91.205, §91.207 or any other rule of Part 91 for the specific kind of flight operation being conducted? (For example, VFR, IFR, day, night.)

d. Are the inoperative instruments or equipment required to be operational by an AD?

If the answer is "Yes" to any of these questions, the aircraft is not airworthy, and maintenance is required before I can fly. If the answer is "No" to any of these questions, then the inoperative instruments or equipment must be removed from the aircraft (by an A&P) or deactivated and placarded INOPERATIVE.

Note: See Appendix 3 for further explanation of this regulation.

Exam Tip: If an instrument or equipment item is inoperative in your aircraft, be able to explain how you will determine if the aircraft is airworthy and legal for flight.

15. What are minimum equipment lists? (FAA-H-8083-25)

The minimum equipment list (MEL) is a precise listing of instruments, equipment and procedures that allows an aircraft to be operated under specific conditions with inoperative equipment. The MEL is the specific inoperative equipment document for a particular make and model aircraft by serial and registration numbers (e.g., BE-200, N12345). The FAA-approved MEL includes only those items of equipment that the FAA deems may be inoperative and still maintain an acceptable level of safety with appropriate conditions and limitations.

Note: Do not confuse an MEL with the aircraft's equipment list. They are not the same.

16. **For an aircraft with an approved MEL, explain the decision sequence a pilot would use after discovering the position lights are inoperative.** (FAA-H-8083-25)

With an approved MEL, if the position lights were discovered inoperative prior to a daytime flight, the pilot would make an entry in the maintenance record or discrepancy record provided for that purpose. The item is then either repaired or deferred in accordance with the MEL. Upon confirming that daytime flight with inoperative position lights is acceptable in accordance with the provisions of the MEL, the pilot would leave the position lights switch OFF, open the circuit breaker (or do whatever action is called for in the procedures document), and placard the position light switch as INOPERATIVE.

17. **Explain the limitations that apply to aircraft operations being conducted using an MEL.** (FAA-H-8083-25)

The use of an MEL for a small, nonturbine-powered airplane operated under Part 91 allows for the deferral of inoperative items or equipment. The FAA considers an approved MEL to be a supplemental type certificate (STC) issued to an aircraft by serial number and registration number. Once an operator requests an MEL, and a letter of authorization (LOA) is issued by the FAA, then the MEL becomes mandatory for that aircraft. All maintenance deferrals must be done in accordance with the terms and conditions of the MEL and the operator-generated procedures document.

18. **What instruments and equipment are required for VFR (visual flight rules) day flight?** (14 CFR 91.205)

For VFR flight during the day, the following instruments and equipment are required:

Anticollision light system—aviation red or white for small airplanes certificated after March 11, 1996

Tachometer for each engine

Oil pressure gauge for each engine

Manifold pressure gauge for each altitude engine

Altimeter

Temperature gauge for each liquid-cooled engine

Oil temperature gauge for each air-cooled engine

Fuel gauge indicating the quantity in each tank

Flotation gear—if operated for hire over water beyond power-off gliding distance from shore

Landing gear position indicator, if the airplane has retractable gear

Airspeed indicator

Magnetic direction indicator

Emergency locator transmitter (if required by 14 CFR §91.207)

Safety belts (shoulder harnesses for each front seat also required in aircraft manufactured after 1978)

Remember: A TOMATO FLAMES

19. What instruments and equipment are required for VFR night flight? (14 CFR 91.205)

For VFR flight at night, all the instruments and equipment for VFR day flight are required, plus the following:

Fuses—one spare set or three fuses of each kind required accessible to the pilot in flight

Landing light—if the aircraft is operated for hire

Anticollision light system—approved aviation red or white

Position lights (navigation lights)—approved forward and rear position

Source of electrical energy—adequate for all installed electrical and radio

Remember: FLAPS

20. Who can perform maintenance on an aircraft? (FAA-H-8083-25)

FAA-certificated A&P mechanic, an A&P mechanic with IA, an appropriately-rated FAA-certificated repair station, or the aircraft manufacturer.

21. **Define** *preventive maintenance.* (FAA-H-8083-25, 14 CFR Part 43, AC 43-12)

Preventive maintenance means simple or minor preservation operations and the replacement of small standard parts not involving complex assembly operations. Certificated pilots, excluding student pilots, sport pilots, and recreational pilots, may perform preventive maintenance on any aircraft that is owned or operated by them provided that aircraft is not used in air carrier service. Part 43 Appendix A identifies typical preventive maintenance operations, which include such basic items as oil changes, wheel bearing lubrication, and hydraulic fluid (brakes, landing gear system) refills.

Exam Tip: Know where to look in the regulations for items approved for preventive maintenance: Part 43, Appendix A, Paragraph C—Preventive Maintenance.

22. **What logbook entry information is required of the person performing preventive maintenance?** (FAA-H-8083-25, 14 CFR 43.3)

All pilots who maintain or perform preventive maintenance must make an entry in the maintenance record of the aircraft. The entry must include a description of the work, the date of completion of the work performed, and an entry of the pilot's name, signature, certificate number, and type of certificate held.

23. **While inspecting the engine logbook of the rental aircraft you are planning to fly, you notice that the engine has exceeded its time between overhaul (TBO). Is it legal to fly this aircraft?** (AC 20-105)

Yes. TBO is computed by the engine manufacturer and is a reliable estimate of the number of hours the engine could perform reliably within the established engine parameters and still not exceed the service wear limits for overhaul for major component parts such as the crankshaft, cam shaft, cylinders, connecting rods, and pistons. TBO times are make and model specific and the recommended overhaul times are usually identified in the engine manufacturer's service bulletin or letter. For Part 91 operations, compliance with the TBO is not a mandatory maintenance requirement.

24. **What are several good reasons for aircraft owners to comply with TBO times recommended by the manufacturer?** (AC 20-105)

    a. An overhaul at TBO will ensure safety and reliability.

    b. An engine overhaul at TBO is usually less expensive than one for an engine that has been run an additional 200 or 300 hours.

    c. Running the engine past TBO usually accelerates the overall wear of the engine due to bearing movement outside tolerances, loss of protective materials such as plating or nitrating on the cylinder walls, and vibration caused by engine reciprocating parts that have worn unevenly and are now out of balance.

    Study Tip: Chapter 2 of the FAA-H-8083-30 provides an excellent overview and as in-depth explanation of the maintenance regulations, publications, forms, and records required to design, build, and maintain aircraft. Consider it as an additional reference when studying the ACS Airworthiness task prior to your checkride.

Additional Study Questions

1. **During preflight, you discover that one of the position lights (installed equipment) is inoperative prior to a daytime flight. Can you legally conduct the flight?** (14 CFR 91.213(d), FAA-H-8083-25)

2. **While en route on a VFR cross-country, you notice that your vertical speed indicator is inoperative during a descent to your first fuel stop. Can you legally continue your cross-country flight? If yes, what actions are required?** (FAA-H-8083-25)

3. **How can a pilot determine if all applicable airworthiness directives have been complied with for an airplane?** (FAA-H-8083-25, 14 CFR 91.417)

4. **Explain how you will deactivate an item or system that has become inoperative in your airplane. Can you deactivate any item or system in the airplane? What is required?** (FAA-H-8083-25)

5. **If the AFM for an aircraft you are about to fly is missing, what substitution may be made, if any?** (14 CFR 91.9, FAA-H-8083-25)

6. **Are the AFM supplements required onboard the airplane?** (FAA-H-8083-25)

7. **As PIC, you have the responsibility for determining whether your aircraft is in a condition for safe flight. When flying rental aircraft, how can procedures regarding discrepancy records or squawk sheets affect the total risk of a flight?** (FAA Safety Briefing)

8. **You have just completed the first leg of a long cross-country and notice that the oil level is approaching the one quart low mark. As a private pilot, can you add the quart of oil yourself or is a mechanic required?** (14 CFR Part 43)

9. **What are Special Airworthiness Safety Bulletins (SAIB)? Are they regulatory?** (FAA-H-8083-25)

10. **During your preflight inspection, you discover that the left main tire on your aircraft has a large flat spot with nylon cord showing. You wisely decide that this is unacceptable, and the tire should be replaced before flight. Do the regulations allow the pilot to perform this maintenance, or must a licensed mechanic (A&P) perform it?** (14 CFR Part 43)

11. **A 100-hour inspection was due at 3,302.5 hours. The 100-hour inspection was actually done at 3,309.5 hours. When is the next 100-hour inspection due?** (FAA-H-8083-25)

Weather
Information

3

A. Weather Sources

1. What service does the FAA provide for pilots to obtain a weather briefing? (AIM 7-1-2)

The FAA provides the Flight Service program, which provides weather briefings to pilots through its Flight Service Stations (FSS) by phone 1-800-WX-BRIEF and online at 1800wxbrief.com (contracted through Leidos Flight Service).

2. What are the two main categories of sources of weather data? (FAA-H-8083-28)

Federal government—The FAA and National Weather Service (NWS) collect weather observations. The NWS analyzes the observations and produces forecasts and the FAA and NWS disseminate observations, analyses, and forecasts through a variety of systems. The federal government is the only approval authority for sources of weather observations (e.g., contract towers and airport operators).

Commercial weather information providers—Repackage proprietary weather products based on NWS information with formatting and layout modification but make no material changes to the weather information. Other commercial providers produce forecasts, analyses, and other proprietary weather products which may substantially differ from the information contained in NWS products.

3. You're planning a cross-country flight. Does the weather data provided by commercial and/or third-party vendors satisfy the preflight action required by 14 CFR §91.103? (AIM 7-1-3)

Pilots and operators should be aware that weather services provided by entities other than the FAA, NWS, or their contractors may not meet FAA/NWS quality control standards. All operators and pilots contemplating using such services should request and/or review an appropriate description of services and provider disclosure. Pilots and operators should be cautious when using unfamiliar products or products not supported by FAA/NWS technical specifications. When in doubt, consult with an FAA Flight Service Specialist.

4. **Does the FAA consider weather self-briefings compliant with the regulations?** (AC 91-92)

For many general aviation (GA) pilots, the FSS remains an important source of comprehensive weather and aeronautical information. However, most pilots have become more accustomed to performing a self-briefing than calling an FSS. According to the FAA a self-briefing may be compliant with current federal aviation regulations. By self-briefing, pilots can often improve their knowledge of weather and aeronautical information. Flight service personnel are available should a pilot need assistance.

5. **What types of weather briefings are available from an AFSS/FSS briefer?** (AIM 7-1-5)

Standard briefing—Request when you are planning a flight and you have not received a previous briefing or have not received preliminary information through online resources.

Abbreviated briefing—Request when you need information to supplement mass disseminated data, update a previous briefing, or when you need only one or two items.

Outlook briefing—Request whenever your proposed time of departure is six or more hours from the time of the briefing, for planning purposes only.

Inflight briefing—Request when needed to update a preflight briefing.

6. **What pertinent information should a weather briefing include?** (AIM 7-1-5)

For a standard briefing, the briefer will automatically provide the following information in the following sequence: adverse conditions, VFR flight not recommended, synopsis, current conditions, enroute forecast, destination forecast, winds aloft, Notices to Air Missions (NOTAMs), ATC delays, and any additional information upon request.

7. **What is a Flight Information Service–Broadcast (FIS-B)?** (FAA-H-8083-25, AIM 7-1-9)

Flight Information Service–Broadcast (FIS-B) is a ground-based broadcast service provided through the Automatic Dependent Surveillance–Broadcast (ADS-B) Universal Access Transceiver

(UAT) network. The service provides users with a 978 MHz data link capability when operating within range and line-of-sight of a transmitting ground station. FIS-B enables users of properly equipped aircraft to receive and display a suite of broadcast weather and aeronautical information products.

8. Can onboard datalink weather (FIS-B) be useful in navigating an aircraft safely around an area of thunderstorms? (FAA-H-8083-28, AIM 7-1-9)

FIS aviation weather products (for example, graphical ground-based radar precipitation depictions) are not appropriate for tactical (typical timeframe of less than 3 minutes) avoidance of severe weather such as negotiating a path through a weather hazard area. FIS supports strategic (typical timeframe of 20 minutes or more) weather decision-making such as route selection to avoid a weather hazard area in its entirety. The misuse of information beyond its applicability may place the pilot and aircraft in jeopardy. In addition, FIS should never be used in lieu of an individual preflight weather and flight planning briefing.

9. While en route, how can a pilot obtain updated weather information? (FAA-H-8083-25)

a. FSS on 122.2 MHz and appropriate RCO (remote communication outlet) frequencies.

b. Automated Terminal Information Service (ATIS)/Automated Surface Observing Systems (ASOS)/Automated Weather Observing Systems (AWOS) broadcasts along your route of flight.

c Listen to Air Route Traffic Control Center (ARTCC) broadcasts—Aviation Watch Notification Messages (formerly AWWs), convective Significant Meteorological Information (SIGMETs), SIGMETs, Airmen's Meteorological Information (AIRMET), urgent Pilot Weather Reports (PIREPs), or Center Weather Advisory (CWA) alerts are broadcast once on all frequencies, except emergency.

d. Datalink weather—Cockpit display of FIS-B information.

e. Air traffic control (ATC) (workload permitting).

Exam Tip: Be prepared to demonstrate how you would obtain in-flight weather advisories and updates, and how you would communicate with a FSS while en route.

B. Weather Products

Observations

1. What is a METAR and what are the two types?
(FAA-H-8083-28)

A METAR (Aviation Routine Weather Report) is an hourly surface observation of conditions observed at an airport. There are two types of METAR reports: a routine METAR report transmitted every hour and an aviation selected special weather report (SPECI). This is a special report that can be given at any time to update the METAR for rapidly changing weather conditions, aircraft mishaps, or other critical information.

2. Describe the basic elements of a METAR.
(FAA-H-8083-28)

A METAR report contains the following elements in order as presented:

a. *Type of reports*—The METAR, and the SPECI (aviation special weather report).

b. *ICAO station identifier*—A 4-letter station identifier from the International Civil Aviation Organization (ICAO); in the contiguous United States (CONUS), the 3-letter identifier is prefixed with K.

c. *Date and time of report*—A 6-digit date/time group appended with Z (UTC; coordinated universal time). The first two digits are the date, then two for the hour, and two for minutes.

d. *Modifier*—As required; if used, the modifier AUTO identifies the report as an automated weather report with no human intervention. If AUTO is shown in the body of the report, AO1 or AO2 will be encoded in the remarks section to indicate the type of precipitation sensor used at the station.

e. *Wind*—5-digit group (6 digits if speed is over 99 knots); first three digits = wind direction, in tens of degrees referenced to true north. Directions less than 100 degrees are preceded with a zero; the next two digits are the average speed in knots, measured or estimated (or, if over 99 knots, the next three digits).

f. *Visibility*—Surface visibility in statute miles, space, fractions of statute miles (as needed), and the letters SM.

(continued)

g. *Runway visual range (RVR)*—As required.

h. *Weather phenomena*—Broken into two categories: qualifiers and weather phenomena.

i. *Sky condition*—Amount/height/type (as required) or indefinite ceiling/height (vertical visibility). Heights are recorded in feet AGL (above ground level).

j. *Temperature/dew point group*—2-digit format in whole degrees Celsius, separated by a solidus (/). Temperatures below zero are prefixed with M.

k. *Altimeter*—4-digit format representing tens, units, tenths, and hundredths of inches of mercury prefixed with A. The decimal point is not reported or stated.

l. *Remarks (RMK)*—As required; operationally significant weather phenomena, location of phenomena, beginning and ending times, and/or direction of movement.

Example:
METAR KLAX 140651Z AUTO 00000KT 1SM
R35L/4500V6000FT -RA BR BKN030 10/10 A2990 RMK AO2

3. **Describe several types of weather observing programs available.** (AIM 7-1-10)

a. *Manual observations*—With only a few exceptions, these reports are from airport locations staffed by FAA personnel who manually observe, perform calculations, and enter their observations into the communication system.

b. *AWOS*—Automated Weather Observing System; consists of various sensors, a processor, a computer-generated voice subsystem, and a transmitter to broadcast local, minute-by-minute weather data directly to the pilot. Observations will include the prefix AUTO in data.

c. *AWOS broadcasts*—Computer-generated voice is used to automate the broadcast of minute-by-minute weather observations.

d. *ASOS/AWOS*—Automated Surface Observing System/ Automated Weather Observing System; the primary U.S. surface weather observing systems. Both systems provide continuous minute-by-minute observations that generate METARs and other aviation weather information. Transmitted over a discrete VHF radio frequency or the voice portion of a local NAVAID (navigational aid), and receivable to a maximum of 25 NM from the station and a maximum altitude of 10,000 feet AGL. Observations made without human intervention will include the modifier "AUTO" in the report data. A maintenance indicator ($) is coded when an automated system detects that maintenance is needed on the system.

4. What are PIREPs (UA), and where are they usually found? (FAA-H-8083-28)

A pilot report (PIREP) provides valuable information regarding the conditions as they actually exist in the air, which cannot be gathered from any other source. Pilots can confirm the height of bases and tops of clouds, locations of wind shear and turbulence, and the location of inflight icing. There are two types of PIREPs: routine or "UA," and urgent or "UUA." PIREPs should be given to the ground facility with which communications are established (i.e., FSS, ARTCC, or terminal ATC). Altitudes are MSL (mean sea level), visibilities SM (statute miles), and distances in NM (nautical miles). PIREPs are available from an ATC, FSS, and on the internet via the ADDS (Aviation Digital Data Service) web page at: aviationweather.gov/airep.

Aviation Weather Forecasts

1. What are terminal aerodrome forecasts (TAFs)? (FAA-H-8083-28)

A terminal aerodrome forecast (TAF) is a concise statement of the expected meteorological conditions significant to aviation for a specified time period within 5 statute miles (SM) of the center of the airport's runway complex (terminal). The TAFs use the same weather codes found in METAR weather reports, in the following format:

a. *Type of reports*—A routine forecast (TAF), an amended forecast (TAF AMD), or a corrected forecast (TAF COR).

b. *ICAO station identifier*—A 4-letter station identifier.

c. *Date and time of origin*—The date/time of forecast follows the terminal's location identifier. It contains the day of the month in two digits and time in four digits when the forecast is completed and ready for transmission, with a Z appended to denote UTC. *Example:* 061737Z (This TAF was issued on the 6th day of the month at 1737 UTC.)

d. *Valid period date and time*—The first two digits are the day of the month for the start of the TAF followed by two digits indicating the starting hour (UTC). The next two digits indicate the day of the month for the end of the TAF, and the last two digits are the ending hour (UTC) of the valid period. Scheduled 24- and 30-hour TAFs are issued four times per day, at 0000, 0600, 1200, and 1800Z. *Example:* A 00Z TAF issued on the 9th of the month and valid for 24 hours would have a valid period of 0900/0924.

e. *Forecasts*—Wind, visibility, significant and vicinity weather, cloud and vertical obscuration, nonconvective low-level wind shear, forecast change indicators (FM, TEMPO and PROB).

2. Define aviation area forecast (FA). (FAA-H-8083-28)

FAs are issued for the Gulf of Mexico, the Caribbean Sea, and Alaska. An FA is an abbreviated plain language forecast concerning the occurrence or expected occurrence of specified enroute weather phenomena. The FA (in conjunction with AIRMETs, SIGMETs, convective SIGMETs, CWAs, etc.) is used to determine forecast enroute weather over a specified geographic region. FAs cover an 18- to 24-hour period, depending on the region, and are issued three to four times daily, depending on the region, and are updated as needed.

3. From which primary source should information be obtained regarding expected weather at estimated time of arrival (ETA) if your destination airport does not have a TAF? (FAA-H-8083-28)

The Graphical Forecasts for Aviation (GFA).

4. Describe the Graphical Forecasts for Aviation (GFA). (AIM 7-1-4, FAA-H-8083-28)

The GFA is a set of web-based graphics that provide observations, forecasts, and warnings that can be viewed from 14 hours in the past to 18 hours in the future. The GFA covers the CONUS from the surface up to FL480. Wind, icing, and turbulence forecasts are available in 3,000-foot increments from the surface up to 30,000 feet MSL, and in 6,000-foot increments from 30,000 feet MSL to 48,000 feet MSL. Turbulence forecasts are also broken into LO (below FL180 [flight level 180]) and HI (at or above 18,000 feet MSL) graphics. A maximum icing graphic and maximum wind velocity graphic (regardless of altitude) are also available. The GFA interactive web tool can be viewed at aviationweather.gov/gfa.

5. What type of aviation forecasts are available when selecting the "Forecast" tab of the GFA? (AIM 7-1-4)

The "Forecast" tab will provide gridded displays of various weather parameters as well as NWS textual weather observations, forecasts, and warnings out to 15 hours. Icing, turbulence, and wind gridded products are three-dimensional. Other gridded products are two-dimensional and may represent a composite of a three-dimensional weather phenomenon or a surface weather variable, such as horizontal visibility. Selecting the "Forecast" tab will provide the following forecasts:

a. TAF—Terminal Aerodrome Forecast
b. CIG/VIS—Ceiling and visibility
c. Clouds
d. PCPN/WX—Precipitation and weather
e. TS—Thunderstorms
f. Winds
g. Turb—Turbulence
h. Ice

6. Describe some of the weather products available when selecting the "Obs/Warn" tab of the GFA. (AIM 7-1-4)

Selecting the "Obs/Warn" tab provides an option to display weather data for the current time and the previous 14 hours (rounded to the nearest hour). Selecting the "Obs/Warn" tab will provide the following observations/warnings:

a. METAR
b. PCPN/WX—Precipitation and weather
c. CIG/VIS—Ceiling and visibility
d. PIREP—Pilot Reports
e. RAD/SAT—Radar and Satellite

7. **What are the four types of Inflight Aviation Weather Advisories?** (AIM 7-1-6, FAA-H-8083-28)

Inflight Aviation Weather Advisories are forecasts to advise enroute aircraft of the development of potentially hazardous weather in four types: the SIGMET (WS), the convective SIGMET (WST), the AIRMET (WA; text or graphical product), and the center weather advisory (CWA). All heights are referenced MSL, except in the case of ceilings (CIG) which indicate AGL.

8. **What is a Convective SIGMET?** (FAA-H-8083-28)

A convective SIGMET (WST) implies severe or greater turbulence, severe icing, and low-level wind shear. They may be issued for any convective situation that the forecaster feels is hazardous to all categories of aircraft. Convective SIGMET bulletins are issued for the Eastern (E), Central (C) and Western (W) United States (convective SIGMETs are not issued for Alaska or Hawaii). Bulletins are issued hourly (at H+55). Special bulletins are issued at any time as required and updated at H+55. The text of the bulletin consists of either an observation and a forecast, or just a forecast. The forecast is valid for up to 2 hours and may include information regarding:

a. Severe thunderstorm due to:
   - Surface winds greater than or equal to 50 knots.
   - Hail at the surface greater than or equal to ¾ inch in diameter.
   - Tornadoes.

b. Embedded thunderstorms.

c. A line of thunderstorms.

d. Thunderstorms producing greater than or equal to heavy precipitation that affects 40% or more of an area of at least 3,000 square miles.

9. **What is a SIGMET (WS)?** (AIM 7-1-6)

A SIGMET (WS) advises of weather that is potentially hazardous to all aircraft. SIGMETs are unscheduled products that are valid for 4 hours; SIGMETs associated with tropical cyclones and volcanic ash clouds are valid for 6 hours. Unscheduled updates and corrections are issued, as necessary. In the CONUS, SIGMETs are issued when the following phenomena occur or are expected to occur:

a. Severe icing not associated with thunderstorms.

b. Severe or extreme turbulence or clear air turbulence (CAT) not associated with thunderstorms.

c. Widespread dust storms or sandstorms lowering surface visibilities to below 3 miles.

d. Volcanic ash.

10. What is a G-AIRMET? (FAA-H-8083-28, AIM 7-1-6)

A G-AIRMET is a graphical advisory of weather that may be hazardous to aircraft but is less severe than a SIGMET. They are only valid at specific time snapshots. G-AIRMETs are issued at discrete times 3 hours apart for a period of up to 12 hours into the future (00, 03, 06, 09, and 12 hours). They are issued at 03:00, 09:00, 15:00 and 21:00 UTC (with updates issued as necessary). AIRMETs are issued by the Aviation Weather Center (AWC) for the contiguous 48 states and adjacent coastal waters. G-AIRMETs provide a higher forecast resolution than text AIRMET products. The aviation hazards depicted in a G-AIRMET are IFR conditions, mountain obscuration, icing, freezing level, turbulence, low-level wind shear (LLWS), and strong surface winds.

11. What is an AIRMET (WA)? (FAA-H-8083-28, AIM 7-1-6)

An AIRMET is a textual advisory of significant weather phenomena that describes conditions at intensities lower than those that require the issuance of SIGMETs. They are issued every 6 hours beginning at 0245 UTC. Pilots should use AIRMETs in the preflight and en route phase of flight to enhance safety. Unscheduled updates and corrections are issued, as necessary. AIRMETs contain details about IFR conditions, mountain obscuration, icing, freezing level, turbulence, low-level wind shear (LLWS), and strong surface winds.

12. What are the different types of AIRMETs? (AIM 7-1-6)

There are three types of AIRMETs, Sierra, Tango, and Zulu:

a. AIRMET Sierra describes IFR conditions and/or extensive mountain obscurations.

b. AIRMET Tango describes moderate turbulence, sustained surface winds of 30 knots or greater, and/or nonconvective low-level wind shear.

c. AIRMET Zulu describes moderate icing and provides freezing level heights.

13. What is a winds and temperatures aloft forecast (FB)? (FAA-H-8083-28)

Winds and temperatures aloft are forecast for specific locations in the CONUS and also for a network of locations in Alaska and Hawaii. These forecasts, called FBs, are issued 4 times daily. In an FB, a 4-digit code group shows wind direction, in reference to true north, and wind speed in knots, with an additional 2-digit code group showing forecast temperatures in degrees Celsius. Wind forecasts are not issued for altitudes within 1,500 feet of a location's elevation.

Note: The AWC's website provides a graphical depiction of the FB Winds/Temps forecasts as well as a text version at aviationweather.gov/windtemp.

14. What valuable information can be determined from winds and temperatures aloft forecasts (FB)? (FAA-H-8083-28)

Most favorable altitude—Based on winds and direction of flight.

Areas of possible icing—By noting air temperatures of +2°C to −20°C.

Temperature inversions—Temperature increases with altitude instead of decreasing.

Turbulence—By observing abrupt changes in wind direction and speed at different altitudes.

15. What are Center Weather Advisories? (FAA-H-8083-28)

A Center Weather Advisory (CWA) is an aviation warning for use by aircrews to anticipate and avoid adverse weather conditions in the en route and terminal environments. The CWA is not a flight planning product; instead, it reflects current conditions expected at the time of issuance and/or is a short-range forecast for conditions expected to begin within 2 hours of issuance. CWAs are valid for a maximum of 2 hours. If conditions are expected to continue beyond the 2-hour valid period, a statement will be included in the CWA.

16. What is a Convective Outlook (AC)? (FAA-H-8083-28)

A Convective Outlook (AC) is a narrative and graphical outlook of the potential for severe (tornado, wind gusts 50 knots or greater, or hail 1 inch or greater in diameter) and non-severe (general) convection and specific severe weather threats during the following 8 days. It defines areas of marginal risk (MRGL), slight risk (SLGT), enhanced risk (ENH), moderate risk (MDT), or high risk (HIGH) of severe weather based on a percentage probability.

Aviation Weather Charts

1. Give some examples of the various NWS weather charts you will use during preflight planning. (FAA-H-8083-28)

a. Surface analysis chart.
b. Weather depiction chart.
c. Short-range surface prognostic chart.
d. Significant weather prognostic chart.
e. Convective outlook chart.
f. Constant pressure analysis chart.
g. Freezing level graphics.

2. What is a surface analysis chart? (FAA-H-8083-28)

A surface analysis chart is an analyzed chart of surface weather observations. It depicts the distribution of multiple items including sea level pressure; the positions of highs, lows, ridges, troughs; the location and character of fronts; and the various boundaries such as drylines, outflow boundaries, sea-breeze fronts, and convergence lines. The chart is produced eight times daily.

3. Define the terms: *LIFR, IFR, MVFR,* and *VFR.* (AIM 7-1-7)

LIFR—Low instrument flight rules (IFR); ceiling less than 500 feet and/or visibility less than 1 mile.

IFR—Ceiling 500 to less than 1,000 feet and/or visibility 1 to less than 3 miles.

MVFR—Marginal visual flight rules (VFR); ceiling 1,000 to 3,000 feet and/or visibility 3 to 5 miles inclusive.

VFR—Ceiling greater than 3,000 feet and visibility greater than 5 miles; includes sky clear.

(continued)

Note: Ceiling means the height above the Earth's surface of the lowest layer of clouds or obscuring phenomena that is reported as "broken," "overcast," or "obscuration," and not classified as "thin" or "partial."

4. What are short-range surface prognostic charts?
(FAA-H-8083-28)

Short-range surface prognostic (prog) charts provide a forecast of surface pressure systems, fronts, and precipitation for a 2½-day period. They cover a forecast area of the 48 contiguous states and coastal waters and are prepared by the NWS Weather Prediction Center (and available on the AWC website). Predicted conditions are divided into five forecast periods: 12, 18, 24, 48 and 60 hours. Each chart depicts a snapshot of weather elements expected at the specified valid time. Charts are issued four times a day and can be used to obtain an overview of the progression of surface weather features during the included periods.

5. Describe a U.S. low-level significant weather prog chart.
(FAA-H-8083-28)

The low-level significant weather (SIGWX) charts provide a forecast of aviation weather hazards primarily intended to be used as guidance products for preflight briefings. The forecast domain covers the CONUS and the coastal waters for altitudes Flight Level 240 (FL240) and below. Each depicts a snapshot of weather expected at the specified valid time. The charts depict weather flying categories, turbulence, and freezing levels, and are issued four times per day in two types: a 12-hour and a 24-hour prog.

6. Describe a mid-level significant weather (SIGWX) chart.
(FAA-H-8083-28)

The mid-level significant weather chart provides a forecast and an overview of significant en route weather phenomena over a range of flight levels from 10,000 feet MSL to FL450, and associated surface weather features. The chart is a snapshot of weather expected at the specified valid time and depicts numerous weather elements that can be hazardous to aviation. The AWC issues the 24-hour mid-level significant weather chart four times daily.

7. What is a convective outlook chart? (FAA-H-8083-28)

The convective outlook (AC) chart depicts areas forecast to have the potential for severe (tornado, wind gusts 50 knots or greater, or hail with a diameter of 1 inch or greater) and nonsevere (general) convection and specific severe weather threats during the following 8 days. The chart defines areas of marginal risk (MRGL), slight risk (SLGT), enhanced risk (ENH), moderate risk (MDT), or high risk (HIGH) of severe weather based on percentage probability, which varies for time periods from 1 day to 3 days, and then two probablistic thresholds for days 4 through 8. The day 1, day 2, and day 3 ACs also depict areas of general thunderstorms (TSTM).

8. What are constant pressure analysis charts? (FAA-H-8083-28)

Any surface of equal pressure in the atmosphere is a constant pressure surface. A constant pressure analysis chart (also known as an upper-air analysis chart) is an upper air weather map where all information depicted is at the specified pressure of the chart. From these charts, a pilot can approximate the observed air temperature, wind, and temperature-dewpoint spread along a proposed route. They also depict highs, lows, troughs, and ridges aloft by the height contour patterns resembling isobars on a surface map. Twice daily, five constant pressure charts are issued from observed data obtained at 00Z and 12Z:

Constant Pressure Level	Approximate Altitude (MSL)
850 millibars (mb)	5,000 ft
700 mb	10,000 ft
500 mb	18,000 ft
300 mb	30,000 ft
200 mb	39,000 ft

Exam Tip: Be prepared to interpret and discuss current and forecast weather along your planned route of flight. The evaluator will want you to demonstrate that you can interpret the various aviation weather reports, forecasts, charts/graphics and make an assessment of how it will affect your planned flight.

9. What information does a freezing level graphics chart provide? (FAA-H-8083-28)

Freezing level graphics are used to assess the lowest freezing level heights and their values relative to flight paths. The chart uses colors to represent the height in hundreds of feet above mean sea level (MSL) of the lowest freezing level(s). The initial analysis and 3-hour forecast graphics are updated hourly. The 6-, 9-, and 12-hour forecast graphics are updated every three hours.

C. Meteorology

1. Briefly describe the composition of the Earth's atmosphere. (FAA-H-8083-28)

The Earth's atmosphere consists of numerous gases with nitrogen, oxygen, argon, and carbon dioxide making up 99.998 percent of all gases.

2. Most of the Earth's weather occurs in what region of the atmosphere? (FAA-H-8083-28)

Most of the Earth's weather occurs in the troposphere, which begins at the Earth's surface and extends up to approximately 36,000 feet. As the gases in this layer decrease with height, the air becomes thinner, and the temperature decreases from about 15°C (59°F) to −56.5°C (−70°F).

3. What are standard atmosphere temperature and pressure lapse rates? (FAA-H-8083-25)

A standard temperature lapse rate is one in which the temperature decreases at the rate of approximately 3.5°F or 2°C per 1,000 feet up to 36,000 feet. Above this point, the temperature is considered constant up to 80,000 feet. A standard pressure lapse rate is one in which pressure decreases at a rate of approximately 1 inHg per 1,000 feet of altitude gain to 10,000 feet.

4. Explain the difference between a stable atmosphere and an unstable atmosphere. Why is the stability of the atmosphere important? (FAA-H-8083-28)

The stability of the atmosphere depends on its ability to resist vertical motion. A stable atmosphere makes vertical movement difficult, and small vertical disturbances dampen out and disappear.

In an unstable atmosphere, small vertical air movements tend to become larger, resulting in turbulent airflow and convective activity. Instability can lead to significant turbulence, extensive vertical clouds, and severe weather.

5. How can you determine the stability of the atmosphere? (FAA-H-8083-28)

When temperature decreases uniformly and rapidly as you climb (approaching 3°C per 1,000 feet), you have an indication of unstable air. If the temperature remains unchanged or decreases only slightly with altitude, the air tends to be stable. When air near the surface is warm and moist, suspect instability.

6. List the effects of stable and unstable air on clouds, turbulence, precipitation, and visibility. (FAA-H-8083-28)

	Stable	Unstable
Clouds	Stratiform	Cumuliform
Turbulence	Smooth	Rough
Precipitation	Steady	Showery
Visibility	Fair to poor	Good

7. What causes the wind? (FAA-H-8083-25)

Differences in air density caused by changes in temperature result in a change in pressure. This, in turn, creates motion in the atmosphere, both vertically and horizontally, in the form of wind and convective currents.

8. What are the three forces that affect the wind? (FAA-H-8083-28)

Pressure gradient force (PGF), Coriolis force, and friction.

9. What are isobars? (FAA-H-8083-28)

An isobar is a line on a weather chart that connects areas of equal or constant barometric pressure.

10. Explain how the pressure gradient force affects the wind. (FAA-H-8083-28)

Wind is driven by pressure differences that create a force called the pressure gradient force (PGF). Whenever a pressure difference develops over an area, the PGF makes the wind blow in an attempt to equalize pressure differences. This force is identified by height contour gradients on constant pressure charts and by isobar gradients on surface charts. PGF is directed from higher height/pressure to lower height/pressure and is perpendicular to contours/isobars. Whenever a pressure difference develops over an area, the PGF begins moving the air directly across the contours/isobars.

11. If the isobars are relatively close together on a surface weather chart or a constant pressure chart, what information does this provide? (FAA-H-8083-28)

The spacing of isobars on these charts defines how steep or shallow a pressure gradient is. When isobars are spaced very close together, a steep pressure gradient exists, which indicates higher wind speeds. A shallow pressure gradient (isobars not close together) usually means wind speeds will be slower.

12. What is the name of the force that deflects winds to the right in the northern hemisphere and left in the southern hemisphere? (FAA-H-8083-28)

The Coriolis force. It is at a right angle to wind direction and is directly proportional to wind speed.

13. What are several examples of local winds that may affect an aircraft in flight? (FAA-H-8083-28)

Local winds include: a sea breeze, land breeze, lake breeze, lake effect, valley breeze, mountain-plains wind circulation, and a mountain breeze.

14. Explain the term *wind shear* and state the areas it is likely to occur. (FAA-H-8083-28)

Wind shear is the sudden, drastic change in wind speed and/or direction a small area, from one level or point to another, usually in the vertical. Wind shear occurs in all directions, but for convenience, it is measured along vertical and horizontal axes, thus becoming horizontal and vertical wind shear. Wind shear can affect any flight at any altitude (e.g., at upper levels near jet steams or near the ground due to convection)

15. What types of weather information will you examine to determine if wind shear conditions might affect your flight? (FAA-H-8083-28)

a. *Terminal forecasts*—Any mention of low-level wind shear (LLWS) or the possibility of severe thunderstorms, heavy rain showers, hail, and wind gusts suggest the potential for LLWS and microbursts.

b. *METARs*—Inspect for any indication of thunderstorms, rain showers, or blowing dust. Additional signs, such as warming trends, gusty winds, cumulonimbus clouds, etc., should be noted.

c. *Severe weather watch reports, SIGMETs, and convective SIGMETs*—Severe convective weather is a prime source for wind shear and microbursts.

d. *LLWAS (low level windshear alert system) reports*—Installed at 110 airports in the U.S.; designed to detect wind shifts between outlying stations and a reference centerfield station.

e. *PIREPs*—Reports of sudden airspeed changes on departure or approach and landing corridors provide a real-time indication of the presence of wind shear.

16. While on a cross-country flight, you notice a lens-shaped cloud over a mountainous area along your route of flight. What does the presence of this type of cloud indicate? (FAA-H-8083-28)

It indicates the presence of a mountain wave, which is an atmospheric wave disturbance formed when stable air flow passes over a mountain or mountain ridge. Mountain waves are a form of mechanical turbulence that develop above and downwind of mountains and frequently produce severe to extreme turbulence. When sufficient moisture is present in the upstream flow, mountain waves produce cloud formations, including cap clouds, cirrocumulus standing lenticular (CCSL) clouds, altocumulus standing lenticular (ACSL) clouds, and rotor clouds. These clouds provide visual proof that mountain waves exist, however, the clouds may be absent if the air is too dry.

17. The amount of moisture in the air is dependent on what factor? (FAA-H-8083-28)

The temperature of the air. Every 20°F increase in temperature doubles the amount of moisture the air can hold. Conversely, a decrease of 20°F cuts the capacity in half.

18. Define the terms *relative humidity* and *dew point*. (FAA-H-8083-28)

Relative humidity—The ratio, usually expressed as a percentage, of water vapor actually in the air parcel compared to the amount of water vapor the air parcel could hold at a particular temperature and pressure.

Dew point—The temperature an air parcel must be cooled at constant pressure and constant water vapor pressure to allow the water vapor in the parcel to condense into water (dew).

19. What are the different precipitation types? (FAA-H-8083-28)

Precipitation types include drizzle, rain, freezing rain, freezing drizzle, snow, snow grains, ice crystals, ice pellets, hail, and small hail and/or snow pellets.

20. What are the three ingredients necessary for precipitation to form? (FAA-H-8083-28)

Precipitation formation requires three ingredients: water vapor, sufficient lift to condense the water vapor into clouds, and a growth process that allows cloud droplets to grow large and heavy enough to fall as precipitation. Significant precipitation usually requires clouds to be at least 4,000 feet thick.

21. Explain the general characteristics in regard to the flow of air around high-pressure and low-pressure systems in the Northern Hemisphere. (FAA-H-8083-28)

Low pressure—inward, upward, and counterclockwise

High pressure—outward, downward, and clockwise

22. **If your route of flight takes you toward a low-pressure system, in general what kind of weather can you expect? What if you were flying toward a high-pressure system?** (FAA-H-8083-28)

A low-pressure system is characterized by rising air, which is conducive to cloudiness, precipitation, and bad weather. A high-pressure system is an area of descending air, which tends to favor dissipation of cloudiness and good weather.

23. **Describe the different types of fronts.** (FAA-H-8083-28)

Cold front—Occurs when a mass of cold, dense, and stable air advances and replaces a body of warmer air.

Occluded front—A frontal occlusion occurs when a fast-moving cold front catches up with a slow-moving warm front. The two types are the cold front occlusion and warm front occlusion.

Warm front—The boundary area formed when a warm air mass contacts and flows over a colder air mass.

Stationary front—When the forces of two air masses are relatively equal, the boundary or front that separates them remains stationary and influences the local weather for days. The weather is typically a mixture of both warm and cold fronts.

24. **What are the general characteristics of the weather a pilot would encounter when operating near a cold front? A warm front?** (FAA-H-8083-28)

Cold front—As the front passes, expected weather can include towering cumulus or cumulonimbus clouds, heavy rain accompanied by lightning, thunder, and/or hail; tornadoes possible; during passage, poor visibility, winds variable and gusting; temperature/dew point and barometric pressure drop rapidly.

Warm front—As the front passes, expected weather can include stratiform clouds, drizzle, low ceilings and poor visibility, variable winds, and a rise in temperature.

Note: The weather associated with a front depends on the amount of moisture available, the degree of stability of the air that is forced upward, the slope of the front, the speed of frontal movement, and the upper wind flow.

25. What is a trough? (FAA-H-8083-28)

A trough (also called a trough line) is an elongated area of relatively low atmospheric pressure. At the surface, when air converges into a low, it cannot go outward against the pressure gradient, and it cannot go downward into the ground; it must go upward. Therefore, a low or trough is an area of rising air. Rising air is conducive to cloudiness and precipitation; hence, the general association of low pressure and bad weather.

26. What is a ridge? (FAA-H-8083-28)

A ridge (also called a ridge line) is an elongated area of relatively high atmospheric pressure. Moving out of a high or ridge depletes the quantity of air; therefore, these are areas of descending air. Descending air favors dissipation of cloudiness; hence the association of high pressure and good weather.

27. What does a cloud consist of and why do they form? (FAA-H-8083-28)

A cloud is a visible aggregate of minute water droplets and/or ice particles in the atmosphere above the Earth's surface. Clouds form in the atmosphere as a result of condensation of water vapor in rising currents of air or by the evaporation of the lowest layer of fog. Rising currents of air are necessary for the formation of vertically deep clouds capable of producing precipitation heavier than light intensity.

28. What factor primarily determines the type and vertical extent of clouds? (FAA-H-8083-28)

The stability of the atmosphere.

29. Describe the four basic cloud forms observed in the Earth's atmosphere. (FAA-H-8083-28)

Cirriform—High-level clouds that form above 20,000 ft, are usually composed of ice crystals, and typically thin and white in appearance.

Nimbo-form—Nimbus is Latin meaning "rain." These clouds form between 7,000 and 15,000 ft and bring steady precipitation. As clouds thicken and precipitation begins, the cloud bases tend to lower toward the ground.

Cumuliform—Clouds that show the vertical motion or thermal uplift of air taking place in the atmosphere. The height of the cloud base depends on the humidity of the rising air. The more humid the air, the lower the cloud base. The tops of these clouds can reach over 60,000 ft.

Stratiform—Stratus is Latin for "layer" or "blanket." These clouds consist of a featureless lower layer that can cover the entire sky like a blanket. The cloud bases are usually only a few hundred feet above the ground.

30. What are the three primary causes of turbulence? (FAA-H-803-28)

a. Convective currents (called convective turbulence)
b. Obstructions in the wind flow (called mechanical turbulence)
c. Wind shear

31. What are the four intensity levels of turbulence? (FAA-H-8083-28)

Light—Causes slight, erratic changes in altitude and/or attitude (pitch, roll, or yaw).

Moderate—Changes in altitude and/or attitude occur, but the aircraft remains in positive control at all times. It usually causes variations in indicated airspeed.

Severe—Causes large, abrupt changes in altitude and/or attitude. It usually causes large variations in indicated airspeed. Aircraft may be momentarily out of control.

Extreme—The aircraft is violently tossed about and is practically impossible to control. It may cause structural damage.

32. Define the term *clear air turbulence*. (FAA-H-8083-28)

Clear air turbulence (CAT) is defined as sudden severe turbulence occurring in cloudless regions that causes violent buffeting of aircraft. CAT is a higher altitude turbulence (normally above 15,000 ft) particularly between the core of a jet stream and the surrounding air. CAT is especially troublesome because it is often encountered unexpectedly and frequently without visual clues to warn pilots of the hazard. The best available information on the location of CAT comes from pilots via PIREPs.

33. What are the factors necessary for a thunderstorm to form and what are the three stages of thunderstorm development? (FAA-H-8083-28)

For a thunderstorm to form, the air must have sufficient water vapor, an unstable lapse rate, and an initial upward boost (lifting) to start the storm process in motion. During its lifecycle, a thunderstorm cell progresses through three stages:

a. *Cumulus*—Characterized by a strong updraft.

b. *Mature*—Precipitation beginning to fall from the cloud base signals that a downdraft has developed, and a cell has entered the mature stage.

c. *Dissipating*—Downdrafts characterize the dissipating stage, and the storm dies rapidly.

34. What are the three principal types of thunderstorms? (FAA-H-8083-28)

Single cell—Also called ordinary cell thunderstorms, this type consists of only one cell; they are easily circumnavigated except at night or when embedded in other clouds. Single cell thunderstorms are rare, as almost all thunderstorms are multi-celled.

Multicell (cluster and line)—Consists of a cluster of cells at different stages of their life cycles. As the first cell matures, it is carried downwind, and a new cell forms upwind to take its place. A multicell may have a lifetime of several hours (or more), which makes it tougher to circumnavigate than a single-cell thunderstorm. May have supercells embedded within them.

Supercell—Consists primarily of a single, quasi-steady rotating updraft that persists for an extended period of time. Updraft speeds may reach 9,000 fpm (100 knots). They may persist for many hours (or longer) and their size and persistence make them tough to circumnavigate.

35. What are microbursts? (AIM 7-1-24)

Microbursts are small-scale, intense downdrafts that, on reaching the surface, spread outward in all directions from the downdraft center. This causes the presence of both vertical and horizontal wind shears that can be extremely hazardous to all types and categories of aircraft, especially at low altitudes. Due to their small size, short life span, and the fact that they can occur over areas without surface precipitation, microbursts are not easily detectable using conventional weather radar or wind shear alert systems.

36. Where are microbursts most likely to occur? (AIM 7-1-24)

Microbursts can be found almost anywhere there is convective activity. They may be embedded in heavy rain associated with a thunderstorm or in light rain in benign-appearing virga. When little or no precipitation accompanies the microburst at the surface, a ring of blowing dust may be the only visual clue of its existence.

37. What are the main types of icing an aircraft may encounter? (FAA-H-8083-28)

Structural, induction system, and instrument icing.

38. Name the three types of structural ice that may occur in flight. (FAA-H-8083-28)

Clear icing—Also called glaze ice, a glossy, clear, or translucent ice formed by the relatively slow freezing of large, supercooled water droplets. Clear icing conditions exist more often in an environment with warmer temperatures, higher liquid water contents, and larger droplets. It forms when only a small portion of the drop freezes immediately while the remaining unfrozen portion flows or smears over the aircraft surface and gradually freezes.

Rime icing—Rough, milky, and opaque ice formed by the instantaneous freezing of small, supercooled water droplets after they strike the aircraft. It is the most frequently reported icing type. Rime icing formation favors colder temperatures, lower liquid water content, and small droplets.

Mixed icing—A mixture of clear ice and rime ice that forms as an airplane collects both rime and clear ice due to small-scale variations in liquid water content, temperature, and droplet sizes.

Note: In general, rime icing tends to occur at temperatures colder than $-15°C$, clear ice when the temperature is warmer than $-10°C$, and mixed ice at temperatures in between. This is only general guidance. The type of icing will vary depending on the liquid water content, droplet size, and aircraft-specific variables.

39. What is the definition of the term *freezing level,* and how can you determine where that level is? (FAA-H-8083-28)

The freezing level is the lowest altitude in the atmosphere over a given location at which the air temperature reaches 0°C. It is possible to have multiple freezing layers when a temperature inversion occurs above the defined freezing level. A pilot can use current icing products (CIP) and forecast icing products (FIP), as well as the freezing level graphics chart to determine the approximate freezing level. Other potential sources of icing information are: GFAs, PIREPs, AIRMETs, SIGMETs, surface analysis charts, low-level significant weather charts, and winds and temperatures aloft (for air temperature at altitude).

40. What action is recommended if you inadvertently encounter icing conditions? (FAA-H-8083-15)

When icing is detected, a pilot should do one of two things, particularly if the aircraft is not equipped with deicing equipment: leave the area of precipitation or go to an altitude where the temperature is above freezing. If neither option is available, consider an immediate landing at the nearest suitable airport.

41. What is a temperature inversion? (FAA-H-8083-28)

An inversion is an increase in temperature with height—a reversal of the normal decrease with height. An inversion aloft permits warm rain to fall through cold air below. Temperature in the cold air can be critical to icing. A ground-based inversion favors poor visibility by trapping fog, smoke, and other restrictions in low levels of the atmosphere. The air is stable, with little or no turbulence.

42. How does fog form? (FAA-H-8083-28)

Fog forms when the temperature and dewpoint of the air become identical (or nearly so). This may occur through cooling of the air to a little beyond its dewpoint (producing radiation fog, advection fog, or upslope fog) or by the addition of moisture elevating the dewpoint (producing frontal fog or steam fog).

43. Name several types of fog. (FAA-H-8083-28)

a. *Radiation fog*—Favorable conditions are clear skies, little or no wind, and small temperature-dew point spread (high relative humidity). This fog forms almost exclusively at night or near daybreak.

b. *Advection fog*—Forms when moist air moves over colder ground or water. It is most common along coastal areas but often develops deep in continental areas. It may occur with winds or cloudy skies, over a wide geographic area, and at any time of the day or night.

c. *Upslope fog*—Forms as a result of moist, stable air being cooled adiabatically as it moves up sloping terrain. Once the upslope wind ceases, the fog dissipates.

d. *Frontal fog or precipitation-induced fog*—When warm, moist air is lifted over a front, clouds and precipitation may form. If the cold air below is near its dew point, evaporation (or sublimation) from the precipitation may saturate the cold air and form fog.

e. *Steam fog*—When very cold air moves across relatively warm water, enough moisture may evaporate from the water surface to produce saturation. As the rising water vapor meets the cold air, it immediately re-condenses and rises with the air that is being warmed from below.

f. *Freezing fog*—Occurs when the temperature falls to 0°C (32°F) or below. Tiny, supercooled liquid water droplets in fog can freeze instantly on exposed surfaces when surface temperatures are at or below freezing.

44. What is frost, and what conditions would be conducive to its formation? (FAA-H-8083-25)

Frost is ice crystal deposits formed by sublimation when the temperature and dewpoint are below freezing. Frost can form on an airplane sitting outside on a clear night when moisture is present in the air, and the airplane's skin temperature falls below freezing due to radiation cooling.

45. Is frost considered to be hazardous to flight? Why or why not? (FAA-H-8083-28)

Yes, because while frost does not change the basic aerodynamic shape of the wing, the roughness of its surface spoils the smooth flow of air, thus causing a slowing of airflow. This slowing of the air causes early airflow separation, resulting in a loss of lift. Even a small amount of frost on airfoils may prevent an aircraft from becoming airborne at normal takeoff speed. It is also possible that, once airborne, an aircraft could have insufficient margin of airspeed above stall, so that moderate gusts or turning flight could produce incipient or complete stalling.

46. Describe several types of obstructions to visibility that may occur in the atmosphere. (FAA-H-8083-28)

Weather and obstructions to visibility include fog, mist, haze, smoke, precipitation, blowing snow, dust storm, sandstorm, and volcanic ash.

Additional Study Questions

1. Describe how a pilot should conduct a preflight self-briefing on the weather, NOTAMS, ATC delays, etc. (AC 91-92)

2. Decode the following pilot weather report (PIREP): (AIM 7-1-18)

KCMH UA/OV KAPE 230010/TM 1516/FL085/TP BE20/SK BKN 065/WX FV03SM HZ FU/TA 20/TB LGT

3. What symbols are used to depict the following frontal systems on surface analysis charts: cold, warm, stationary, and occluded. (FAA-H-8083-28)

4. What is a sea breeze and why do they occur? (FAA-H-8083-28)

5. Define the term *ceiling*. (FAA-H-8083-28)

6. **Give examples of charts and reports useful in determining the potential for and location of thunderstorms along your route.** (FAA-H-8083-28)

7. **During your preflight planning, what type of meteorological information should you be aware of with respect to icing?** (FAA-H-8083-28)

8. **If your destination has no terminal forecast, which primary source of information should be referenced for forecasted weather at the estimated time of arrival?** (FAA-H-8083-28)

Cross Country
Flight Planning

A. Flight Planning

1. **Preflight action as required by regulation for all flights away from the vicinity of the departure airport shall include a review of what specific information?** (14 CFR 91.103)

   For a flight under IFR or a flight not in the vicinity of an airport:

   NOTAMs

   Weather reports and forecasts

   Known ATC traffic delays

   Runway lengths at airports of intended use

   Alternatives available if the planned flight cannot be completed

   Fuel requirements

   Takeoff and landing distance data

   Remember: NW KRAFT

2. **What are the three types of VFR aeronautical charts commonly used by pilots?** (FAA-H-8083-25, AIM 9-1-4)

   a. *Sectional charts*—designed for visual navigation of slow to medium speed aircraft. One inch equals 6.86 nautical miles (NM). They are revised every 56 days.

   b. *VFR terminal area charts (TAC)*—TACs depict the Class B airspace. While similar to sectional charts, TACs have more detail because the scale is larger. One inch equals 3.43 NM. Charts are revised every 56 days.

   c. *VFR flyway planning charts*—This chart is printed on the reverse side of selected TAC charts. The coverage is the same as the associated TAC. They depict flight paths and altitudes recommended for use to bypass high traffic areas. One inch equals 3.43 NM.

   Exam Tip: Prior to your checkride, plan on studying the FAA's *Aeronautical Chart User's Guide* (USRGD) for a thorough, in-depth review of all of the chart terms and symbols provided on all of the FAA's aeronautical charts and publications.

3. **How can a pilot determine that their printed aeronautical charts are current?** (USRGD)

   Aeronautical information changes rapidly, so it is important that pilots check the effective dates on each aeronautical chart and publication. To confirm that a chart or publication is current, refer to the next scheduled effective date printed on the cover. Pilots should also check NOTAMs for important updates between chart and publication cycles that are essential for safe flight.

4. Are electronic flight bags (EFBs) approved for use as a replacement for paper reference material (POH and Supplements, charts, etc.) in the cockpit? (AC 91-78)

Yes. EFBs can be used during all phases of flight operations in lieu of paper reference material when the information displayed is the functional equivalent of the paper reference material replaced and is current, up-to-date, and valid. It is recommended that a secondary or back-up source of aeronautical information necessary for the flight be available.

5. What publication provides pilots with updates to visual charts between edition dates? (AIM 9-1-4)

The *Chart Supplement U.S.* is published every 56 days while Sectional Aeronautical Charts and VFR Terminal Area Charts are generally revised every six months. Safety alerts and charting notices are also available for free download at the AIS website: www.faa.gov/air_traffic/flight_info/aeronav/

6. Describe the type of information a pilot should review in the *Chart Supplement U.S.* prior to flight. (FAA-H-8083-25)

A pilot should review information about each airport at which a landing is intended. This includes location, elevation, runway and lighting facilities, available services, UNICOM availability, types of fuel available (use to decide on refueling stops), control tower and ground control frequencies, traffic information, remarks, and other pertinent information.

7. What are NOTAMs? (AIM 5-1-3)

The Notice to Air Missions (NOTAM) system provides pilots with time critical aeronautical information that is temporary, information to be published on aeronautical charts at a later date, or information from another operational publication. The NOTAM is cancelled when the information in the NOTAM is published on the chart or when the temporary condition is returned to normal status. NOTAMs may be disseminated up to 7 days before the start of activity. Pilots can access NOTAM information online via FNS NOTAM Search at: notams.aim.faa.gov/notamSearch/ or from an FSS.

8. **Describe the following classes of NOTAMs?** (AIM 5-1-3)

   a. *Domestic NOTAM (D)*—Information disseminated for all navigational facilities that are part of the NAS, all public use aerodromes, seaplane bases, and heliports listed in the *Chart Supplement U.S.*, NOTAM (D) information includes taxiway closures, personnel and equipment near or crossing runways, and airport lighting aids that do not affect instrument approach criteria (e.g., VGSI).

   b. *FDC NOTAMs*—Issued when it is necessary to disseminate regulatory information, FDC NOTAMs include amendments to published IAPs and other current aeronautical charts, TFRs, high barometric pressure warnings, laser light activity, ADS-B, TIS-B, and FIS-B service availability, satellite-based systems such as WAAS or GPS, and special notices. Additionally, U.S. Domestic Security NOTAMs are FDC NOTAMs that inform pilots of certain U.S. security activities or requirements.

   c. *International NOTAMs*—Published in ICAO format per Annex 15, International NOTAMs are distributed to multiple countries. International NOTAMs basically duplicate data found in a U.S. NOTAM. International NOTAMs received by the FAA from other countries are stored in the U.S. NOTAM System.

   d. *Military NOTAMs*—Originated by the U.S. Air Force, Army, Marine, or Navy, Military NOTAMs pertain to military or joint-use navigational aids/airports that are part of the NAS. Military NOTAMs are published in the International NOTAM format and should be reviewed by users of a military or joint-use facility.

9. **Where can NOTAM information be found?** (AIM 5-1-3)

   a. Call the FSS at 1-800-WX-BRIEF
   b. NOTAM Search at notams.aim.faa.gov/notamSearch
   c. FSS briefing website at 1800wxbrief.com
   d. In flight, FIS-B via ADS-B In

   Note: The NOTAM (D) and FDC NOTAM products broadcast via FIS-B are limited to those issued or effective within the past 30 days. Except for TFRs, NOTAMs older than 30 days are not provided.

B. Pilotage and Dead Reckoning

1. What are three common ways to navigate?
(FAA-H-8083-25)

To navigate successfully, pilots must know their approximate position at all times or be able to determine it whenever they wish. Position may be determined by:

a. Pilotage (by reference to visible landmarks);

b. Dead reckoning (by computing direction and distance from a known position); or

c. Radio navigation (by use of radio aids).

2. Explain how a pilot navigates using pilotage.
(FAA-H-8083-25)

Pilotage is navigation by reference to landmarks or checkpoints. It is a method of navigation that can be used on any course that has adequate checkpoints, but it is more commonly used in conjunction with dead reckoning and VFR radio navigation. The pilot visually identifies landmarks outside the aircraft and compares their position with their position on a chart relative to the plotted course line.

3. Define the term *dead reckoning*. (FAA-H-8083-25)

Dead reckoning is navigation solely by means of computations based on time, airspeed, distance, and direction. The products derived from these variables, when adjusted by wind speed and velocity, are heading and ground speed (GS). The predicted heading takes the aircraft along the intended path and the GS establishes the time to arrive at each checkpoint and the destination. Except for flights over water, dead reckoning is usually used with pilotage for cross-country flying.

4. Explain what type of landmarks will make good checkpoints. (FAA-H-8083-25)

Appropriate checkpoints should be selected along the route and noted in some way. These should be easy-to-locate points, such as large towns, large lakes and rivers, or combinations of recognizable points such as towns with an airport, towns with a network of highways, and railroads entering and departing. Normally, choose only towns indicated by splashes of yellow on the chart. Do not choose towns represented by a small circle—these may turn out to be only a half-dozen houses. (In isolated areas, however, towns represented by a small circle can be prominent checkpoints.)

5. **Describe several factors a pilot should consider when planning the route of flight for a VFR cross country flight.** (FAA-H-8083-25)

   a. *Airspace*—Various classes of airspace and requirements to operate within; avoidance of certain Special Use airspace such as restricted areas, alert areas, CFAs, TFRs, active MOAs.

   b. *Airports*—Availability of airports or suitable landing areas in case of an emergency or need for diversion, availability of fuel and services.

   c. *Terrain and obstacle clearance*—Can the aircraft safely overfly, or must it divert around it? Also, avoidance of rugged or hostile terrain.

   d. *Navigation/communication capability*—Availability of landmarks; VOR signal reception if using VOR navigation; communication availability for contacting FSS, ATC, etc.

6. **Describe several factors a pilot should consider when selecting the cruise altitude for a VFR cross country flight.** (FAA-H-8083-25)

   a. *Trip length*—Longer distances make higher altitudes more desirable for better fuel consumption; shorter distances make lower altitudes more desirable; less time in climb results in faster ground speed, less fuel used.

   b. *Winds aloft*—Headwinds and tailwinds significantly affect time enroute, fuel used.

   c. *Aircraft performance*—Time to climb; optimum TAS/fuel consumption; airplane altitude limitations.

   d. *Terrain and obstacles*—Mountainous and rising terrain; antenna towers.

   e. *Gliding distance*—Higher altitudes provide longer glides in case of an emergency.

   f. *VFR cruising altitude*—Hemispheric rule applies if operating above 3,000 ft AGL.

   g. *Airspace*—Fly above rather than through Class B, C, D
      airspace.

   h. *Weather*—Turbulence level, cloud bases, freezing level.

7. Explain what maximum elevation figures depicted on VFR sectional charts indicate? Is a MEF stated in AGL or MSL? (USRGD)

The maximum elevation figure (MEF) represents the highest elevation, including terrain and other vertical obstacles (towers, trees, etc.), within a quadrant. MEF figures are depicted to the nearest 100-foot value. The last two digits of the number are not shown. Elevations are indicated in thousands and hundreds of feet above mean sea level.

8. What is the lowest altitude an aircraft may be operated over an area designated as a U.S. wildlife refuge, park, or Forest Service Area? (AIM 7-4-6)

All aircraft are requested to maintain a minimum altitude of 2,000 feet above the surface.

9. Explain what the lines of latitude and longitude found on charts indicate. (FAA-H-8083-25)

Latitude—Also known as parallels, latitudes are a measurement north or south of the equator in degrees, minutes, and seconds.

Longitude—Also known as meridians, longitudes are a measurement east or west of the Prime Meridian in degrees, minutes, and seconds. The Prime Meridian is 0° longitude and runs through Greenwich, England.

10. How do you convert from standard time to coordinated universal time (UTC)? (AIM 4-2-12)

You should take the local time (converted to military time) and add the time differential to convert to UTC.

Eastern Standard Time—add 5 hours
Central Standard Time—add 6 hours
Mountain Standard Time—add 7 hours
Pacific Standard Time—add 8 hours
Alaska Standard Time—add 9 hours
Hawaii Standard Time—add 10 hours

Note: For Daylight Savings Time subtract 1 hour from above.

11. **Determine the ETA at your destination airport given the following information:**

    Your aircraft departs an airport in the Central Standard Time Zone at 0830 CST for a 2-hour flight to an airport located in the Mountain Standard Time Zone. At what Universal Coordinated Time will you land at your destination?

    - Convert departure time to UTC by adding 6 hours: 0830 + 6:00 = 1430.
    - Add flight time of 2 hours to find arrival time. 1430 + 2 = 1630Z.

12. **Explain how to measure direction on a sectional chart.** (FAA-H-8083-25)

    By using the meridians, direction from one point to another can be measured in degrees, in a clockwise direction from true north. To indicate a course to be followed in flight, draw a line on the chart from the point of departure to the destination and measure the angle that this line forms with a meridian.

13. **Which meridian along the course line should be used to measure the true course? Why?** (FAA-H-8083-25)

    Because meridians converge toward the poles, course measurement should be taken at a meridian near the midpoint of the course rather than at the point of departure. The course measured on the chart is known as the true course (TC). This is the direction measured by reference to a meridian or true north (TN). It is the direction of intended flight as measured in degrees clockwise from TN.

14. **Explain the difference between a course and a heading.** (FAA-H-8083-25)

    A course is the intended path of an aircraft over the Earth. A heading is the direction in which the airplane's nose is pointing during flight. The heading has the WCA applied to the course.

15. **What is magnetic variation?** (FAA-H-8083-25)

    Variation is the compass error caused by the difference in the physical locations of the magnetic north pole and the geographic north pole. It is expressed as east variation or west variation depending upon whether magnetic north (MN) is to the east or west of true north (TN), respectively.

16. What is an isogonic line? (FAA-H-8083-25)

Shown on most aeronautical charts as broken magenta lines, isogonic lines connect points of equal magnetic variation. They show the amount and direction of magnetic variation, which from time to time may vary.

17. How do you convert a true course or heading to a magnetic course or heading? (FAA-H-8083-25)

To convert true course or heading to magnetic course or heading, note the variation shown by the nearest isogonic line. If variation is west, add; if east, subtract.

Remember: East is Least (Subtract), West is Best (Add)

18. What is magnetic deviation? (FAA-H-8083-25)

Because of magnetic influences within the airplane itself (electrical circuits, radios, lights, tools, engine, magnetized metal parts, etc.) the compass needle is frequently deflected from its normal reading. This deflection is called deviation. Deviation is different for each airplane, and also varies for different headings of the same airplane. The deviation value may be found on a deviation card located in the airplane.

19. Explain how you would determine the following: (FAA-H-8083-25)

True course (TC)—The course measured on the aeronautical chart. It is measured clockwise in degrees from TN on the mid-meridian.

Magnetic course (MC)—The true course with variation applied.

Magnetic heading (MH)—Magnetic course with wind correction angle (WCA) applied. It is the direction in which the nose of the aircraft points during the flight relative to magnetic north.

True heading (TH)—The true course with the wind correction angle (WCA) applied. It is the direction in which the nose of the aircraft points during the flight relative to true north.

Variation—Obtained from the isogonic line on the chart (added if West; subtracted if East).

Deviation—Obtained from the deviation card in the aircraft (added or subtracted from MH, as indicated).

Compass heading (CH)—The magnetic heading corrected for deviation.

20. What is the formula for determining the final compass heading? (FAA-H-8083-25)

$TC \pm WCA = TH \pm V = MH \pm D = CH$

21. Explain how to obtain a preflight briefing, complete a flight log, and file a simulated flight plan.
(FAA-H-8083-25)

a. Call 1800WXBRIEF for a briefing consisting of the latest/most current weather, airport, and enroute NAVAID information. Also, self-brief using online automated weather resources.

b. Draw course lines and mark checkpoints on the chart.

c. Enter checkpoints on the log. Measure distances between checkpoints and total leg length.

d. Enter NAVAIDs on the log.

e. Enter VOR courses on the log.

f. Enter altitude on the log—consider hemispherical rule, winds aloft, airspace, terrain elevation etc.

g. Enter the wind (direction/velocity) and temperature on the log.

h. Measure the true course on the chart and enter it on the log.

i. Compute the true airspeed and enter it on the log.

j. Compute the WCA and groundspeed and enter them on the log.

k. Determine variation from chart and enter it on the log.

l. Determine deviation from compass correction card and enter it on the log.

m. Enter compass heading on the log.

n. Measure distances on the chart and enter them on the log.

o. Figure ETE and ETA and enter them on the log.

p. Calculate fuel burn and usage; enter them on the log.

q. Compute weight and balance. (Ensure use of current W&B data from your aircraft's POH/AFM.)

r. Compute takeoff and landing performance.

s. Complete a Flight Plan form.

t. File the Flight Plan with FSS.

Exam Tip: Be sure to either print or save your weather briefing so that the information used for flight planning is available on the day of the checkride. Highlighting pertinent NOTAMs, information etc. will make a favorable impression on the examiner. If required, updated weather can be obtained via computer, EFB, etc. on the actual day of the checkride.

C. Basic Calculations

Review the following time, speed, distance, and fuel consumption problems. Several groundspeed/true heading problems are also included.

Time, speed, and distance problems:

1. If time equals 25 minutes and distance equals 47 NM, what will ground speed be?

113 knots

2. If distance equals 84 NM and ground speed equals 139 knots, what will time be?

36 minutes

3. If ground speed is 85 knots and time is 51 minutes, what will the distance be?

72 NM

Fuel consumption problems:

4. If gallons-per-hour is 9.3 and time is 1 hour, 27 minutes, how many gallons will be consumed?

13.5 gallons

5. If the time is 2 hours, 13 minutes and gallons consumed is 32, what will the gallons-per-hour be?

14.4 gph

6. If gallons consumed is 38 and gallons-per-hour is 10.8, what will the time be?

3 hours, 31 minutes

True airspeed problems:

7. **If altitude is 10,000 feet, temperature is 0°C, and IAS is 115 knots, what will the TAS be?**

   135 knots TAS

8. **If IAS is 103 knots, altitude is 6,000 feet, and the temperature is –10°C, what will the TAS be?**

   110 knots TAS

9. **If the temperature is 40°F, the IAS is 115 knots, and the altitude is 11,000 feet, what will the TAS be?**

   139 knots TAS

Density altitude problems:

10. **If pressure altitude is 1,500 feet and the temperature is 35°C, what will the density altitude be?**

    4,100 feet

11. **If pressure altitude is 5,000 feet and the temperature is –10°C, what will the density altitude be?**

    3,150 feet

12. **If the pressure altitude is 2,000 feet and the temperature is 30°C, what will the density altitude be?**

    4,160 feet

Conversion problems:

13. **100 nautical miles = _____ statute miles**

    115 SM

14. **12 quarts oil = _____ pounds**

    22.5 pounds

15. **45 gallons fuel = _____ pounds**

    270 pounds

16. 80°F = _____ °C

27°C

17. 20 knots = _____ miles per hour

23 mph

Ground speed/true heading problems:

18. If wind direction is 220, wind speed is 030, true course is 146, and TAS is 135, what will ground speed and true heading be?

Ground speed is 124 knots, true heading is 158°.

19. If wind direction is 240, wind speed is 025, true course is 283 and TAS is 165, what will ground speed and true heading be?

Ground speed is 146 knots, true heading is 277°.

20. If wind direction is 060, wind speed is 030, true course is 036 and TAS is 140, what will ground speed and true heading be?

Ground speed is 112 knots, true heading is 041°.

D. VFR Flight Plan

1. What information is required by regulation in a VFR flight plan? (14 CFR 91.153)

Unless otherwise authorized by ATC, each person filing a VFR flight plan shall include in it the following information:

a. The aircraft identification number and, if necessary, its radio call sign.

b. The type of the aircraft or, in the case of a formation flight, the type of each aircraft and the number of aircraft in the formation.

c. The full name and address of the pilot in command or, in the case of a formation flight, the formation commander.

d. The point and proposed time of departure.

e. The proposed route, cruising altitude (or flight level), and true airspeed at that altitude.

(continued)

    f. The point of first intended landing and the estimated elapsed time until over that point.

    g. The amount of fuel on board (in hours).

    h. The number of persons in the aircraft, except where that information is otherwise readily available to the FAA.

    i. Any other information the pilot in command or ATC believes is necessary for ATC purposes.

2. How can a pilot file a VFR flight plan? Will an ATC tower automatically activate a VFR flight plan? (AIM 5-1-5)

It is strongly recommended that a VFR flight plan be filed with a Flight Service Station or equivalent flight plan filing service. Pilots are responsible for activating flight plans with a Flight Service Station. Control tower personnel do not automatically activate VFR flight plans.

3. When are VFR flight plans required to be filed? (AIM 5-1-5)

The requirements for the filing and activation of VFR flight plans can vary depending in which airspace the flight is operating. Within the continental U.S., a VFR flight plan is not normally required. VFR flights (except for DOD and law enforcement flights) into an air defense identification zone (ADIZ) are required to file DVFR flight plans. Flights within the Washington, DC, Special Flight Rules Area (DC SFRA) have additional requirements that must be met. VFR flight to an international destination requires a filed and activated flight plan.

4. What is a DVFR flight plan? (AIM 5-1-8)

Defense VFR; VFR flights (except for DOD and law enforcement flights) into an ADIZ are required to file DVFR flight plans for security purposes. The IFR or DVFR aircraft must depart within 5 minutes of the estimated departure time contained in the flight plan. DVFR flight plans must be filed using FAA Form 7233-4 or DD Form 1801.

5. How can a flight plan that has been filed with flight service be activated? (AIM 5-1-5)

Pilots are encouraged to activate their VFR flight plans with Flight Service by the most expeditious means possible. This may be via radio or other electronic means. Pilots may also activate a VFR flight plan by using an assumed departure time. This assumed departure time will cause the flight plan to become active at the designated time. VFR flight plan proposals are normally retained for two hours following the proposed time of departure.

Note: A pilot can call 1800WXBRIEF on the ground and have them activate at ETD or call the FSS in the air on a designated frequency and activate.

6. How can a pilot determine what frequency is appropriate for activating a VFR flight plan once airborne? (FAA-H-8083-25)

Two ways:

a. Ask the FSS briefer during the preflight weather briefing.

b. Consult the communications section under flight service for the airport of departure in the *Chart Supplement U.S.*

7. When you land at an airport with an ATC tower in operation, will the tower automatically close your flight plan? (AIM 5-1-14)

Control towers do not automatically close VFR or DVFR flight plans since they do not know if a particular VFR aircraft is on a flight plan. A pilot is responsible for ensuring that his/her VFR or DVFR flight plan is canceled. You should close your flight plan with the nearest FSS, or if one is not available, you may request any ATC facility to relay your cancellation.

8. If your flight is behind schedule, and you do not report the delay, or you forget to close your flight plan, how much time from the ETA does the FSS allow before search and rescue efforts are begun? (AIM 5-1-14)

If you fail to report or cancel your flight plan within one-half hour after your ETA, search and rescue procedures are started.

E. Navigation Systems and Radar Services

1. Name several types of navigational aids. (AIM 1-1-3 through 1-1-7, 1-1-17)

a. VOR (Very High Frequency Omnidirectional Range)

b. VORTAC (VHF Omnidirectional Range/Tactical Air Navigation)

c. DME (Distance Measuring Equipment)

d. RNAV (Area Navigation) includes INS, VOR/DME-referenced, and GPS.

e. PBN (performance-based navigation) includes RNP (Required Navigation Performance).

2. What is a VOR or VORTAC? (FAA-H-8083-25)

VORs are VHF radio stations that project radials in all directions (360°) from the station, like spokes from the hub of a wheel. Each of these radials is denoted by its outbound magnetic direction. Almost all VOR stations will also be VORTACs. A VORTAC (VOR Tactical Air Navigation) provides the standard bearing information of a VOR, plus distance information to pilots of airplanes which have distance measuring equipment (DME).

3. Within what frequency range do VORs operate? (FAA-H-8083-25)

Transmitting frequencies of omnirange stations are in the VHF (very high frequency) band between 108 and 117.95 MHz, which are immediately below aviation communication frequencies.

4. What is a VOR radial? (FAA-H-8083-25)

A radial is defined as a line of magnetic bearing extending from an omnidirectional range (VOR). A VOR projects 360 radials from the station. These radials are always identified by their direction "from" the station. Regardless of heading, an aircraft on the 360° radial will always be located north of the station.

5. How are VOR NAVAIDs designated? (AIM 1-1-8)

VOR's are designated by their standard service volumes (SSV). The three legacy SSV designations are Terminal (T), Low (L), and High (H). The two new SSV are VOR Low (VL) and VOR High (VH).

6. What reception distances can be expected from the various SSV designators for VORs? (AIM 1-1-8)

SSV Designator	Altitude	Range
Terminal (T)	1,000 up to and including 12,000 feet	25 NM
Low Altitude (L)	1,000 up to and including 18,000 feet	40 NM
High Altitude (H)	1,000 up to and including 14,500 feet 14,500 up to and including 60,000 feet 18,000 up to and including 45,000 feet	40 NM 100 NM 130 NM
VOR Low (VL)	1,000 up to but not including 5,000 feet 5,000 up to but not including 18,000 feet	40 NM 70 NM
VOR High (VH)	1,000 up to but not including 5,000 feet 5,000 up to but not including 14,500 feet 14,500 up to and including 60,000 feet 18,000 up to and including 45,000 feet	40 NM 70 NM 100 NM 130 NM

Note: All altitudes reflected are above transmitter height (ATH). The two new VOR SSV's were established in 2020 to allow for additional off-route navigation capabilities.

7. What limitations, if any, apply to VOR reception distances? (AIM 1-1-3)

VORs are subject to line-of-sight restrictions, and the range varies proportionally to the altitude of the receiving equipment.

8. What are the different methods for checking the accuracy of VOR receiver equipment? (AIM 1-1-4, 14 CFR 91.171)

a. *VOT check*—plus or minus 4°

b. *Ground checkpoint*—plus or minus 4°

c. *Airborne checkpoint*—plus or minus 6°

d. *Dual VOR check*—4° between each other

e. *Selected radial over a known ground point*—plus or minus 6°

Note: Locations of airborne check points, ground check points and VOTs are published in the *Chart Supplement U.S.*

9. What is DME? (FAA-H-8083-25)

Distance measuring equipment (DME) is an ultra-high frequency (UHF) navigational aid present with VOR/DMEs and VORTACs. It measures, in nautical miles (NM), the slant range distance of an airplane from a VOR/DME or VORTAC (both hereafter referred to as a VORTAC). DME operates on frequencies in the UHF spectrum between 960 MHz and 1215 MHz. Reliable signals may be received at distances up to 199 NM at line-of-sight altitude.

10. What are the two new DME Standard Service Volumes (SSV)? (AIM 1-1-8)

DME Low (DL)—For altitudes up to 12,900 feet ATH at a radial distance corresponding to the line of sight to the NAVAID. From 12,900 feet ATH up to but not including 18,000 feet ATH at radial distances out to 130 NM.

DME High (DH)—For altitudes up to 12,900 feet ATH at a radial distance corresponding to the line of sight to the NAVAID. From 12,900 ATH up to and including 60,000 feet at radial distances out to 100 NM. From 12,900 feet ATH up to and including 45,000 feet ATH at radial distances out to 130 NM.

Note: ATH = Altitude Above Transmitter Height

11. Give a brief explanation of the Global Positioning System (GPS). (AIM 1-1-17)

GPS is a satellite-based radio navigation system that broadcasts a signal used by receivers to determine a precise position anywhere in the world. The receiver tracks multiple satellites and determines a pseudo-range measurement that is then used to determine the user's location.

12. What are the different types of GPS receivers available for use? (AIM 1-1-17)

GPS receivers used for VFR navigation vary from fully integrated IFR/VFR installations used to support VFR operations, to handheld devices. Pilots must understand the limitations of the receivers prior to using them in flight to avoid misusing navigation information.

13. What is the purpose of RAIM? (FAA-H-8083-25, AIM 1-1-17)

Receiver autonomous integrity monitoring (RAIM) is a self-monitoring function performed by a GPS receiver to ensure that adequate GPS signals are being received from the satellites at all times. This function requires adequate simultaneous reception of at least five GPS satellites for IFR navigation reliability, works independently, and notifies the pilot when there is a problem with GPS signal reception.

14. Where can a pilot obtain RAIM availability information? (AIM 1-1-17)

Pilots may obtain GPS RAIM availability information by using a manufacturer-supplied RAIM prediction tool or using the Service Availability Prediction Tool (SAPT) on the FAA enroute and terminal RAIM prediction website. Pilots can also request GPS RAIM aeronautical information from an FSS during preflight briefings.

15. If RAIM capability is lost in-flight, can you continue to use GPS for navigation? (FAA-H-8083-25, AIM 1-1-17)

Without RAIM capability, the pilot has no assurance of the accuracy of the GPS position. VFR GPS panel-mount receivers and handheld units have no RAIM alerting capability. This prevents the pilot from being alerted to the loss of the required number of satellites in view, or the detection of a position error.

16. Before conducting a flight using GPS equipment for navigation, what basic preflight checks should be made? (FAA-H-8083-16)

a. Verify that the GPS equipment is properly installed and certified for the planned operation.

b. Verify that the databases (navigation, terrain, obstacle, etc.) have not expired.

c. Review GPS NOTAM/RAIM information related to the planned route of flight.

d. Review operational status of ground-based NAVAIDs and related aircraft equipment (e.g., 30-day VOR check) appropriate to route of flight.

e. Determine that the GPS receiver operation manual or airplane flight manual supplement is onboard and available for use.

17. How can a pilot determine what type of operation a GPS receiver is approved for? (POH/AFM)

The pilot should reference the POH/AFM and supplements to determine the limitations and operating procedures for the particular GPS equipment installed. Most systems require that the avionics operations manual/handbook be on board as a limitation of use.

18. Where can a pilot obtain current GPS NOTAMs? (AIM 1-1-17)

The Federal NOTAM System (FNS) website (notams.aim.faa .gov/notamSearch) provides a single, authoritative source for all NOTAMs including current GPS NOTAMs.

19. How many satellites does a GPS receiver require to compute its position? (FAA-H-8083-15)

3 satellites—yields a latitude and longitude position only (2D)

4 satellites—yields latitude, longitude, and altitude position (3D)

5 satellites—3D and RAIM

6 satellites—3D and RAIM (isolates corrupt signal and removes from navigation solution)

20. What is WAAS? (FAA-H-8083-15, AIM 1-1-18)

The wide area augmentation system (WAAS) is a ground and satellite integrated navigational error correction system that provides accuracy enhancements to signals received from the global positioning system. WAAS provides extremely accurate lateral and vertical navigation signals to aircraft equipped with GPS/WAAS-enabled certified (TSO C-146) equipment.

21. What limitations should you be aware of when using a panel-mount VFR GPS or a hand-held VFR GPS system for navigation? (AIM 1-1-17)

a. *RAIM capability*—Many VFR GPS receivers and all hand-held units have no RAIM alerting capability. Loss of the required number of satellites in view, or the detection of a position error, cannot be displayed to the pilot by such receivers.

b. *Database currency*—In many receivers, an updatable database is used for navigation fixes, airports, and instrument procedures.

These databases must be maintained to the current update for IFR operation, but no such requirement exists for VFR use.

c. *Antenna location*—In many VFR installations of GPS receivers, antenna location is more a matter of convenience than performance. Handheld GPS receiver antenna location is limited to the cockpit or cabin only and is rarely optimized to provide a clear view of available satellites. Loss of signal, coupled with a lack of RAIM capability, could present erroneous position and navigation information with no warning to the pilot.

22. What are VFR waypoints? (FAA-H-8083-25)

VFR waypoints provide pilots with a supplementary tool to assist with position awareness while navigating visually in aircraft equipped with area navigation receivers (such as GPS). They provide navigational aids for pilots unfamiliar with an area, waypoint definition of existing reporting points, enhanced navigation in and around Class B and Class C airspace, and around special use airspace. VFR waypoint names consist of a five-letter identifier beginning with "VP" and are retrievable from navigation databases; they should be used only when operating under VFR conditions.

23. What is ADS-B? (P/CG)

Automatic dependent surveillance–broadcast (ADS-B) is a surveillance system in which an aircraft to be detected is fitted with cooperative equipment in the form of a data link transmitter. The aircraft broadcasts its GPS-derived position and other information such as position, altitude, and velocity over the data link, which is received by a ground-based transmitter/receiver (transceiver) for processing and display at an ATC facility. In addition, aircraft equipped with ADS-B In capability can also receive these broadcasts and display the information to improve the pilot's situational awareness of other traffic. ADS-B is automatic because no external interrogation is required. It is dependent because it relies on onboard position sources and broadcast transmission systems to provide surveillance information to ATC and other users.

24. Explain how a transponder operates. (P/CG, FAA-H-8083-25)

A transponder is the airborne radar beacon receiver/transmitter portion of the Air Traffic Control Radar Beacon System (ATCRBS) which automatically receives radio signals from interrogators on the ground, and selectively replies with a specific reply pulse or pulse group only to those interrogations being received on the mode to which it is set to respond.

25. Describe the four types of radar services available. (P/CG)

a. *Basic radar service*—These services are provided for VFR aircraft by all commissioned terminal radar facilities. Basic radar service includes safety alerts, traffic advisories, limited radar vectoring when requested by the pilot, and sequencing at locations where procedures have been established for this purpose and/or when covered by a letter of agreement.

b. *TRSA service*—Provides, in addition to basic radar service, sequencing of all IFR and participating VFR aircraft to the primary airport and separation between all participating VFR aircraft. The purpose of this service is to provide separation between all participating VFR aircraft and all IFR aircraft operating within the area defined as a TRSA.

c. *Class C service*—Provides, in addition to basic radar service, approved separation between IFR and VFR aircraft, and sequencing of VFR aircraft, and sequencing of VFR arrivals to the primary airport.

d. *Class B service*—Provides, in addition to basic radar service, approved separation of aircraft based on IFR, VFR, and/or weight, and sequencing of VFR arrivals to the primary airport(s).

26. Explain the difference between Mode A, Mode C, and Mode S transponders. (AC 90-114, FAA-H-8083-25)

Mode A transmits position as a 4-digit identifying code only.

Mode C transmits position and pressure altitude information automatically.

Mode S transmits position, pressure altitude information and permits data exchange.

27. What are the following transponder codes? (AIM 4-1-20, 6-2-2, 6-3-4, 6-4-2)

1200—VFR operations
7500—Hijack
7600—Communications failure
7700—Emergency

Note: ADS-B systems integrated with the transponder will automatically set the applicable emergency status when 7500, 7600, or 7700 are entered into the transponder. ADS-B systems not integrated with the transponder, or systems with optional emergency codes, will require that the appropriate emergency code is entered through a pilot interface. (AIM 4-5-7)

F. Diversion and Lost Procedures

1. While en route on a cross-country flight, the weather has deteriorated, and it has become necessary to divert to an alternate airport. Assuming no GPS or DME capability, describe how you will navigate to the alternate. (FAA-H-8083-25)

- After selecting my alternate, I will approximate the magnetic course to the alternate using a straight edge and a compass rose from a nearby VOR or an airway that closely parallels my direction to the alternate.
- I can use the straight edge and scale at the bottom of the chart to approximate a distance to the alternate. I can fine-tune this course and distance later, as time permits, with a plotter.
- If time permits, I'll start my diversion over a prominent ground feature. However, in an emergency, I will divert promptly toward my alternate. *Note:* Attempting to complete all plotting, measuring, and computations involved before diverting to the alternate destination may only aggravate an actual emergency.
- Once established on course, I'll note the time, and then use the winds aloft nearest to my diversion point to calculate a heading and GS. Once I have my GS, I'll determine my ETA and fuel consumption to the alternate.
- I'll give priority to flying the aircraft while dividing attention between navigation and planning.
- When determining my altitude to use while diverting, I'll consider cloud heights, winds, terrain, and radio reception.

2. What are several reasons a pilot might need to divert during a flight? (FAA-H-8083-25)

Unpredicted weather conditions, a system malfunction, poor preflight planning, passenger emergency, runway/airport closed.

3. Explain how a pilot can prepare for a potential diversion before takeoff. (FAA-H-8083-25)

a. Check the charts for airports or suitable landing areas along or near the route of flight.

b. Check for navigational aids that can be used during a diversion.

c. Carry additional reserve fuel for the possibility of a diversion.

d. Ensure updated weather will be available in flight (FSS, FIS-B, etc.).

4. What actions should be taken if you become disoriented or lost on a cross-country flight (no GPS available)?

Condition I: Plenty of fuel and weather conditions good.

- Fly a specific heading in a direction you believe to be correct (or circle, if unsure); don't wander aimlessly.

- If you have been flying a steady compass heading and keeping a relatively accurate navigation log, it's not likely you will have a problem locating your position.

- If several VORs are within reception distance, use them for a cross-bearing to determine position (even a single VOR can be of enormous help in narrowing down your possible position); or, fly to the station—there's no doubt where you are then.

- Use knowledge of your last known position, elapsed time, approximate wind direction and ground speed, to establish how far you may have traveled since your last checkpoint.

- Use this distance as a radius and draw a semicircle ahead of your last known position on chart. For example, you estimate your ground speed at 120 knots. If you have been flying 20 minutes since your last checkpoint, then the no-wind radius of your semicircle is 40 miles projected along the direction of your estimated track.

- If still unsure of your position, loosen up the eyeballs and start some first-class pilotage. Look for something big. Don't concern yourself with the minute or trivial at this point. Often, there will be linear features such as rivers, mountain ranges, or prominent highways and railroads that are easy to identify. You can use them simply as references for orientation purposes and thus find them of great value in fixing your approximate position.

Condition II: Low on fuel; weather deteriorating; inadequate experience; darkness imminent; and/or equipment malfunctioning.

Get it on the ground! Most accidents are the product of mistakes which have multiplied over a period of time and getting lost is no exception: don't push your luck. It may well be that in doing so you have added the final mistake which will add another figure to the accident statistics. If terrain or other conditions make landing impossible at the moment, don't waste time, for it is of the essence: don't search for the perfect field—anything usable will do. Remember, most people on the ground know where they are, and you know that you do not.

5. If it becomes apparent that you cannot locate your position, what actions are recommended at this point?

The FAA recommends the use of the 4 Cs:

- *Climb*—The higher altitude allows better communication capability as well as better visual range for identification of landmarks.
- *Communicate*—Use the system. Use 121.5 MHz if no other frequency produces results. It is guarded by FSS's, control towers, military towers, approach control facilities, and Air Route Traffic Control Centers.
- *Confess*—Once communications are established, let them know your problem.
- *Comply*—Follow instructions.

6. What is an ARTCC, and what useful service can it provide to VFR flights? (P/CG)

An Air Route Traffic Control Center (ARTCC) is a facility established to provide air traffic control service primarily to aircraft operating on IFR flight plans within controlled airspace and principally during the en route phase of flight. Air Route Surveillance Radar allows them the capability to detect and display an aircraft's position while en route between terminal areas. When equipment capabilities and controller workload permit, certain advisory/ assistance service may be provided to VFR aircraft (VFR Flight Following). Frequencies may be obtained from FSS or the *Chart Supplement U.S.* Also, IFR enroute charts have ARTCC sector frequencies depicted. If departing from an airport with a control tower, you can request the appropriate frequency from them.

7. What is an emergency locator transmitter (ELT)?
(AIM 6-2-4)

An ELT is a radio transmitter attached to the aircraft structure which operates from its own power source on 121.5, 243.0 MHz, and the newer 406 MHz. It aids in locating downed aircraft by radiating a downward-sweeping audio tone, 2 – 4 times a second. It is designed to function without human action after an accident. It can be operationally tested during the first 5 minutes after any hour. (*Note:* Digital 406 MHz ELTs should only be tested per the manufacturer's instructions.)

Note: Pilots and their passengers should know how to activate the aircraft's ELT if manual activation is required. They should also be able to verify the aircraft's ELT is functioning and transmitting an alert after a crash or manual activation.

8. What is the universal VHF emergency frequency?
(AIM 6-3-1 and 5-6-13)

121.5 MHz; Both 121.5 MHz and 243.0 MHz are guarded by military towers, most civil towers, and radar facilities. If an ARTCC does not respond when called on 121.5 MHz or 243.0 MHz, call the nearest tower.

Note: All aircraft operating in U.S. national airspace are highly encouraged to maintain a listening watch on VHF/UHF guard frequencies (121.5 or 243.0 MHz).

G. Federal Aviation Regulations Part 91

1. If an inflight emergency requires immediate action by the pilot, what authority and responsibilities does a pilot have? (14 CFR 91.3)

a. The PIC is directly responsible for, and is the final authority as to, the operation of that aircraft.

b. In an inflight emergency requiring immediate action, the PIC may deviate from any rule in Part 91 to the extent required to meet that emergency.

c. Each PIC who deviates from a Part 91 rule shall, upon request from the Administrator, send a written report of that deviation to the Administrator.

2. Under what conditions can an object be dropped from an aircraft? (14 CFR 91.15)

No pilot-in-command of a civil aircraft may allow any object to be dropped from that aircraft in flight that creates a hazard to persons or property. However, this section does not prohibit the dropping of any object if reasonable precautions are taken to avoid injury or damage to persons or property.

3. If operating an aircraft in close proximity to another, such as formation flight, what regulations apply? (14 CFR 91.111)

a. No person may operate an aircraft so close to another aircraft as to create a collision hazard.

b. No person may operate an aircraft in formation flight except by arrangement with the pilot-in-command of each aircraft in the formation.

c. No person may operate an aircraft, carrying passengers for hire, in formation flight.

4. Unless otherwise authorized or required by ATC, what is the maximum indicated airspeed at which a person may operate an aircraft below 10,000 feet MSL? (14 CFR 91.117)

No person may operate an aircraft below 10,000 feet MSL at an indicated airspeed of more than 250 knots (288 MPH).

5. **What is the minimum safe altitude that an aircraft may be operated over a congested area of a city?** (14 CFR 91.119)

Except when necessary for takeoff or landing, no person may operate an aircraft over a congested area of a city, town, or settlement, or over any open-air assembly of persons, below an altitude of 1,000 feet above the highest obstacle within a horizontal radius of 2,000 feet of the aircraft.

6. **In areas other than congested areas, what minimum safe altitudes shall be used?** (14 CFR 91.119)

Except when necessary for takeoff or landing, an aircraft shall be operated no lower than 500 feet above the surface, except over open water or sparsely populated areas. In those cases, the aircraft may not be operated closer than 500 feet to any person, vessel, vehicle, or structure.

7. **Define *minimum safe altitude*.** (14 CFR 91.119)

An altitude allowing, if a power unit fails, an emergency landing without undue hazard to persons or property on the surface.

8. **When flying below 18,000 feet MSL, cruising altitude must be maintained by reference to an altimeter set using what procedure?** (14 CFR 91.121)

When the barometric pressure is 31.00 inHg or less, each person operating an aircraft must maintain the cruising altitude of that aircraft by reference to an altimeter that is set to the current reported altimeter setting of a station along the route and within 100 NM of the aircraft. If there is no station within this area, the current reported altimeter setting of an available station may be used. If the barometric pressure exceeds 31.00 inHg, consult the *Aeronautical Information Manual* for correct procedures.

9. **If an altimeter setting is not available before flight, what procedure should be used?** (14 CFR 91.121)

Use the same procedure as in the case of an aircraft not equipped with a radio: the elevation of the departure airport or an appropriate altimeter setting available before departure should be used.

10. What is the fuel requirement for VFR flight during the day? (14 CFR 91.151)

During the day, you must be able to fly to the first point of intended landing, and assuming normal cruising speed, to fly after that for at least 30 minutes.

11. What is the fuel requirement for VFR flight at night? (14 CFR 91.151)

No person may begin a flight in an airplane under VFR conditions unless (considering wind and forecast weather conditions) there is enough fuel to fly to the first point of intended landing and, assuming normal cruising speed, at night, to fly after that for at least 45 minutes.

12. When operating an aircraft under VFR in level cruising flight at an altitude of more than 3,000 feet above the surface, what rules apply concerning specific altitudes flown? (14 CFR 91.159)

When operating above 3,000 feet AGL but less than 18,000 feet MSL on a *magnetic course* of 0° to 179°, fly at an odd-thousand-foot MSL altitude plus 500 feet. When on a *magnetic course* of 180° to 359°, fly at an even-thousand-foot MSL altitude plus 500 feet.

13. Is an emergency locator transmitter (ELT) required on all aircraft? (14 CFR 91.207)

No person may operate a U.S. registered civil airplane unless there is attached to the airplane an automatic-type emergency locator transmitter that is in operable condition. Several exceptions exist, including the following:

a. Aircraft engaged in training operations conducted entirely within a 50 NM radius of the airport from which such local flight operations began.

b. Aircraft engaged in design and testing.

c. New aircraft engaged in manufacture, preparation, and delivery.

d. Aircraft engaged in agricultural operations.

14. When must the batteries in an emergency locator transmitter be replaced or recharged, if rechargeable? (14 CFR 91.207)

Batteries used in ELTs must be replaced (or recharged, if the batteries are rechargeable):

a. When the transmitter has been in use for more than 1 cumulative hour; or

b. When 50 percent of their useful life (or, rechargeable batteries, 50 percent of their useful life of charge), has expired.

Note: The new expiration date for replacing (or recharging) the battery must be legibly marked on the outside of the transmitter and entered in the aircraft maintenance record. This date indicates 50% of the battery's useful life.

15. What are the regulations concerning use of supplemental oxygen on board an aircraft? (14 CFR 91.211)

a. At cabin pressure altitudes above 12,500 feet MSL up to and including 14,000 feet MSL: for that part of the flight at those altitudes that is more than 30 minutes, the required minimum flight crew must be provided with and use supplemental oxygen.

b. At cabin pressure altitudes above 14,000 feet MSL: for the entire flight time at those altitudes, the required flight crew is provided with and uses supplemental oxygen.

c. At cabin pressure altitudes above 15,000 feet MSL: each occupant is provided with supplemental oxygen.

16. According to regulations, where is aerobatic flight of an aircraft not permitted? (14 CFR 91.303)

No person may operate an aircraft in aerobatic flight:

a. Over any congested area of a city, town, or settlement;

b. Over an open-air assembly of persons;

c. Within the lateral boundaries of the surface areas of Class B, Class C, Class D, or Class E airspace designated for an airport;

d. Within 4 NM of the center line of a Federal airway;

e. Below an altitude of 1,500 feet above the surface; or

f. When flight visibility is less than 3 SM.

17. Define *aerobatic flight*. (14 CFR 91.303)

For the purposes of this section, aerobatic flight means an intentional maneuver involving an abrupt change in an aircraft's attitude, an abnormal attitude, or abnormal acceleration, not necessary for normal flight.

18. When are parachutes required on board an aircraft? (14 CFR 91.307)

a. Unless each occupant of the aircraft is wearing an approved parachute, no pilot of a civil aircraft carrying any person (other than a crewmember) may execute any intentional maneuver that exceeds:

- A bank angle of 60° relative to the horizon; or
- A nose-up or nose-down attitude of 30° relative to the horizon.

b. The above regulation does not apply to:

- Flight tests for pilot certification or rating; or
- Spins and other flight maneuvers required by the regulations for any certificate or rating when given by a CFI or ATP instructing in accordance with 14 CFR §61.67.

Additional Study Questions

1. When navigating by VOR, when will you have reverse sensing? (FAA-H-8083-25)

2. What is the VOR Minimum Operational Network? (AIM 1-1-3)

3. Explain the factors you considered when selecting the landmarks you used for your checkpoints on your cross-country flight plan. (FAA-H-8083-25)

4. During your cross-country flight, explain how you will verify that you have identified the correct landmark that you selected as your checkpoint. (FAA-H-8083-25)

5. Where can a pilot find information on the location of the nearest VOT testing station? (AIM 1-1-4)

6. **During your cross-country flight, explain how you will obtain in-flight weather updates for your specific route of flight.** (FAA-H-8083-25)

7. **How can you determine if there are any known ATC delays for your cross-country flight today?** (AIM 7-1-5)

8. **When referencing a sectional chart, explain why the 360-degree radial on a VORTAC compass rose is not pointing towards the top of the chart?** (FAA-H-8083-25)

9. **What factors should be considered when evaluating the type of survival equipment to carry for a flight over uninhabited terrain?** (AIM 6-2-6, CAMI OK-06-033)

10. **While studying the sectional chart about your destination airport, you notice a small blue star after the control tower frequency. What is the significance of the blue star?** (Chart Legend)

National Airspace System 5

A. General

1. What are the two categories of airspace in the National Airspace system? (FAA-H-8083-25)

Regulatory and non-regulatory.

2. Within the two categories, what are the four types of airspace? (FAA-H-8083-25)

a. Controlled airspace
b. Uncontrolled airspace
c. Special Use airspace
d. Other airspace

3. Explain the factors that determine the category and type of airspace an area will have. (FAA-H-8083-25)

The categories and types of airspace are dictated by the complexity or density of aircraft movements, nature of the operations conducted within the airspace, the level of safety required, and national and public interest.

Exam Tip: Be prepared to explain the type of airspace your planned route of flight will take you through from departure to arrival at your destination. Know the required visibility, cloud clearance and communication requirements at any point and altitude along your route of flight. Also, expect the "what if you're here" questions concerning special use airspace, special VFR clearances, etc.

4. Briefly describe the terms *controlled* and *uncontrolled airspace*. (FAA-H-8083-25)

Controlled airspace—A generic term that covers the different classifications of airspace and defined dimensions within which air traffic control (ATC) service is provided in accordance with the airspace classification. Controlled airspace consists of: Class A, Class B, Class C, Class D, and Class E.

Uncontrolled airspace—Or Class G airspace, is the portion of the airspace that has not been designated as Class A, B, C, D, or E. It is therefore designated uncontrolled airspace. Class G airspace extends from the surface to the base of the overlying Class E airspace. Although ATC has no authority or responsibility to control air traffic, pilots should remember there are visual flight rules (VFR) minimums that apply to Class G airspace.

B. Controlled Airspace

1. What is Class A airspace? (AIM 3-2-2)

Generally, that airspace from 18,000 ft MSL up to and including FL600, including that airspace overlying the waters within 12 NM of the coast of the 48 contiguous states and Alaska; and designated international airspace beyond 12 NM of the coast of the 48 contiguous states and Alaska within areas of domestic radio navigational signal or ATC radar coverage, and within which domestic procedures are applied.

2. Can a flight under VFR be conducted within Class A airspace? (14 CFR 91.135)

No, unless otherwise authorized by ATC, each person operating an aircraft in Class A airspace must operate that aircraft under instrument flight rules (IFR).

3. What is the minimum pilot certification for operations conducted within Class A airspace? (14 CFR 91.135)

The pilot must be at least a private pilot with an instrument rating.

4. What minimum equipment is required for flight operations within Class A airspace? (14 CFR 91.135, 91.215, 91.225)

a. A two-way radio capable of communicating with ATC on the frequency assigned.

b. A Mode C altitude encoding transponder.

c. ADS-B and TIS-B equipment operating on 1090 MHz ES frequency.

d. Equipped with instruments and equipment required for IFR operations.

5. How is Class A airspace depicted on navigational charts? (AIM 3-2-2)

Class A airspace is not specifically charted.

6. What is the definition of Class B airspace? (AIM 3-2-3)

Generally, that airspace from the surface to 10,000 ft MSL surrounding the nation's busiest airports in terms of IFR operations or passenger enplanements. The configuration of each Class B airspace area is individually tailored and consists of a surface area and two or more layers (some Class B airspace areas resemble upside down wedding cakes) and is designated to contain all published instrument procedures once an aircraft enters the airspace.

7. What minimum pilot certification is required to operate an aircraft within Class B airspace? (14 CFR 91.131)

No person may take off or land a civil aircraft at an airport within a Class B airspace area or operate a civil aircraft within a Class B airspace area unless:

a. The pilot-in-command holds at least a private pilot certificate.

b. The pilot-in-command holds a recreational pilot certificate and has met the requirements of 14 CFR §61.101; or for a student pilot seeking a recreational pilot certificate met the requirements of 14 CFR §61.94.

c. The pilot-in-command holds a sport pilot certificate and has met the requirements of 14 CFR §61.325; or the requirements for a student pilot seeking a recreational pilot certificate in 14 CFR §61.94.

d. The aircraft is operated by a student pilot who has met the requirements of 14 CFR §61.94 or §61.95 of this chapter, as applicable.

Note: Certain Class B airspace areas do not allow pilot operations to be conducted to or from the primary airport unless the pilot-in-command holds at least a private pilot certificate (example: Dallas/ Fort Worth International).

8. What is the minimum equipment required for operations of an aircraft within Class B airspace? (14 CFR 91.131, 91.215, 91.225)

a. An operable two-way radio capable of communications with ATC on the appropriate frequencies for that area.

b. A Mode C altitude encoding transponder.

c. ADS-B Out equipment—operating on UAT 978 MHz or 1090 MHz ES frequency.

d. If IFR, an operable VOR or TACAN receiver or an operable and suitable RNAV system.

9. **Before operating an aircraft into Class B airspace, what basic requirement must be met?** (14 CFR 91.131)

Arriving aircraft must obtain an ATC clearance from the ATC facility having jurisdiction for that area prior to operating an aircraft in that area.

10. **What minimum weather conditions are required when conducting VFR flight operations within Class B airspace?** (14 CFR 91.155)

VFR flight operations must be conducted clear of clouds with at least 3 SM flight visibility.

11. **How is Class B airspace depicted on navigational charts?** (AIM 3-2-3)

Class B airspace is charted on Sectional Charts, IFR En Route Low Altitude, and Terminal Area Charts. A solid shaded blue line depicts the lateral limits of Class B airspace. Numbers indicate the base and top, e.g., 100/25, 100/SFC.

12. **What basic ATC services are provided to all aircraft operating within Class B airspace?** (AIM 3-2-3)

VFR pilots will be provided sequencing and separation from other aircraft while operating within Class B airspace.

13. **It becomes apparent that wake turbulence may be encountered while ATC is providing sequencing and separation services in Class B airspace. Whose responsibility is it to avoid this turbulence?** (AIM 3-2-3)

The pilot-in-command is responsible. The services provided by ATC do not relieve pilots of their responsibilities to see and avoid other traffic operating in basic VFR weather conditions, to adjust their operations and flight path as necessary to preclude serious wake turbulence encounters, to maintain appropriate terrain and obstruction clearance, or to remain in weather conditions equal to or better than the minimums required by 14 CFR §91.155.

14. **What is the maximum speed allowed when operating inside Class B airspace, under 10,000 ft and within a Class D surface area?** (14 CFR 91.117)

    Unless otherwise authorized or required by ATC, no person may operate an aircraft at or below 2,500 ft above the surface within 4 NM of the primary airport of a Class C or Class D airspace area at an indicated airspeed of more than 200 knots. This restriction does not apply to operations conducted within a Class B airspace area. Such operations shall comply with the below 10,000 ft MSL restriction: "No person shall operate an aircraft below 10,000 ft MSL, at an indicated airspeed of more than 250 knots."

15. **When operating beneath the lateral limits of Class B airspace, or in a VFR corridor designated through Class B airspace, what maximum speed is authorized?** (14 CFR 91.117)

    No person may operate an aircraft in the airspace underlying a Class B airspace area designated for an airport or in a VFR corridor designated through such a Class B airspace area, at an indicated airspeed of more than 200 knots (230 MPH).

16. **What is Class C airspace?** (AIM 3-2-4)

    Generally, that airspace from the surface to 4,000 ft above the airport elevation (charted in MSL) surrounding those airports that have an operational control tower, are serviced by a radar approach control, and that have a certain number of IFR operations or passenger enplanements.

17. **What are the basic dimensions of Class C airspace?** (AIM 3-2-4)

    Although the configuration of each Class C airspace area is individually tailored, the airspace usually consists of a 5 NM radius core surface area that extends from the surface up to 4,000 ft above the airport elevation, and a 10 NM radius shelf area that extends from 1,200 ft to 4,000 ft above the airport elevation. The outer area radius will be 20 NM, with some variations based on site specific requirements. The outer area extends outward from the primary airport and extends from the lower limits of radar/radio coverage up to the ceiling of the approach control airspace.

18. **What minimum pilot certification is required to operate an aircraft within Class C airspace?** (AIM 3-2-4)

    A student pilot certificate.

19. **What minimum equipment is required to operate an aircraft within Class C airspace?** (14 CFR 91.130, 91.215, 91.225)

    Unless otherwise authorized by the ATC having jurisdiction over the Class C airspace area, no person may operate an aircraft within a Class C airspace area designated for an airport unless that aircraft is equipped with the following:

    a. A two-way radio.

    b. Automatic pressure altitude reporting equipment with Mode C capability.

    c. ADS-B Out equipment—operating on UAT 978 MHz or 1090 MHz ES frequency.

20. **When operating an aircraft through Class C airspace or to an airport within Class C airspace, what basic requirement must be met?** (14 CFR 91.130)

    Each person must establish two-way radio communications with the ATC facilities providing air traffic services prior to entering that airspace and thereafter maintain those communications while within that airspace.

21. **Define what is meant by *established* in this context: "Two-way radio communications must be established prior to entering Class C airspace."** (AIM 3-2-4)

    If a controller responds to a radio call with, "(aircraft call sign) standby," radio communications have been established. It is important to understand that if the controller responds to the initial radio call *without* using the aircraft identification, radio communications have *not* been established and the pilot may not enter the Class C airspace.

22. **When departing a satellite airport without an operative control tower located within Class C airspace, what requirement must be met?** (14 CFR 91.130)

Each person must establish and maintain two-way radio communications with the ATC facilities having jurisdiction over the Class C airspace area as soon as practicable after departing.

23. **What minimum weather conditions are required when conducting VFR flight operations within Class C airspace?** (14 CFR 91.155)

VFR flight operations within Class C airspace require 3 SM flight visibility and cloud clearances of at least 500 ft below, 1,000 ft above and 2,000 ft horizontal to clouds.

24. **How is Class C airspace depicted on navigational charts?** (AIM 3-2-4)

A solid magenta line is used to depict Class C airspace. Class C airspace is charted on Sectional Charts, IFR En Route Low Altitude, and Terminal Area Charts where appropriate.

25. **What type of Air Traffic Control services are provided when operating within Class C airspace?** (AIM 3-2-4)

When two-way radio communications and radar contact are established, all VFR aircraft are:

a. Sequenced to the primary airport.

b. Provided Class C services within the Class C airspace and the outer area.

c. Provided basic radar services beyond the outer area on a workload permitting basis. This can be terminated by the controller if workload dictates.

26. **Describe the various types of terminal radar services available for VFR aircraft.** (AIM 4-1-18)

Basic radar service—Safety alerts, traffic advisories, limited radar vectoring (on a workload-permitting basis) and sequencing at locations where procedures have been established for this purpose and/or when covered by a letter of agreement.

TRSA service—Radar sequencing and separation service for VFR aircraft in a TRSA.

Class C service—This service provides, in addition to basic radar service, approved separation between IFR and VFR aircraft, and sequencing of VFR arrivals to the primary airport.

Class B service—Provides, in addition to basic radar service, approved separation of aircraft based on IFR, VFR, and/or weight, and sequencing of VFR arrivals to the primary airport(s).

27. Where is Mode C transponder and ADS-B Out equipment required? (AIM 4-1-20, 14 CFR 91.215, 91.225, 99.13)

In general, the regulations require aircraft to be equipped with an operable Mode C transponder and ADS-B Out equipment when operating:

a. In Class A, Class B, or Class C airspace areas.

b. Above the ceiling and within the lateral boundaries of Class B or Class C airspace up to 10,000 ft MSL.

c. Class E airspace at and above 10,000 ft MSL within the 48 contiguous states and the District of Columbia, excluding the airspace at and below 2,500 ft AGL.

d. Within 30 miles of a Class B airspace primary airport, below 10,000 ft MSL (Mode C Veil).

e. For ADS-B Out: Class E airspace at and above 3,000 ft MSL over the Gulf of Mexico from the coastline of the United States out to 12 nautical miles.

f. All aircraft flying into, within, or across the contiguous United States ADIZ.

Note: Civil and military aircraft should operate with the transponder in the altitude reporting mode and ADS-B Out transmissions enabled (if equipped) at all airports, any time the aircraft is positioned on any portion of an airport movement area. This includes all defined taxiways and runways.

28. What is the maximum speed an aircraft may be operated within Class C airspace? (AIM 3-2-4)

Unless otherwise authorized or required by ATC, no person may operate an aircraft at or below 2,500 ft above the surface within 4 NMs of the primary airport of a Class C airspace area at an indicated speed of more than 200 knots (230 MPH).

29. What is Class D airspace? (AIM 3-2-5)

Generally, Class D airspace extends upward from the surface to 2,500 ft above the airport elevation (charted in MSL) surrounding those airports that have an operational control tower. The configuration of each Class D airspace area is individually tailored and when instrument procedures are published, the airspace will normally be designed to contain those procedures.

30. When operating an aircraft through Class D airspace or to an airport within Class D airspace, what requirement must be met? (14 CFR 91.129)

Each person must establish two-way radio communications with the ATC facilities providing air traffic services prior to entering that airspace and thereafter maintain those communications while within that airspace.

Note: ADS-B Out equipment is not required in Class D airspace provided that the Class D airspace is not located within a 30 NM Mode C Veil.

31. When departing a satellite airport without an operative control tower located within Class D airspace, what requirement must be met? (14 CFR 91.129)

Each person must establish and maintain two-way radio communications with the ATC facility having jurisdiction over the Class D airspace area as soon as practicable after departing.

32. Is an ATC clearance required if flight operations are conducted through a Class E surface area arrival extension? (AIM 3-2-5, 3-2-6)

Class E airspace may be designated as extensions to Class B, Class C, Class D, and Class E surface areas. Class E airspace extensions begin at the surface and extend up to the overlying controlled airspace. The extensions provide controlled airspace to contain standard instrument approach procedures without imposing a communications requirement on pilots operating under VFR. Surface area arrival extensions become part of the surface area and are in effect during the same times as the surface area.

33. **What minimum weather conditions are required when conducting VFR flight operations within Class D airspace?** (14 CFR 91.155)

VFR flight operations within Class D airspace require 3 SM flight visibility and cloud clearances of at least 500 ft below, 1,000 ft above and 2,000 ft horizontal to clouds.

34. **How is Class D airspace depicted on navigational charts?** (AIM 3-2-5)

Class D airspace areas are depicted on Sectional and Terminal charts with blue segmented lines, and on IFR Enroute Lows with a boxed [D].

35. **What type of Air Traffic Control services are provided when operating within Class D airspace?** (AIM 3-2-5, 5-5-8, 5-5-10)

No separation services are provided to VFR aircraft. When meteorological conditions permit, regardless of the type of flight plan or whether or not under the control of a radar facility, the pilot is responsible to see and avoid other traffic, terrain or obstacles. A controller, on a workload permitting basis, will provide radar traffic information, safety alerts and traffic information for sequencing purposes.

36. **What is the maximum speed an aircraft may be operated within Class D airspace?** (AIM 3-2-5)

Unless otherwise authorized or required by ATC, no person may operate an aircraft at or below 2,500 ft above the surface within 4 NM of the primary airport of a Class D airspace area at an indicated airspeed of more than 200 knots (230 MPH).

37. **When a control tower, located at an airport within Class D airspace, ceases operation for the day, what happens to the lower limit of the controlled airspace?** (AIM 3-2-5)

During the hours the tower is not in operation, Class E surface area rules, or a combination of Class E rules down to 700 ft AGL and Class G rules to the surface, will become applicable. Check the *Chart Supplement U.S.* for specifics.

38. Will all airports with an operating control tower always have Class D airspace surrounding them? (AIM 4-3-2)

No; some airports do not have the required weather reporting capability necessary for surface based controlled airspace. The controlled airspace over these airports normally begins at 700 ft or 1,200 ft AGL and can be determined from visual aeronautical charts.

39. What is the definition of *controlled airspace*? (P/CG)

Controlled airspace is airspace of defined dimensions within which air traffic control service is provided to IFR flights and to VFR flights in accordance with the airspace classification. Controlled airspace is a generic term that covers Class A, Class B, Class C, Class D, and Class E airspace.

40. State several examples of Class E airspace. (AIM 3-2-6)

a. *Surface area designated for an airport where a control tower is not in operation*—Class E surface areas extend upward from the surface to a designated altitude, or to the adjacent or overlying controlled airspace and are configured to contain all instrument procedures.

b. *Extension to a surface area*—Class E airspace may be designated as extensions to Class B, Class C, Class D, and Class E surface areas. Class E airspace extensions begin at the surface and extend up to the overlying controlled airspace. The extensions provide controlled airspace to contain standard instrument approach procedures without imposing a communications requirement on pilots operating under VFR.

c. *Airspace used for transition*—Class E airspace areas may be designated for transitioning aircraft to/from the terminal or enroute environment. They extend upward from either 700 ft AGL or 1,200 ft AGL and are designated for airports with an approved instrument procedure. The 700 ft/1,200 ft AGL Class E airspace transition areas remain in effect continuously, regardless of airport operating hours or surface area status.

d. *Enroute domestic areas*—Class E airspace areas that extend upward from a specified altitude and provide controlled airspace in those areas where there is a requirement to provide

IFR enroute ATC services, but the Federal airway system is inadequate.

e. *Federal airways and low-altitude RNAV routes*—Federal airways and low-altitude RNAV routes are Class E airspace areas and, unless otherwise specified, extend upward from 1,200 ft AGL to, but not including 18,000 ft MSL.

f. *Offshore airspace areas*—Class E airspace areas that extend upward from a specified altitude to, but not including 18,000 ft MSL. These areas provide controlled airspace beyond 12 miles from the coast of the U.S. in those areas where there is a requirement to provide IFR enroute ATC services, and within which the U.S. is applying domestic procedures.

g. *Unless designated at a lower altitude*—Class E airspace in the U.S. consists of the airspace extending upward from 14,500 ft MSL to, but not including 18,000 ft MSL overlying the 48 contiguous states, the District of Columbia and Alaska, including the waters within 12 NM from the coast of the 48 contiguous states and Alaska.

h. *The airspace above FL 600 is Class E airspace.*

41. What are the operating rules and pilot/equipment requirements to operate within Class E airspace? (AIM 3-2-6)

a. Pilot certification—student pilot certificate.

b. Equipment:

   i. An operable radar beacon transponder with automatic altitude reporting capability and operable ADS-B Out equipment is required at and above 10,000 ft MSL within the 48 contiguous states and the District of Columbia, excluding the airspace at and below 2,500 ft above the surface; and

   ii. Operable ADS-B Out equipment at and above 3,000 ft MSL over the Gulf of Mexico from the coastline of the United States out to 12 NM offshore.

42. **When a Class C or Class D surface area is not in effect continuously (for example, where a control tower only operates part-time), what will happen to the surface area airspace when the tower closes?** (AIM 3-2-6)

The surface area airspace will change to either a Class E surface area or Class G airspace. In such cases, the "Airspace" entry for the airport in the *Chart Supplement U.S.* will state "other times Class E" or "other times Class G." When a part-time surface area changes to Class E airspace, the Class E arrival extensions will remain in effect as Class E airspace. If a part-time Class C, Class D, or Class E surface area becomes Class G airspace, the arrival extensions will change to Class G at the same time.

43. **Explain the purpose of Class E transition areas.** (AIM 3-2-6)

Class E transition areas extend upward from either 700 ft AGL (magenta vignette) or 1,200 ft AGL (blue vignette) and are designated for airports with an approved instrument procedure. Class E transition areas exist to help separate (via cloud clearance) arriving and departing IFR traffic from VFR aircraft operating in the vicinity.

Note: Do not confuse the 700-foot and 1,200-foot Class E transition areas with surface areas or surface area extensions. Class E Surface (SFC) Airspace is symbolized with a magenta dashed line.

44. **Are you required to establish communications with a tower located within Class E airspace?** (14 CFR 91.127)

Yes, unless otherwise authorized or required by ATC, no person may operate an aircraft to, from, through, or on an airport having an operational control tower unless two-way communications are maintained between that aircraft and the control tower. Communications must be established prior to 4 NM from the airport, up to and including 2,500 ft AGL.

45. **How is Class E airspace depicted on navigational charts?** (AIM 3-2-6, USRGD)

Class E airspace below 14,500 ft MSL is charted on Sectional, Terminal, and IFR Enroute Low Altitude charts. The lateral and vertical limits of all Class E controlled airspace up to but not including 18,000 ft are shown by narrow bands of vignette on Sectional and Terminal Area charts. Controlled airspace floors of 700 ft AGL are defined by a magenta vignette; floors other than 700 ft that abut uncontrolled airspace are defined by a blue vignette; differing floors greater than 700 ft AGL are annotated by a symbol and a number indicating the floor. If the ceiling is less than 18,000 ft MSL, the value (prefixed by the word "ceiling") is shown along the limits of the controlled airspace.

46. How are Class E surface extension areas depicted on navigational charts? (USRGD)

Class E airspace areas that serve as extensions to Class B, Class C, and Class D airspace are depicted by a magenta segmented line.

47. What minimum flight visibility and clearance from clouds are required for VFR flight in the following situations? (14 CFR 91.155)

Class C, D, or E Airspace

Less than 10,000 feet MSL:
- Visibility—3 SM.
- Cloud clearance—500 feet below, 1,000 feet above, 2,000 feet horizontal.

At or above 10,000 feet MSL:
- Visibility—5 SM.
- Cloud clearance—1,000 feet below, 1,000 feet above, 1 SM horizontal.

Class G Airspace

1,200 feet or less above the surface (regardless of MSL altitude):
Day:
- Visibility—1 SM.
- Cloud clearance—Clear of clouds.

Night:
- Visibility—3 SM.
- Cloud clearance—500 feet below, 1,000 feet above, 2,000 feet horizontal.

(continued)

More than 1,200 feet above the surface but less than 10,000 feet MSL:

Day:
- Visibility—1 SM.
- Cloud clearance—500 feet below, 1,000 feet above, 2,000 feet horizontal.

Night:
- Visibility—3 SM.
- Cloud clearance—500 feet below, 1,000 feet above, 2,000 feet horizontal.

More than 1,200 feet above the surface and at or above 10,000 feet MSL:
- Visibility—5 SM.
- Cloud clearance—1,000 feet below, 1,000 feet above, 1 SM horizontal.

48. What are the basic VFR weather minimums required for operation of an aircraft into Class B, Class C, Class D, or Class E airspace? (14 CFR 91.155)

1,000-foot ceiling and 3 miles visibility. Except as provided in 14 CFR §91.157 (special VFR), no person may:

a. Operate an aircraft beneath the ceiling under VFR within the lateral boundaries of controlled airspace designated to the surface for an airport when the ceiling is less than 1,000 ft.

b. Take off or land an aircraft, or enter the traffic pattern of an airport, under VFR, within the lateral boundaries of the surface areas of Class B, Class C, Class D, or Class E airspace designated for an airport unless ground visibility at that airport is at least 3 SM or, if ground visibility is not reported, unless flight visibility during landing or takeoff, or while operating in the traffic pattern is at least 3 SM.

49. If VFR flight minimums cannot be maintained, can a VFR flight be made into Class B, C, D, or E airspace? (AIM 4-4-6)

No, with one exception. A "Special VFR clearance" may be obtained from ATC prior to operating within a Class B, Class C, Class D, or Class E surface area provided the flight can remain clear of clouds with at least 1 SM ground visibility if taking off or landing or, 1 SM flight visibility for operations within Class B, Class C, Class D, and Class E surface areas.

50. Are Special VFR clearances always available to pilots in all classes of airspace? (AIM 4-4-6)

A VFR pilot may request and be given a clearance to enter, leave, or operate within most Class D and Class E surface areas and some Class B and Class C surface areas traffic permitting and providing such flight will not delay IFR operations.

Note: Special VFR operations by fixed wing aircraft are prohibited in some Class B and Class C surface areas due to the volume of IFR traffic. A list of these Class B and Class C surface areas is contained in Part 91. They are also depicted on Sectional Aeronautical Charts.

51. If it becomes apparent that a special VFR clearance will be necessary, what facility should the pilot contact in order to obtain one? (AIM 4-4-6)

When a control tower is located within a Class B, Class C, or Class D surface area, requests for clearances should be made to the tower. In a Class E surface area, clearance may be obtained from the nearest tower, FSS, or center.

52. Can a Special VFR clearance be obtained into or out of Class B, C, D, or E airspace at night? (AIM 4-4-6)

Special VFR operations by fixed-wing aircraft are prohibited between sunset and sunrise unless the pilot is instrument rated and the aircraft is equipped for IFR flight.

C. Uncontrolled Airspace

1. What is the definition of Class G airspace?
(FAA-H-8083-25, AIM 3-3-1)

Uncontrolled airspace or Class G airspace is the portion of the airspace that has not been designated as Class A, B, C, D, or E. It is therefore designated uncontrolled airspace. Class G airspace extends from the surface to the base of the overlying Class E airspace. Although ATC has no authority or responsibility to control air traffic, pilots should remember there are visual flight rules (VFR) minimums that apply to Class G airspace.

2. **Are you required to establish communications with a tower located within Class G airspace?** (14 CFR 91.126)

Yes, unless otherwise authorized or required by ATC, no person may operate an aircraft to, from, through, or on an airport having an operational control tower unless two-way communications are maintained between that aircraft and the control tower. Communications must be established prior to 4 NM from the airport, up to and including 2,500 AGL.

3. **What are the vertical limits of Class G airspace?** (FAA-H-8083-25)

Class G airspace begins at the surface and continues up to the overlying controlled (Class E) airspace, not to exceed 14,500 ft MSL.

4. **What is the minimum cloud clearance and visibility required when conducting flight operations in a traffic pattern at night in Class G airspace below 1,200 ft AGL?** (14 CFR 91.155)

When the visibility is less than 3 statute miles (SM) but not less than 1 SM during night hours, an airplane may be operated clear of clouds if operated in an airport traffic pattern within one-half mile of the runway.

D. Special Use Airspace

1. **What is a prohibited area?** (AIM 3-4-2)

Prohibited areas contain certain airspace of defined dimensions identified by an area on the surface of the earth within which flight of aircraft is prohibited. Such areas are established for security or other reasons associated with national welfare.

2. **What is a restricted area?** (AIM 3-4-3)

Restricted areas contain airspace identified by an area on the surface of the earth within which the flight of aircraft, while not wholly prohibited, is subject to restrictions. These areas denote the existence of unusual, often invisible, hazards to aircraft such as artillery firing, aerial gunnery, or guided missiles. Penetration of restricted areas without authorization from the using or controlling agency may be extremely hazardous to the aircraft and its occupants.

3. **Under what conditions, if any, may pilots enter restricted or prohibited areas?** (14 CFR 91.133)

   No person may operate an aircraft within a restricted area contrary to the restrictions imposed, or within a prohibited area, unless that person has permission of the using or controlling agency. Normally *no* operations are permitted within a prohibited area and *prior* permission must always be obtained before operating within a restricted area.

4. **What is a warning area?** (AIM 3-4-4)

   A warning area is airspace of defined dimensions extending from 3 NM outward from the coast of the United States, containing activity that may be hazardous to nonparticipating aircraft. The purpose of such an area is to warn nonparticipating pilots of the potential danger. A warning area may be located over domestic or international waters, or both.

5. **What is a Military Operating Area (MOA)?** (AIM 3-4-5)

   A MOA consists of airspace of defined vertical and lateral limits established for the purpose of separating certain military training activities from IFR traffic. Pilots operating under VFR should exercise extreme caution while flying within an MOA when military activity is being conducted. The activity status (active/ inactive) of MOAs may change frequently. Therefore, pilots should contact any FSS within 100 miles of the area to obtain accurate real-time information concerning the MOA hours of operation. Prior to entering an active MOA, pilots should contact the controlling agency for traffic advisories.

6. **What is an alert area?** (AIM 3-4-6)

   Alert areas are depicted on aeronautical charts to inform nonparticipating pilots of areas that may contain a high volume of pilot training or an unusual type of aerial activity. Pilots should be particularly alert when flying in these areas. All activity within an Alert Area shall be conducted in accordance with regulations, without waiver, and pilots of participating aircraft as well as pilots transiting the area shall be equally responsible for collision avoidance.

7. What is a controlled firing area (CFA)? (AIM 3-4-7)

CFAs contain activities that, if not conducted in a controlled environment, could be hazardous to nonparticipating aircraft. The distinguishing feature of the CFA, as compared to other special use airspace, is that its activities are suspended immediately when spotter aircraft, radar or ground lookout positions indicate an aircraft might be approaching the area. CFAs are not charted.

8. What is a national security area (NSA)? (AIM 3-4-8)

NSAs consist of airspace of defined vertical and lateral dimensions established at locations where there is a requirement for increased security and safety of ground facilities. Pilots are requested to voluntarily avoid flying through the depicted NSA. When is it necessary to provide a greater level of security and safety, flight in NSAs may be temporarily prohibited by regulation under the provisions of 14 CFR §99.7.

9. Where can information on special use airspace be found? (AIM 3-4-1, 3-4-9)

The frequency for the controlling agency is tabulated in the margins of the applicable IFR and VFR charts. Permanent SUAs (except CFAs) are charted on sectional aeronautical, VFR terminal area, and applicable en route charts, and include the hours of operation, altitudes, and the controlling agency. For temporary restricted areas and MOAs, pilots should review the Domestic Notices found on the Federal NOTAM System website at notams.aim.faa.gov/notamSearch/ or the FAA SUA website at sua.faa.gov.

E. Other Airspace Areas

1. What are examples of "other" airspace areas? (AIM 3-5-1 thru 3-5-7)

Other airspace areas is a general term referring to the majority of the remaining airspace. It includes:

- Local airport advisory
- Military training route (MTR)
- Temporary flight restriction (TFR)
- Parachute jump aircraft operations

- Published VFR routes
- Terminal radar service area (TRSA)
- Special Air Traffic Rules (SATR) and Special Flight Rules Area (SFRA)

2. What are Military Training Routes? (AIM 3-5-2)

Military Training Routes are developed for use by the military for the purpose of conducting low-altitude, high speed training. The routes above 1,500 ft AGL are developed to be flown, to the maximum extent possible, under IFR. The routes at 1,500 ft AGL and below are generally developed to be flown under VFR. Routes below 1,500 ft AGL use four-digit identifiers (e.g., IR 1004, VR 1008). Routes above 1,500 ft AGL use three-digit identifiers (e.g., IR 003, VR 004). IR is for IFR routes and VR is for VFR routes.

3. What is a Temporary Flight Restriction (TFR)? (AC 91-63, AIM 3-5-3)

A TFR is a regulatory action issued via the U.S. NOTAM system to restrict certain aircraft from operating within a defined area, on a temporary basis, to protect persons or property in the air or on the ground. They may be issued due to a hazardous condition, a special event, or as a general warning for the entire FAA airspace. TFR information can be obtained from an FSS or on the internet at tfr.faa.gov.

4. Where can a pilot find information on Parachute Jump Aircraft Operations? (AIM 3-5-4, FAA-H-8083-25)

Procedures relating to parachute jump areas are contained in 14 CFR Part 105. Parachute jump aircraft operations are published in the Chart Supplement U.S and jump sites that are used frequently are depicted on sectional charts.

5. What is the purpose of Published VFR Routes? (AIM 3-5-5, FAA-H-8083-25)

Published VFR routes are for transitioning around, under, or through some complex airspace. Terms such as VFR flyway, VFR corridor, Class B airspace VFR transition route, and terminal area VFR route have been applied to such routes. These routes are generally found on VFR terminal area planning charts.

6. **Where can a pilot find information on VFR flyways, VFR Corridors, and Class B airspace transition routes used to transition busy terminal airspace?** (AIM 3-5-5)

   Information will normally be depicted on the reverse side of VFR Terminal Area Charts, commonly referred to as Class B airspace charts.

7. **What is a Terminal Radar Service Area (TRSA)?** (AIM 3-5-6, P/CG)

   A TRSA consists of airspace surrounding designated airports wherein ATC provides radar vectoring, sequencing, and separation on a full-time basis for all IFR and participating VFR aircraft. Pilot participation is urged but not mandatory.

8. **What class of airspace is a TRSA?** (AIM 3-5-6)

   TRSAs do not fit into any of the U.S. airspace classes and are not contained in Part 71 nor are there any operating rules in Part 91. The primary airport(s) within the TRSA become Class D airspace. The remaining portion of a TRSA overlies other controlled airspace which is normally Class E airspace beginning at 700 or 1,200 ft and established to transition to/from the enroute/terminal environment. TRSAs will continue to be an airspace area where participating pilots can receive additional radar services which have been redefined as TRSA service.

9. **How are TRSAs depicted on navigational charts?** (AIM 3-5-6)

   TRSAs are depicted on VFR sectional and terminal area charts with a solid black line and altitudes for each segment. The Class D portion is charted with a blue segmented line.

10. **Explain the requirements to operate an aircraft within airspace designated as a SATR area or SFRA.** (AIM 3-5-7)

    Special Air Traffic Rules (SATR)—Rules that govern procedures for conducting flights in certain areas listed in 14 CFR Part 93. The term *SATR* is used in the United States to describe the rules for operations in specific areas designated in the Code of Federal Regulations.

    Special Flight Rules Area (SFRA)—Airspace of defined dimensions, above land areas or territorial waters, within which the flight of aircraft is subject to the rules set forth in Part 93, unless otherwise authorized by ATC. Not all areas listed in Part 93 are designated SFRA, but special air traffic rules apply to all areas described in Part 93.

Note: Procedures, nature of operations, configuration, size, and density of traffic vary among the identified areas.

11. What is an ADIZ, and where are they located? (P/CG)

An Air Defense Identification Zone is an area of airspace over land or water, in which the ready identification, location, and control of all aircraft (except Department of Defense and law enforcement aircraft) is required in the interest of national security.

12. What requirements must be satisfied prior to operations into, within or across an ADIZ? (AIM 5-6-4, 14 CFR Part 99)

Operational requirements for aircraft operations associated with an ADIZ are as follows:

Flight plan—An IFR or DVFR flight plan must be filed and activated with the appropriate aeronautical facility.

Two-way radio—An operating two-way radio is required.

Transponder—Aircraft must be equipped with an operable radar beacon transponder having altitude reporting (Mode C) capabilities. The transponder must be turned on and set to the assigned ATC code.

Position reports—For IFR flights, normal position reporting. For DVFR flights, an estimated time of ADIZ penetration must be filed at least 15 minutes prior to entry.

Land-based ADIZ—are activated and deactivated over U.S. metropolitan areas as needed, with dimensions, activation dates, etc., disseminated via NOTAM. Pilots unable to comply with all NOTAM requirements must remain clear of Land-Based ADIZ. Pilots entering a Land-Based ADIZ without authorization or who fail to follow all requirements risk interception by military fighter aircraft.

F. Airspace Classification Summary

The following section summarizes the requirements for operations within the various airspace classes.

1. Discuss Class A airspace. (AIM 3-2-2, 14 CFR 91.135)

Vertical dimensions	18,000 ft MSL up to and including FL600
Operations permitted	IFR
Entry prerequisites	ATC clearance
Minimum pilot qualifications	Instrument rating
Two-way radio communications	Yes
VFR minimum visibility	N/A
VFR minimum distance from clouds	N/A
Aircraft separation	All
Conflict resolution	N/A
Traffic advisories	N/A
Safety advisories	Yes

2. Discuss Class B airspace. (AIM 3-2-3, 14 CFR 91.131)

Vertical dimensions	Surface to 10,000 ft MSL
Operations permitted	IFR and VFR
Entry prerequisites	ATC clearance
Minimum pilot qualifications	Private/Student
Two-way radio communications	Yes
VFR Minimum visibility	3 SM
VFR Minimum distance from clouds	Clear of clouds
Aircraft separation	All
Conflict resolution	Yes
Traffic advisories	Yes
Safety advisories	Yes

3. Discuss Class C airspace. (AIM 3-2-4, 14 CFR 91.130)

Vertical dimensions	Surface to 4,000 ft AGL (charted MSL)
Operations permitted	IFR and VFR
Entry prerequisites	ATC clearance for IFR; radio contact for all
Minimum pilot qualifications	Student certificate
Two-way radio communications	Yes
VFR Minimum visibility	3 SM
VFR Minimum distance from clouds	500 ft below, 1,000 ft above, and 2,000 ft horizontal
Aircraft separation	IFR, SVFR and runway operations
Conflict resolution	Between IFR and VFR operations
Traffic advisories	Yes
Safety advisories	Yes

4. Discuss Class D airspace. (AIM 3-2-5, 14 CFR 91.129)

Vertical dimensions	Surface to 2,500 ft AGL (charted MSL)
Operations permitted	IFR and VFR
Entry prerequisites	ATC clearance for IFR; radio contact for all
Minimum pilot qualifications	Student certificate
Two-way radio communications	Yes
VFR Minimum visibility	3 SM
VFR Minimum distance from clouds	500 ft below, 1,000 ft above, and 2,000 ft horizontal
Aircraft separation	IFR, SVFR and runway operations
Conflict resolution	No
Traffic advisories	Workload permitting
Safety advisories	Yes

5. Discuss Class E airspace. (AIM 3-2-6, 14 CFR 91.127)

Vertical dimensions: Except for 18,000 ft MSL, no defined vertical limit. Extends upward from either the surface or a designated altitude to the overlying or adjacent controlled airspace.

Operations permitted	IFR and VFR
Entry prerequisites	ATC clearance for IFR
Minimum pilot qualifications	Student certificate
Two-way radio communications	Yes for IFR
VFR minimum visibility	3 SM*
VFR minimum distance from clouds	500 ft below, 1,000 ft above, and 2,000 ft horizontal*
Aircraft separation	IFR and SVFR
Conflict resolution	No
Traffic advisories	Workload permitting
Safety advisories	Yes

6. Discuss Class G airspace. (AIM 3-3-1, 14 CFR 91.126, 91.155)

Vertical dimensions	Surface up to the overlying controlled (Class E) airspace, not to exceed 14,500 ft MSL
Operations permitted	IFR and VFR
Entry prerequisites	None
Minimum pilot qualifications	Student certificate
Two-way radio communications	No
VFR minimum visibility	1 SM*
VFR minimum distance from clouds	500 ft below, 1,000 ft above and 2,000 ft horizontal*
Aircraft separation	None
Conflict resolution	No
Traffic advisories	Workload permitting
Safety advisories	Yes

Different visibility minima and distance from cloud requirements exist for night operations, operations above 10,000 ft MSL, and operations below 1,200 ft AGL.

Additional Study Questions

1. If your Mode C transponder/ADS-B Out equipment fails while en route, can you continue flight into Class B or Class C airspace? (AIM 4-1-20)

2. Is Mode C transponder/ADS-B Out equipment required for flight over Class C airspace if operating below 10,000 feet MSL? (AIM 4-1-20)

3. Why do the Class E airspace cloud clearance and visibility requirements change above 10,000 ft? (FAA Safety ALC-25)

4. Are there any restrictions when flying through an alert area? Can you fly through one at any time? (AIM 3-4-6)

5. Your cross-country route of flight takes you through a restricted area. Will you have to fly around it? (AIM 3-4-3, 14 CFR 91.133)

6. Are you required to have an ATC clearance when operating within the lateral boundaries of a TRSA? (AIM 3-5-6)

7. How can you determine the vertical limits of a Military Operations Area? (Chart Legend)

8. You're planning a VFR cross country flight that will take you through busy Class B airspace. ATC usually routes you around the Class B airspace which you would like to avoid. Is there a procedure for transiting the Class B airspace without an ATC clearance or communication with air traffic control? (AIM 3-5-5)

9. What is a FAA-Recognized Identification Area or FRIA? (AC 89-3)

Performance and Limitations 6

A. Aerodynamics

1. What are the four dynamic forces that act on an airplane during all maneuvers? (FAA-H-8083-25)

Lift—The upward acting force.

Gravity (or weight)—The downward acting force.

Thrust—The forward acting force.

Drag—The backward acting force.

2. What flight condition will result in the sum of the opposing forces being equal? (FAA-H-8083-25)

In steady-state, straight-and-level, unaccelerated flight, the sum of the opposing forces is equal to zero. There can be no unbalanced forces in steady, straight flight (Newton's Third Law). This is true whether flying level or when climbing or descending. It does not mean the four forces are equal. It means the opposing forces are equal to, and thereby cancel the effects of each other.

3. What is an airfoil? State some examples. (FAA-H-8083-25)

An airfoil is a device which gets a useful reaction from air moving over its surface, namely LIFT. Wings, horizontal tail surfaces, vertical tail surfaces, and propellers are examples of airfoils.

4. What is the angle of incidence? (FAA-H-8083-25)

The angle of incidence is the angle formed by the longitudinal axis of the airplane and the chord of the wing. It is measured by the angle at which the wing is attached to the fuselage. The angle of incidence is fixed and cannot be changed by the pilot.

5. What is a relative wind? (FAA-H-8083-25)

The relative wind is the direction of the airflow with respect to the wing. When a wing is moving forward and downward the relative wind moves backward and upward. The flight path and relative wind are always parallel but travel in opposite directions.

6. What is the angle of attack? (FAA-H-8083-25)

The angle of attack is the angle between the wing chord line and the direction of the relative wind; it can be changed by the pilot.

7. What is Bernoulli's Principle? (FAA-H-8083-25)

Bernoulli's Principle—The pressure of a fluid (liquid or gas) decreases at points where the speed of the fluid increases. In the case of airflow, high speed flow is associated with low pressure and low speed flow with high pressure. The airfoil of an aircraft is designed to increase the velocity of the airflow above its surface, thereby decreasing pressure above the airfoil. Simultaneously, the impact of the air on the lower surface of the airfoil increases the pressure below. This combination of pressure decrease above and increase below produces lift.

8. What are several factors which will affect both lift and drag?

Wing area—Lift and drag acting on a wing are roughly proportional to the wing area. A pilot can change wing area by using certain types of flaps (e.g., Fowler flaps).

Shape of the airfoil—As the upper curvature of an airfoil is increased (up to a certain point) the lift produced increases. Lowering an aileron or flap device can accomplish this. Also, ice or frost on a wing can disturb normal airflow, changing its camber, and disrupting its lifting capability.

Angle of attack—As angle of attack is increased, both lift and drag are increased, up to a certain point.

Velocity of the air—An increase in velocity of air passing over the wing increases lift and drag.

Air density—Lift and drag vary directly with the density of the air. As air density increases, lift and drag increase. As air density decreases, lift and drag decrease. Air density is affected by these factors: pressure, temperature, and humidity.

9. What is torque effect? (FAA-H-8083-25)

Torque effect involves Newton's Third Law of Physics: For every action, there is an equal and opposite reaction. Applied to the airplane, this means that as the internal engine parts and the propeller are revolving in one direction, an equal force is trying to rotate the airplane in the opposite direction. It is greatest when at low airspeeds with high power settings and a high angle of attack.

10. What effect does torque reaction have on an airplane on the ground and in flight? (FAA-H-8083-25)

In flight—Torque reaction is acting around the longitudinal axis, tending to make the airplane roll. To compensate, some of the older airplanes are rigged in a manner to create more lift on the wing that is being forced downward. The more modern airΩplanes are designed with the engine offset to counteract this effect of torque.

On the ground—During the takeoff roll, an additional turning moment around the vertical axis is induced by torque reaction. As the left side of the airplane is being forced down by torque reaction, more weight is being placed on the left main landing gear. This results in more ground friction, or drag, on the left tire than on the right, causing a further turning moment to the left.

11. What are the four factors that contribute to torque effect? (FAA-H-8083-25)

Torque reaction of the engine and propeller—For every action there is an equal and opposite reaction. The rotation of the propeller (from the cockpit) to the right tends to roll or bank the airplane to the left.

Gyroscopic effect of the propeller—Gyroscopic precession applies here: the resultant action or deflection of a spinning object when a force is applied to the outer rim of its rotational mass. If the axis of a propeller is tilted, the resulting force will be exerted 90° ahead in the direction of rotation and in the same direction as the applied force. It is most noticeable on takeoffs in taildraggers when the tail is raised.

Corkscrewing effect of the propeller slipstream—High-speed rotation of an airplane propeller results in a corkscrewing rotation to the slipstream as it moves rearward. At high propeller speeds and low forward speeds (as in a takeoff), the slipstream strikes the vertical tail surface on the left side pushing the tail to the right and yawing the airplane to the left.

Asymmetrical loading of the propeller (P-Factor)—When an airplane is flying with a high angle of attack, the bite of the downward moving propeller blade is greater than the bite of the upward moving blade. This is due to the downward moving blade meeting the oncoming relative wind at a greater angle of attack than the upward moving blade. Consequently, there is greater thrust on the downward moving blade on the right side, and this forces the airplane to yaw to the left.

12. What is centrifugal force? (FAA-H-8083-25)

Centrifugal force is the equal and opposite reaction of the airplane to the change in direction, and it acts equal and opposite to the horizontal component of lift.

13. What is load factor? (FAA-H-8083-25)

Load factor is the ratio of the total load supported by the airplane's wing to the actual weight of the airplane and its contents. In other words, it is the actual load supported by the wings divided by the total weight of the airplane. It can also be expressed as the ratio of a given load to the pull of gravity, e.g., to refer to a load factor of three as 3 Gs. In this case the weight of the airplane is equal to 1 G, and if a load of three times the actual weight of the airplane were imposed upon the wing due to curved flight, the load factor would be equal to 3 Gs.

14. For what two reasons is load factor important to pilots? (FAA-H-8083-25)

a. Because of the obviously dangerous overload that it is possible for a pilot to impose on the aircraft structure.

b. Because an increased load factor increases the stalling speed and makes stalls possible at seemingly safe flight speeds.

15. What situations may result in load factors reaching the maximum or being exceeded? (FAA-H-8083-25)

Level turns—The load factor increases at a terrific rate after a bank has reached 45° or 50°. The load factor in a 60°-bank turn is 2 Gs. The load factor in an 80°-bank turn is 5.76 Gs. The wing must produce lift equal to these load factors if altitude is to be maintained.

Turbulence—Severe vertical gusts cause a sudden increase in angle of attack, resulting in large loads which are resisted by the inertia of the airplane.

Speed—The amount of excess load that can be imposed upon the wing depends on how fast the airplane is flying. At speeds below maneuvering speed, the airplane will stall before the load factor can become excessive. At speeds above maneuvering speed, the limit load factor for which an airplane is stressed can be exceeded by abrupt or excessive application of the controls or by strong turbulence.

16. What are the different operational categories for aircraft and within which category does your aircraft fall? (FAA-H-8083-25)

The maximum safe load factors (limit load factors) specified for airplanes in the various categories are as follows:

Normal	+3.8 to −1.52
Utility (mild aerobatics including spins)	+4.4 to −1.76
Aerobatic	+6.0 to −3.00

17. What effect does an increase in load factor have on stalling speed? (FAA-H-8083-25)

As load factor increases, stalling speed increases. Any airplane can be stalled at any airspeed within the limits of its structure and the strength of the pilot. At a given airspeed the load factor increases as angle of attack increases, and the wing stalls because the angle of attack has been increased to a certain angle. Therefore, there is a direct relationship between the load factor imposed upon the wing and its stalling characteristics. A rule for determining the speed at which a wing will stall is that the stalling speed increases in proportion to the square root of the load factor.

18. Define the term *maneuvering speed*. (FAA-H-8083-25, SAIB CE-11-17)

Maneuvering speed is the maximum speed at which the limit load can be imposed (either by gusts or full deflection of the control surfaces) without causing structural damage. It is the speed below which you can, in smooth air, move a single flight control one time, to its full deflection, for one axis of airplane rotation only (pitch, roll or yaw) without risk of damage to the airplane. Speeds up to, but not exceeding the maneuvering speed allow an aircraft to stall prior to experiencing an increase in load factor that would exceed the limit load of the aircraft.

Note: Operating at or below maneuvering speed does not provide structural protection against multiple full control inputs in one axis or full control inputs in more than one axis at the same time.

19. Discuss the effect on maneuvering speed of an increase or decrease in weight. (FAA-H-8083-25)

Maneuvering speed increases with an increase in weight and decreases with a decrease in weight. An aircraft operating at a reduced weight is more vulnerable to rapid accelerations encountered during flight through turbulence or gusts. Design limit load factors could be exceeded if a reduction in maneuvering speed is not accomplished. An aircraft operating at or near gross weight in turbulent air is much less likely to exceed design limit load factors and may be operated at the published maneuvering speed for gross weight if necessary.

20. Define *loss-of-control-inflight* (LOC-I) and describe several situations that might increase the risk of an LOC-I accident occurring. (FAA-H-8083-3)

LOC-I is defined as a significant deviation of an aircraft from the intended flight path, and it often results from an airplane upset. Maneuvering is the most common phase of flight for LOC-I accidents to occur; however, LOC-I accidents occur in all phases of flight. Situations that increase the risk of this include uncoordinated flight, equipment malfunctions, pilot complacency, distraction, turbulence, and poor risk management, such as attempting to fly in IMC when the pilot is not qualified or proficient in it.

21. What causes an airplane to stall? (FAA-H-8083-25)

The direct cause of every stall is an excessive angle of attack. Each airplane has a particular angle of attack where the airflow separates from the upper surface of the wing and the stall occurs. This critical angle of attack varies from 16° to 20° depending on the airplane's design, but each airplane has only one specific angle of attack where the stall occurs, regardless of airspeed, weight, load factor, or density altitude.

22. What is a spin? (AC 61-67)

A spin in a small airplane or glider is a controlled (recoverable) or uncontrolled (possibly unrecoverable) maneuver in which the airplane or glider descends in a helical path while flying at an angle of attack greater than the critical angle of attack. Spins result from aggravated stalls in either a slip or a skid. If a stall does not occur, a spin cannot occur.

23. What causes a spin? (AC 61-67)

The primary cause of an inadvertent spin is exceeding the critical angle of attack while applying excessive or insufficient rudder, and to a lesser extent, aileron.

24. When are spins most likely to occur? (AC 61-67)

A stall/spin situation can occur in any phase of flight but is most likely to occur in the following situations:

a. *Engine failure on takeoff during climbout*—Pilot tries to stretch glide to landing area by increasing back pressure or makes an uncoordinated turn back to departure runway at a relatively low airspeed.

b. *Crossed-control turn from base to final (slipping or skidding turn)*—Pilot overshoots final (possibly due to a crosswind) and makes uncoordinated turn at a low airspeed.

c. *Engine failure on approach to landing*—Pilot tries to stretch glide to runway by increasing back pressure.

d. *Go-around with full nose-up trim*—Pilot applies power with full flaps and nose-up trim combined with uncoordinated use of rudder.

e. *Go-around with improper flap retraction*—Pilot applies power and retracts flaps rapidly resulting in a rapid sink rate followed by an instinctive increase in back pressure.

25. What procedure should be used to recover from an inadvertent spin? (AC 61-67)

a. Close the throttle (if not already accomplished).

b. Neutralize the ailerons.

c. Apply full opposite rudder.

d. Briskly move the elevator control forward to approximately the neutral position. (Some aircraft require merely a relaxation of back pressure; others require full forward elevator pressure).

e. Once the stall is broken the spinning will stop. Neutralize the rudder when the spinning stops.

f. When the rudder is neutralized, gradually apply enough aft elevator pressure to return to level flight.

Remember: P A R E

Power—Reduce to idle.

Ailerons—Position to neutral.

Rudder—Apply full opposite against rotation.

Elevator—Apply positive, forward of neutral, movement to break stall.

Once the spin rotation stops, neutralize the rudder, and begin applying back pressure to return to level flight.

Note: Always reference your airplane's POH/AFM for the appropriate spin recovery procedure.

26. What causes adverse yaw? (FAA-H-8083-25)

When turning an airplane to the left for example, the downward deflected aileron on the right produces more lift on the right wing. Since the downward deflected right aileron produces more lift, it also produces more drag, while the opposite left aileron has less lift and less drag. This added drag attempts to pull or veer the airplane's nose in the direction of the raised wing (right); that is, it tries to turn the airplane in the direction opposite to that desired. This undesired veering is referred to as adverse yaw.

27. What is ground effect? (FAA-H-8083-3)

Ground effect is a condition of improved performance the airplane experiences when it is operating near the ground. A change occurs in the three-dimensional flow pattern around the airplane because the airflow around the wing is restricted by the ground surface. This reduces the wing's upwash, downwash, and wingtip vortices. In order for ground effect to be of a significant magnitude, the wing must be quite close to the ground.

28. What major problems can be caused by ground effect? (FAA-H-8083-3)

During landing—At a height of approximately one-tenth of a wingspan above the surface, drag may be 40 percent less than when the airplane is operating out of ground effect. Therefore, any excess speed during the landing phase may result in a significant float distance. In such cases, if care is not exercised by the pilot, he/she may run out of runway and options at the same time.

During takeoff—Due to the reduced drag in ground effect, the aircraft may seem capable of takeoff well below the recommended speed. However, as the airplane rises out of ground effect with a deficiency of speed, the greater induced drag may result in very marginal climb performance, or the inability of the airplane to fly at all. In extreme conditions, such as high temperature, high gross weight, and high-density altitude, the airplane may become airborne initially with a deficiency of speed and then settle back to the runway.

B. Weight and Balance

1. Define the following: (FAA-H-8083-1, FAA-H-8083-25)

Empty weight—The weight of the airframe, engines, all permanently installed equipment, and unusable fuel. Depending on the FARs under which the aircraft was certificated, either the undrainable oil or full reservoir of oil is included.

Gross weight—The maximum allowable weight of both the airplane and its contents.

Useful load—The weight of the pilot, copilot, passengers, baggage, usable fuel, and drainable oil.

Arm—The horizontal distance in inches from the reference datum line to the center of gravity of the item.

Moment—The product of the weight of an item multiplied by its arm. Moments are expressed in pound-inches.

Center of gravity—The point about which aircraft would balance if it were possible to suspend it at that point. Expressed in inches from datum.

Datum—An imaginary vertical plane or line from which all measurements of arm are taken. Established by the manufacturer.

2. What basic equation is used in all weight and balance problems to find the center of gravity location of an airplane and/or its components? (FAA-H-8083-25)

Weight × Arm = Moment

By rearrangement of this equation to the forms:

Weight = Moment/Arm

Arm (CG) = (Total) Moment/(Total) Weight

With any two known values, the third value can be found.

Remember: W A M

(Weight × Arm = Moment)

3. When shifting weight from one location to another on an airplane (forward or aft), what happens to the total moments? (FAA-H-8083-25)

When weight is shifted from one location to another, the total weight of the aircraft is unchanged. The total moments, however, do change in relation and proportion to the direction and distance the weight is moved. When weight is moved forward, the total moments decrease; when weight is moved aft, total moments increase. The moment change is proportional to the amount of weight moved.

4. What is the formula for a weight shift? (FAA-H-8083-25)

$$\frac{\text{Weight shifted}}{\text{Total weight}} = \frac{\text{Change in CG}}{\text{Distance weight is shifted}}$$

5. What performance characteristics will be adversely affected when an aircraft has been overloaded? (FAA-H-8083-1)

a. Higher takeoff speed.
b. Longer takeoff run.
c. Reduced rate and angle of climb.
d. Lower maximum altitude.
e. Shorter range.
f. Reduced cruising speed.
g. Reduced maneuverability.
h. Higher stalling speed.
i. Higher landing speed.
j. Longer landing roll.
k. Excessive weight on the nosewheel.

6. What effect does a forward center of gravity have on an aircraft's flight characteristics? (FAA-H-8083-1)

Higher stall speed—Stalling angle of attack is reached at a higher speed due to increased wing loading.

Slower cruise speed—Increased drag; greater angle of attack is required to maintain altitude.

More stable—The center of gravity is farther forward from the center of pressure which increases longitudinal stability.

Greater back elevator pressure required—Longer takeoff roll; higher approach speeds and problems with landing flare.

7. What effect does a rearward center of gravity have on an aircraft's flight characteristics? (FAA-H-8083-1)

Lower stall speed—Less wing loading.

Higher cruise speed—Reduced drag; smaller angle of attack is required to maintain altitude.

Less stable—Stall and spin recovery more difficult; the center of gravity is closer to the center of pressure, causing longitudinal instability.

8. What are the standard weights assumed for the following when calculating weight and balance problems? (FAA-H-8083-25, AC 120-27)

Crew and passengers	190 lbs each
AvGas	6 lbs/U.S. gal
Jet A	6.75 lbs/U.S. gal
Oil	7.5 lbs/U.S. gal
Water	8.35 lbs/U.S. gal

9. The rental aircraft you normally fly has just returned from the avionics shop with newer, lighter-weight avionics. When reviewing the aircraft weight and balance record, you don't see an A&P entry reflecting this change. Is this normal? Why? (FAA-H-8083-1)

No. Changes of fixed equipment may have a major effect upon the weight of the aircraft. Many aircraft are overloaded by the installation of extra radios or instruments. Fortunately, the replacement of older, heavy electronic equipment with newer, lighter types results in a weight reduction. This weight change, however helpful, can cause the CG to shift, which must be computed and annotated in the weight and balance record. It is the responsibility of the A&P mechanic or technician making any repair or alteration to know the weight and location of these changes, and to compute the CG and record the new empty weight and empty weight center of gravity (EWCG) in the aircraft weight and balance record.

Exam Tip: When reviewing your weight and balance computations, the examiner may ask to see the aircraft document you referenced to obtain the aircraft's actual weight and balance data (empty weight, moment, etc.) for the aircraft (make, model, serial number) used for the test. Make sure that you have that information readily available and that it represents the aircraft's most recent/current weight and balance data.

C. Aircraft Performance

1. What are some of the main elements of aircraft performance? (FAA-H-8083-25)

a. Takeoff and landing distance.
b. Rate of climb.
c. Ceiling.
d. Payload.
e. Range.
f. Speed.
g. Fuel economy.
h. Maneuverability.
i. Stability.

2. What factors affect the performance of an aircraft during takeoffs and landings? (FAA-H-8083-25)

a. Air density (density altitude).
b. Surface wind.
c. Runway surface.
d. Upslope or downslope of runway.
e. Weight.

3. What effect does wind have on aircraft performance? (FAA-H-8083-25)

Takeoff—The effect of a headwind is to allow the aircraft to reach the lift-off speed at a lower ground speed, which will increase airplane performance by shortening the takeoff distance and increasing the angle of climb. The effect of a tailwind is the aircraft needs to achieve greater ground speed to get to lift-off speed. This decreases aircraft performance by increasing takeoff distance and reducing the angle of climb.

Landing—The effect of wind on landing distance is identical to its effect on takeoff distance. A headwind will lower ground speed and increase airplane performance by steepening the approach angle and reducing the landing distance. A tailwind will increase ground speed and decrease performance, by decreasing the approach angle and increasing the landing distance.

Cruise flight—Winds aloft have somewhat an opposite effect on airplane performance. A headwind will decrease performance by reducing ground speed, which in turn increases the fuel requirement for the flight. A tailwind will increase performance by increasing the ground speed, which in turn reduces the fuel requirement for the flight.

4. How does weight affect takeoff and landing performance? (FAA-H-8083-25)

Increased gross weight can have a significant effect on takeoff performance:

a. Higher liftoff speed;
b. Greater mass to accelerate (slow acceleration);
c. Increased retarding force (drag and ground friction); and
d. Longer takeoff distance.

The effect of gross weight on landing distance is that the airplane will require a greater speed to support the airplane at the landing angle of attack and lift coefficient resulting in an increased landing distance.

5. What effect does an increase in density altitude have on takeoff and landing performance? (FAA-P-8740-2)

An increase in density altitude results in:

a. Increased takeoff distance (greater takeoff TAS required).
b. Reduced rate of climb (decreased thrust and reduced acceleration).
c. Increased true airspeed on approach and landing (same IAS).
d. Increased landing roll distance.

6. Define the term *density altitude*. (FAA-H-8083-25)

Density altitude is pressure altitude corrected for nonstandard temperature. Under standard atmospheric conditions, air at each level in the atmosphere has a specific density, and under standard conditions, pressure altitude and density altitude identify the same level. Therefore, density altitude is the vertical distance above sea level in the standard atmosphere at which a given density is found.

7. How does air density affect aircraft performance? (FAA-H-8083-25)

The density of the air has a direct effect on:

a. Lift produced by the wings;
b. Power output of the engine;
c. Propeller efficiency; and
d. Drag forces.

8. What factors affect air density? (FAA-P-8740-2)

Altitude—The higher the altitude, the less dense the air.

Temperature—The warmer the air, the less dense it is.

Humidity—More humid air is less dense.

9. How do temperature, altitude, and humidity affect density altitude? (FAA-P-8740-2)

a. Density altitude will increase (low air density) when one or more of the following occurs:
   • High air temperature
   • High altitude
   • High humidity

b. Density altitude will decrease (high air density) when one or more of the following occurs:
   • Low air temperature
   • Low altitude
   • Low humidity

10. Know the following speeds for your airplane!

V_{S0}—Stall speed in landing configuration; the calibrated power-off stalling speed or the minimum steady flight speed at which the airplane is controllable in the landing configuration.

V_{S1}—Stall speed clean or in specified configuration; the calibrated power-off stalling speed or the minimum steady flight speed at which the airplane is controllable in a specified configuration.

V_Y—Best rate-of-climb speed; the calibrated airspeed at which the airplane will obtain the maximum increase in altitude per unit of time. This best rate-of-climb speed normally decreases slightly with altitude.

V_X—Best angle-of-climb speed; the calibrated airspeed at which the airplane will obtain the highest altitude in a given horizontal distance. This best angle-of-climb speed normally increases with altitude.

V_{LE}—Maximum landing gear extension speed; the maximum calibrated airspeed at which the airplane can be safely flown with the landing gear extended. This is a problem involving stability and controllability.

V_{LO}—Maximum landing gear operating speed; the maximum calibrated airspeed at which the landing gear can be safely extended or retracted. This is a problem involving the air loads imposed on the operating mechanism during extension or retraction of the gear.

V_{FE}—Maximum flap extension speed; the highest calibrated airspeed permissible with the wing flaps in a prescribed extended position. This is a problem involving the air loads imposed on the structure of the flaps.

V_A—Maneuvering speed; the calibrated design maneuvering airspeed. This is the maximum speed at which the limit load can be imposed (either by gusts or full deflection of the control surfaces) without causing structural damage.

V_{NO}—Normal operating speed; the maximum calibrated airspeed for normal operation or the maximum structural cruise speed. This is the speed above which exceeding the limit load factor may cause permanent deformation of the airplane structure.

V_{NE}—Never exceed speed; the calibrated airspeed which should never be exceeded. If flight is attempted above this speed, structural damage or structural failure may result.

11. Explain the difference between best glide speed and minimum sink speed. (FAA-H-8083-3)

Best glide speed—The speed and configuration that provides the greatest forward distance for a given loss of altitude. In most airplanes, best glide airspeed will be roughly halfway between V_X (best angle of climb speed) and V_Y (best rate of climb speed).

Minimum sink speed—Used to maximize the time that the airplane remains in flight. Use of minimum sink speed results in the airplane losing altitude at the lowest rate. It is important that pilots realize that flight at the minimum sink airspeed results in less distance traveled and is useful in flight situations where time in flight is more important than distance flown (e.g., more time to fix problem, ditching at sea). Minimum sink speed is not an often-published airspeed but generally is a few knots less than best glide speed.

12. How many miles can you glide in your aircraft per 1,000 feet of altitude lost? (POH/AFM)

A rule of thumb for Cessna 152s and 172s is 1.5 NM per 1,000 feet of altitude lost above ground level. Reference your aircraft's POH/AFM and also consider experimenting to determine how far your aircraft can glide.

13. During flight planning, explain how to determine the time, fuel, and distance to climb for the departure leg of the flight plan. (FAA-H-8083-25)

The chart to check for climb performance is the time, fuel, and distance-to-climb chart. This chart will give the time it will take to accomplish the climb, the fuel amount used during the climb, and the ground distance that will be covered during the climb. To use this chart, obtain the information for the departing airport and for the cruise altitude.

14. During flight planning, explain how to determine the planned TAS and fuel burn (GPH) during cruise flight. (FAA-H-8083-25)

The aircraft's POH/AFM provides cruise and range performance charts which are designed to give TAS, fuel consumption, endurance in hours, and range in miles at specific cruise configurations and under the specified conditions. Select the pressure altitude and temperature that is closest to the planned altitude and expected temperature. Choose the planned engine speed to obtain power, true airspeed, and cruise fuel flow numbers.

15. Explain the factors that affect the airplane's rate of fuel consumption. (FAA-H-8083-25)

The rate of fuel consumption depends on many factors: condition of the engine, propeller RPM, richness of the mixture, and the percentage of horsepower used for flight at cruising speed.

16. What information can you obtain from the following charts? (FAA-H-8083-25)

a. *Takeoff charts*—These allow you to compute the takeoff distance of the airplane with no flaps or with a specific flap configuration. You can also compute distances for a no flap takeoff over a 50-foot obstacle scenario as well as with flaps over a 50-foot obstacle. The takeoff distance chart provides for various airplane weights, altitudes, temperatures, winds, and obstacle heights.

b. *Crosswind and headwind component chart*—This allows for figuring the headwind and crosswind component for any given wind direction and velocity.

c. *Landing charts*—Provide normal landing distance as well as landing distance over a 50-foot obstacle.

d. *Stall speed performance charts*—These are designed to give an understanding of the speed at which the airplane will stall in a given configuration. It will typically take into account the angle of bank, the position of the gear and flaps, and the throttle position.

17. Define the term *pressure altitude*, and state why it is important. (FAA-H-8083-3)

Pressure altitude—The altitude indicated when the altimeter setting window (barometric scale) is adjusted to 29.92 inHg. This is the altitude above the standard datum plane, a theoretical plane where air pressure (corrected to 15°C) equals 29.92 inHg. Pressure altitude is used to compute density altitude, true altitude, true airspeed, and other performance data.

18. The following questions are designed to provide pilots with a general review of the basic information they should know about their specific airplane before taking a flight check or review.

1. *What is the normal climb-out speed?*

2. *What is the best rate-of-climb speed?*

3. *What is the best angle-of-climb speed?*

4. *What is the maximum flap extension speed?*

5. *What is the maximum gear extension speed?*

6. *What is the stall speed in the normal landing configuration?*

7. *What is the stall speed in the clean configuration?*

8. *What is the normal approach-to-land speed?*

9. *What is maneuvering speed?*

10. *What is red-line speed?*

11. *What engine-out glide speed will give you maximum range?*

12. *What is the make and horsepower of the engine?*

13. *How many usable gallons of fuel can you carry?*

14. *Where are the fuel tanks located, and what are their capacities?*

15. *Where are the fuel vents for your aircraft?*

16. *What is the octane rating of the fuel used by your aircraft?*

17. *Where are the fuel sumps located on your aircraft? When should you drain them?*

18. *What are the minimum and maximum oil capacities?*

19. *What weight of oil is being used?*

20. *What is the maximum oil temperature and pressure?*

21. *Do the aircraft avionics have any limitations placed on them?*

22. *What limitations does the autopilot have?*

23. *What are the nosewheel turning limitations for your aircraft?*

24. *What is the maximum allowable/demonstrated crosswind component for the aircraft?*

25. *How many people will this aircraft carry safely with a full fuel load?*

26. *What is the maximum allowable weight the aircraft can carry with baggage in the baggage compartment?*

27. *What takeoff distance is required if a takeoff were made from a sea-level pressure altitude?*

28. *What is your maximum allowable useful load?*

29. *Solve a weight and balance problem for the flight you plan to make with one passenger at 170 pounds.*

 a. *Does your load fall within the weight and balance envelope?*

 b. *What is the final gross weight?*

 c. *How much fuel can be carried?*

 d. *How much baggage can be carried with full fuel?*

 e. *Know the function of the various types of antennae on your aircraft.*

Exam Tip: Make sure to perform a weight and balance calculation for both departure and arrival fuel weights to ensure the aircraft remains within the CG envelope for the entire flight.

Additional Study Questions

1. **You have just landed on a 2,100-foot grass strip to pick up two passengers and you plan to depart in the early afternoon. The temperature will be warmer than expected, so you compute the density altitude and determine that the required takeoff distance over a 50-foot obstacle will be 2,000 feet. Your weight and balance calculation indicates you will be 100 pounds under gross weight. If you decide to take off, explain the potential hazards, the overall risk, and the actions you could take to mitigate that risk.** (FAA-H-8083-2)

2. **Why are some aircraft not allowed to perform forward slips with flaps extended?** (AFM)

3. While enroute, will the CG change as your aircraft uses fuel? (FAA-H-8083-25)

4. What causes an airplane (except a T-tail) to pitch nose down when power is reduced and controls are not adjusted? (FAA-H-8083-25)

5. Will the indicated airspeed at which an aircraft stalls change as altitude is increased? (FAA-H-8083-25)

6. What force causes an airplane to turn? (FAA-H-8083-25)

7. The amount of excess load that can be imposed on the structure of an airplane is dependent on what factor? (FAA-H-8083-25)

8. Define the terms *service ceiling* and *absolute ceiling*. What are their values for your aircraft? (FAA-H-8083-25)

9. The performance chart numbers for your aircraft are based on test flights conducted in a new aircraft. During preflight planning, how can a pilot minimize risk when using the charts to make performance calculations for takeoff, enroute cruise, and landing? (FAA-H-8083-25)

10. You're planning a VFR departure from Durango Colorado KDRO (elevation 6,689 feet MSL) in a Cessna 172. Explain the potential hazards that exist when departing KDRO as compared to departing KLAX (elevation 127 feet MSL). Is there anything you can do to mitigate the risk? (FAA-H-8083-2)

Operation of Systems

7

Notice: Some of the following questions reference the systems of a Cessna 152. Be sure to review your aircraft's POH/AFM for specific information regarding the systems in your aircraft type.

A. Aircraft and Engine Operations

1. What are the four main control surfaces and what are their functions? (FAA-H-8083-25)

Elevators—The elevators control the movement of the airplane about its lateral axis. This motion is called pitch.

Ailerons—The ailerons control the airplane's movement about its longitudinal axis. This motion is called roll.

Rudder—The rudder controls movement of the airplane about its vertical axis. This motion is called yaw.

Trim tabs—Trim tabs are small, adjustable hinged-surfaces on the aileron, rudder, or elevator control surfaces. They are labor-saving devices that enable the pilot to release manual pressure on the primary control.

2. How are the various flight controls operated? (POH/AFM)

The flight control surfaces are manually actuated through use of either a rod or cable system. A control wheel actuates the ailerons and elevator, and rudder/brake pedals actuate the rudder.

3. What are flaps and what is their function? (FAA-H-8083-25)

The wing flaps are movable panels on the inboard trailing edges of the wings. They are hinged so that they may be extended downward into the flow of air beneath the wings to increase both lift and drag. Their purpose is to permit a slower airspeed and a steeper angle of descent during a landing approach. In some cases, they may also be used to shorten the takeoff distance.

4. Describe the landing gear system on this airplane. (POH/AFM)

The landing gear consists of a tricycle-type system utilizing two main wheels and a steerable nosewheel. Tubular spring steel main gear struts provide main gear shock absorption, while nose gear shock absorption is provided by a combination air/oil shock strut.

5. Describe the braking system on this aircraft. (POH/AFM)

Hydraulically actuated disc-type brakes are utilized on each main gear wheel. A hydraulic line connects each brake to a master cylinder located on each pilot's rudder pedals. By applying pressure to the top of either the pilot's or copilot's set of rudder pedals, the brakes may be applied.

6. What type of hydraulic fluid does your aircraft use and what color is it? (FAA-H-8083-25, FAA-H-8083-31)

Refer to your POH/AFM; a mineral-based hydraulic fluid (MIL-H-5606) is the most widely used type for small aircraft. It has an odor similar to penetrating oil and is dyed red. A newer, fire-resistant fluid (MIL-H-83282) is also used in small aircraft and is dyed red.

7. How is steering accomplished on the ground? (POH/AFM)

Light airplanes are generally provided with nosewheel steering capabilities through a simple system of mechanical linkage connected to the rudder pedals. When a rudder pedal is depressed, a spring-loaded bungee (push-pull rod) connected to the pivotal portion of a nosewheel strut will turn the nosewheel.

8. What type of engine does your aircraft have? (POH/AFM)

A normally aspirated, direct drive, air-cooled, horizontally opposed, four-cylinder, overhead-valve, carbureted engine. The engine is manufactured by Lycoming and rated at 110 HP.

9. What four strokes must occur in each cylinder of a typical four stroke engine in order for it to produce full power? (FAA-H-8083-25)

The four strokes are:

Intake—Begins as the piston starts its downward travel causing the intake valve to open and the fuel-air mixture to be drawn into the cylinder.

Compression—Begins when the intake valve closes, and the piston starts moving back to the top of the cylinder. This phase of the cycle is used to obtain a much greater power output from the fuel-air mixture once it is ignited.

Power—Begins when the fuel-air mixture is ignited which causes a tremendous pressure increase in the cylinder and forces the piston downward away from the cylinder head, creating the power that turns the crankshaft.

Exhaust—Used to purge the cylinder of burned gases and begins when the exhaust valve opens, and the piston starts to move toward the cylinder head once again.

Remember: Suck, squeeze, bang, blow.

10. What is the purpose of a carburetor? (FAA-H-8083-25)

Carburetion may be defined as the process of mixing fuel and air in the correct proportions so as to form a combustible mixture. The carburetor vaporizes liquid fuel into small particles and then mixes it with air. It measures the airflow and meters fuel accordingly.

11. Explain how the carburetor heat system operates. (POH/AFM)

A carburetor heat valve, controlled by the pilot, allows unfiltered, heated air from a shroud located around an exhaust riser or muffler to be directed to the induction air manifold prior to the carburetor. Carburetor heat should be used anytime suspected or known carburetor icing conditions exist.

12. What change occurs to the fuel/air mixture when applying carburetor heat? (FAA-H-8083-25)

Normally, the introduction of heated air into the carburetor will result in a richer mixture. Warm air is less dense, resulting in less air for the same amount of fuel. Use of carburetor heat can cause a decrease in engine power of up to 15 percent.

13. What is the purpose of the throttle control? (FAA-H-8083-25)

The throttle allows the pilot to manually control the amount of fuel/air charge entering the cylinders. This in turn regulates the engine speed and power.

14. What is the purpose of the mixture control?
(FAA-H-8083-25)

It regulates the fuel-to-air ratio. All airplane engines incorporate a device called a mixture control, by which the fuel/air ratio can be controlled by the pilot during flight. The purpose of a mixture control is to prevent the mixture from becoming too rich at high altitudes, due to decreasing air density. It is also used to lean the mixture during cross-country flights to conserve fuel and provide optimum power.

15. Describe a fuel injection system installed in some aircraft. (FAA-H-8083-25)

The fuel injection system injects fuel directly into the cylinders, or just ahead of the intake valve. It incorporates six basic components:

a. *Engine-driven fuel pump*—Provides fuel under pressure from the fuel tank to the fuel/air control unit.

b. *Fuel/air control unit*—Meters fuel based on the mixture control setting and sends it to the fuel manifold valve at a rate controlled by the throttle.

c. *Fuel manifold valve*—Distributes fuel to the individual fuel discharge nozzles.

d. *Discharge nozzles*—Located in each cylinder head, these inject the fuel/air mixture at the precise time for each cylinder directly into each cylinder intake port.

e. *Auxiliary fuel pump*—Provides fuel under pressure to fuel/air control unit for engine starting and/or emergency use.

f. *Fuel pressure/flow indicators*—Measures metered fuel pressure/flow.

16. What type of ignition system does your airplane have?
(POH/AFM)

Engine ignition is provided by two engine-driven magnetos, and two spark plugs per cylinder. The ignition system is completely independent of the aircraft electrical system. The magnetos are engine-driven self-contained units supplying electrical current without using an external source of current. However, before they can produce current, the magnetos must be actuated, as the engine crankshaft is rotated by some other means. To accomplish this, the aircraft battery furnishes electrical power to operate a starter which, through a series of gears, rotates the engine crankshaft. This in turn actuates the armature of the magneto to produce the sparks for ignition of the fuel in each cylinder. After the engine starts, the starter system is disengaged, and the battery no longer contributes to the actual operation of the engine.

17. What are the two main advantages of a dual ignition system? (FAA-H-8083-25)

a. Increased safety, in case one system fails the engine may be operated on the other until a landing is safely made.

b. More complete and even combustion of the mixture, and consequently, improved engine performance, i.e., the fuel/air mixture will be ignited on each side of the combustion chamber and burn toward the center.

18. What type of fuel system does your aircraft have? (POH/AFM)

The fuel system is a gravity feed system. Using gravity, the fuel flows from two wing fuel tanks to a fuel shutoff valve that, in the On position, allows fuel to flow through a strainer and then to the carburetor. From there, the fuel is mixed with air and then flows into the cylinders through the intake manifold tubes.

19. What purpose do the fuel tank vents have? (POH/AFM)

As the fuel level in an aircraft fuel tank decreases, a vacuum would be created within the tank which would eventually result in a decreasing fuel flow and finally engine stoppage. Fuel system venting provides a way of replacing fuel with outside air, preventing formation of a vacuum.

20. Does your aircraft use a fuel pump? (POH/AFM)

No, the fuel is transferred from the wing tanks to the carburetor by the gravity feed system. The gravity system does not require a fuel pump because the fuel is always under positive pressure to the carburetor. For some aircraft where for some reason it is not possible to place the wings above the carburetor, or for which a greater pressure is required than what gravity feed can supply, it is necessary to utilize engine-driven fuel pumps and auxiliary fuel pumps as backups.

21. What type of fuel does your aircraft require (minimum octane rating and color)? (POH/AFM)

The approved fuel grade used is 100LL and the color is blue.

22. Can other types of fuel be used if the specified grade is not available? (FAA-H-8083-25)

Airplane engines are designed to operate using a specific grade of fuel as recommended by the manufacturer. If the proper grade of fuel is not available, it is possible, but not desirable, to use the next higher grade as a substitute. Always reference the aircraft's POH/AFM. Auto gas should *never* be used in aircraft engines unless the aircraft has been modified with an FAA-issued Supplemental Type Certificate (STC).

23. What color of dye is added to the following fuel grades: 80, 100, 100LL, Jet A? (FAA-H-8083-25, FAA-P-8740-35)

Grade	Color
80 (obsolete)	Red
100 (obsolete)	Green
100LL	Blue
Jet A	Colorless or Straw

24. If a non-turbine piston engine powered airplane is accidentally fueled with Jet A fuel, will it start? (FAA-H-8083-25, FAA-P-8740-35)

Yes. Reciprocating engines may run briefly on jet fuel, but detonation and overheating will soon cause power failure. When an aircraft that requires Avgas is inadvertently fueled with Jet A, there is usually a small amount of Avgas remaining in the aircraft's fuel system (tanks, fuel lines, carburetor, etc.). This remaining fuel can enable an aircraft to taxi, perform an engine run-up, and possibly even take off before experiencing a catastrophic engine failure.

Note: Other than the kerosene smell and the oily feel when rubbed between the fingers, it can be very difficult to visually identify an accidental mixture of 100LL Avgas (blue) and Jet A (straw color).

25. What is the function of the manual primer, and how does it operate? (POH/AFM)

The manual primer's main function is to provide assistance in starting the engine. The primer draws fuel from the fuel strainer and injects it directly into the cylinder intake ports. This usually results in a quicker, more efficient engine start.

26. Describe the electrical system on your aircraft. (POH/AFM)

Electrical energy is provided by a 28-volt, direct-current system powered by an engine-driven 60-amp alternator and a 24-volt battery.

27. How are the circuits for the various electrical accessories within the aircraft protected? (POH/AFM)

Most of the electrical circuits in an airplane are protected from an overload condition by either circuit breakers or fuses or both. Circuit breakers perform the same function as fuses except that when an overload occurs, a circuit breaker can be reset.

28. The electrical system provides power for what equipment in the airplane? (POH/AFM)

Normally, the following:
a. Radio equipment
b. Turn coordinator
c. Fuel gauges
d. Pitot heat
e. Landing light
f. Taxi light
g. Strobe lights
h. Interior lights
i. Instrument lights
j. Position lights
k. Flaps (maybe)
l. Stall warning system (maybe)
m. Oil temperature gauge
n. Electric fuel pump (maybe)

29. What does the ammeter indicate? (POH/AFM)

The ammeter indicates the flow of current, in amperes, from the alternator to the battery or from the battery to the electrical system. With the engine running and master switch on, the ammeter will indicate the charging rate to the battery. If the alternator has gone off-line and is no longer functioning, or the electrical load exceeds the output of the alternator, the ammeter indicates the discharge rate of the battery.

30. What function does the voltage regulator have? (POH/AFM)

The voltage regulator is a device which monitors system voltage, detects changes, and makes the required adjustments in the output of the alternator to maintain a constant regulated system voltage. It must do this at low RPM, such as during taxi, as well as at high RPM in flight. In a 28-volt system, it will maintain 28 volts ±0.5 volts.

31. Why is the generator/alternator voltage output slightly higher than the battery voltage? (FAA-H-8083-25)

The difference in voltage keeps the battery charged. For example, a 12-volt battery would be supplied with 14 volts.

32. How does the aircraft cabin heat work? (POH/AFM)

Fresh air, heated by an exhaust shroud, is directed to the cabin through a series of ducts.

33. How does the pilot control the temperature in the cabin? (POH/AFM)

Temperature is controlled by mixing outside air (cabin air control) with heated air (cabin heat control) in a manifold near the cabin firewall. This air is then ducted to vents located on the cabin floor.

34. What are the five basic functions of aircraft engine oil? (FAA-H-8083-25)

Lubricates the engine's moving parts.
Cools the engine by reducing friction.
Removes heat from the cylinders.
Seals provide a seal between the cylinder walls and pistons.
Cleans by carrying off metal and carbon particles and other oil contaminants.

B. System and Equipment Malfunctions

1. What causes carburetor icing, and what are the first indications of its presence? (FAA-H-8083-25)

The vaporization of fuel, combined with the expansion of air as it passes through the carburetor, causes a sudden cooling of the mixture. The temperature of the air passing through the carburetor may drop as much as 60°F within a fraction of a second. Water vapor is squeezed out by this cooling, and if the temperature in the carburetor reaches 32°F or below, the moisture will be deposited as frost or ice inside the carburetor. For airplanes with a fixed-pitch propeller, the first indication of carburetor icing is loss of RPM. For airplanes with controllable-pitch (constant-speed) propellers, the first indication is usually a drop in manifold pressure.

2. What method is used to determine that carburetor ice has been eliminated? (FAA-H-8083-25)

When heat is first applied, there will be a drop in RPM in airplanes equipped with a fixed-pitch propeller; there will be a drop in manifold pressure in airplanes equipped with a controllable-pitch propeller. If ice is present there will be a rise in RPM or manifold pressure after the initial drop (often accompanied by intermittent engine roughness); and then, when the carburetor heat is turned off, the RPM or manifold pressure will rise to a setting greater than that before application of heat. The engine should run more smoothly after the ice has been removed.

3. What conditions are favorable for carburetor icing? (FAA-H-8083-25)

Carburetor ice is most likely to occur when temperatures are below 70°F (21°C) and the relative humidity is above 80 percent. However, due to the sudden cooling that takes place in the carburetor, icing can occur even with temperatures as high as 100°F (38°C) and humidity as low as 50 percent. This temperature drop can be as much as 60° to 70°F.

4. Define the terms *anti-icing equipment* and *deicing equipment* and state several examples of each.
(FAA-H-8083-3; FAA-H-8083-25)

Anti-icing equipment—Prevents ice from forming on certain protected surfaces. Examples are heated pitot tubes and static ports, carburetor heat, heated fuel vents, propeller blades with electro-thermal boots, and heated windshields. It is normally actuated prior to flight into suspected icing conditions. Reference your POH/AFM.

Deicing equipment—Removes ice that has already formed on protected surfaces. It is generally limited to pneumatic boots on the wing and tail leading edges.

5. Describe how an aircraft deicing system works.
(FAA-H-8083-3)

Upon pilot actuation, boots attached to the wing leading edges inflate with air from a pneumatic pump(s) to break off accumulated ice. After a few seconds of inflation, they are deflated back to their normal position with vacuum assistance. The pilot monitors the buildup of ice and cycles the boots as directed in the POH/AFM.

6. If an airplane has anti-icing and/or deicing equipment installed, can it be flown into icing conditions?
(FAA-H-8083-3)

Even though it may appear elaborate and complete, the presence of anti-icing and deicing equipment does not necessarily mean that an airplane is approved for flight in icing conditions. The POH/AFM, placards, and even the manufacturer should be consulted for specific determination of approvals and limitations.

7. What is detonation? (FAA-H-8083-25)

Detonation is an uncontrolled, explosive ignition of the fuel/air mixture within the cylinder's combustion chamber. It causes excessive temperature and pressure which, if not corrected, can quickly lead to failure of the piston, cylinder, or valves. In less severe cases, detonation causes engine overheating, roughness, or loss of power. Detonation is characterized by high cylinder head temperatures and is most likely to occur when operating at high power settings.

8. **What are some of the most common operational causes of detonation?** (FAA-8083-25)

   a. Using a lower fuel grade than that specified by the aircraft manufacturer.

   b. Operating with extremely high manifold pressures in conjunction with low RPM.

   c. Operating the engine at high power settings with an excessively lean mixture.

   d. Extended ground operations or steep climbs where cylinder cooling is reduced.

9. **What action should be taken if detonation is suspected?** (FAA-H-8083-25)

   Detonation may be avoided by following these basic guidelines during the various phases of ground and flight operations:

   a. Ensure that the proper grade of fuel is used.

   b. Keep the cowl flaps (if available) in the full-open position while on the ground to provide the maximum airflow through the cowling.

   c. Use an enriched fuel mixture, as well as a shallow climb angle, to increase cylinder cooling during takeoff and initial climb.

   d. Avoid extended, high power, steep climbs.

   e. Develop the habit of monitoring the engine instruments to verify proper operation according to procedures established by the manufacturer.

10. **What is preignition?** (FAA-H-8083-25)

    Preignition occurs when the fuel/air mixture ignites prior to the engine's normal ignition event resulting in reduced engine power and high operating temperatures. Premature burning is usually caused by a residual hot spot in the combustion chamber, often created by a small carbon deposit on a spark plug, a cracked spark plug insulator, or other damage in the cylinder that causes a part to heat sufficiently to ignite the fuel/air charge. As with detonation, preignition may also cause severe engine damage, because the expanding gases exert excessive pressure on the piston while still on its compression stroke.

11. What action should be taken if preignition is suspected? (FAA-H-8083-25)

Corrective actions for preignition include any type of engine operation which would promote cooling such as:

a. Reduce power.

b. Reduce the climb rate for better cooling.

c. Enrich the fuel/air mixture.

d. Open cowl flaps if available.

12. During the before-takeoff runup, you switch the magnetos from the BOTH position to the RIGHT position and notice there is no RPM drop. What condition does this indicate?

The left P-lead is not grounding, or the engine has been running only on the right magneto because the left magneto has totally failed.

13. Interpret the following ammeter indications.

a. Ammeter indicates a right deflection (positive).

- *After starting*—Power from the battery used for starting is being replenished by the alternator; or, if a full-scale charge is indicated for more than 1 minute, the starter is still engaged, and a shutdown is indicated.
- *During flight*—A faulty voltage regulator is causing the alternator to overcharge the battery. Reset the system and if the condition continues, terminate the flight as soon as possible.

b. Ammeter indicates a left deflection (negative).

- *After starting*—It is normal during start. At other times this indicates the alternator is not functioning or an overload condition exists in the system. The battery is not receiving a charge.
- *During flight*—The alternator is not functioning, or an overload exists in the system. The battery is not receiving a charge. Possible causes: the master switch was accidentally shut off, or the alternator circuit breaker tripped.

14. What action should be taken if the ammeter indicates a continuous discharge while in flight?

The alternator has quit producing a charge, so the alternator circuit breaker should be checked and reset if necessary. If this does not correct the problem, the following should be accomplished:

a. The alternator should be turned off; pull the circuit breaker (the field circuit will continue to draw power from the battery).

b. All electrical equipment not essential to flight should be turned off (the battery is now the only source of electrical power).

c. The flight should be terminated, and a landing made as soon as possible.

15. What action should be taken if the ammeter indicates a continuous charge while in flight (more than two needle widths)?

If a continuous excessive rate of charge were allowed for any extended period of time, the battery would overheat and evaporate the electrolyte at an excessive rate. A possible explosion of the battery could result. Also, electronic components in the electrical system would be adversely affected by higher than normal voltage. Protection is provided by an overvoltage sensor which will shut the alternator down if an excessive voltage is detected. If this should occur the following should be done:

a. The alternator should be turned off; pull the circuit breaker (the field circuit will continue to draw power from the battery).

b. All electrical equipment not essential to flight should be turned off (the battery is now the only source of electrical power).

c. The flight should be terminated, and a landing made as soon as possible.

Exam tip: Expect the examiner to test your knowledge of the aircraft's electrical system by asking several "what if" type of questions such as: What if your alternator failed in flight? What systems, instruments and equipment would be operative/ inoperative? After an alternator failure, what systems and equipment will the battery supply power to? How long will the battery supply power? When the battery finally dies, will the engine continue to operate? You get the idea; know your aircraft's electrical system well.

16. **During a cross-country flight you notice that the oil pressure is low, but the oil temperature is normal. What is the problem and what action should be taken?**

A low oil pressure in flight could be the result of any one of several problems, the most common being that of insufficient oil. If the oil temperature continues to remain normal, a clogged oil pressure relief valve or an oil pressure gauge malfunction could be the culprit. In any case, a landing at the nearest airport is advisable to check for the cause of trouble.

17. **What procedures should be followed concerning a partial loss of power in flight?** (POH/AFM)

If a partial loss of power occurs, the first priority is to establish and maintain a suitable airspeed (best glide airspeed if necessary). Then, select an emergency landing area and remain within gliding distance. As time allows, attempt to determine the cause and correct it.

Complete the following checklist:

a. Check the carburetor heat.

b. Check the amount of fuel in each tank and switch fuel tanks if necessary.

c. Check the fuel selector valve's current position.

d. Check the mixture control.

e. Check that the primer control is all the way in and locked.

f. Check the operation of the magnetos in all three positions; both, left, or right.

18. **What procedures should be followed if an engine fire develops in flight?** (POH/AFM)

In the event of an engine fire in flight, the following procedures should be used:

a. Set the mixture control to Idle cutoff.

b. Set the fuel selector valve to Off.

c. Turn the master switch to Off.

d. Set the cabin heat and air vents to Off; leave the overhead vents On.

(continued)

e. Establish an airspeed of 100 KIAS and increase the descent, if necessary, to find an airspeed that will provide for an incombustible mixture.

f. Execute a forced landing procedures checklist.

19. What procedures should be followed if an engine fire develops on the ground during starting? (POH/AFM)

Continue to attempt an engine start as a start will cause flames and excess fuel to be sucked back through the carburetor.

a. If the engine starts:
  • Increase the power to a higher RPM for a few moments; and
  • Shut down the engine and inspect it.

b. If the engine does not start:
  • Set the throttle to the Full position.
  • Set the mixture control to Idle cutoff.
  • Continue to try an engine start in an attempt to put out the fire by vacuum.

c. If the fire continues:
  • Turn the ignition switch to Off.
  • Turn the master switch to Off.
  • Set the fuel selector to Off.

In all cases, evacuate the aircraft and obtain a fire extinguisher and/or assistance.

C. Pitot/Static Flight Instruments

1. What instruments operate off of the pitot/static system? (FAA-H-8083-15)

Altimeter, vertical speed, and airspeed indicator.

2. How does an altimeter work? (FAA-H-8083-15)

A sensitive altimeter is an aneroid barometer that measures the absolute pressure of the ambient air and displays it in terms of feet above a selected pressure level. The sensitive element in a sensitive altimeter is a stack of evacuated, corrugated bronze aneroid capsules. The air pressure acting on these aneroids tries to compress them against their natural springiness, which tries to expand them. The result is that their thickness changes as the air pressure changes. Stacking several aneroids increases the dimension change as the pressure varies over the usable range of the instrument.

3. What are the limitations of a pressure altimeter? (FAA-H-8083-15)

Nonstandard pressure and temperature; temperature variations expand or contract the atmosphere and raise or lower pressure levels that the altimeter senses.

On a warm day—The pressure level is higher than on a standard day. The altimeter indicates lower than actual altitude.

On a cold day—The pressure level is lower than on a standard day. The altimeter indicates higher than actual altitude.

Changes in surface pressure also affect pressure levels at altitude.

Higher than standard pressure—The pressure level is higher than on a standard day. The altimeter indicates lower than actual altitude.

Lower than standard pressure—The pressure level is lower than on a standard day. The altimeter indicates higher than actual altitude.

Remember: High to low or hot to cold, look out below!

4. Define and state how you would determine the following altitudes: absolute, indicated, pressure, true, and density. (FAA-H-8083-25)

Absolute altitude—The vertical distance of an aircraft above the terrain.

Indicated altitude—The altitude read directly from the altimeter (uncorrected) after it is set to the current altimeter setting.

Pressure altitude—The altitude when the altimeter setting window is adjusted to 29.92. Pressure altitude is used for computer solutions to determine density altitude, true altitude, true airspeed, etc.

True altitude—The true vertical distance of the aircraft above sea level. Airport, terrain, and obstacle elevations found on aeronautical charts are true altitudes.

Density altitude—Pressure altitude corrected for nonstandard temperature variations. Directly related to an aircraft's takeoff, climb, and landing performance.

5. How does the airspeed indicator operate?
(FAA-H-8083-25)

The airspeed indicator is a sensitive, differential pressure gauge which measures the difference between impact pressure from the pitot head and undisturbed atmospheric pressure from the static source. The difference is registered by the airspeed pointer on the face of the instrument.

6. What is the limitation of the airspeed indicator?
(FAA-H-8083-15)

The airspeed indicator is subject to proper flow of air in the pitot/static system.

7. What are the errors of the airspeed indicator?

Position error—Caused by the static ports sensing erroneous static pressure; slipstream flow causes disturbances at the static port preventing actual atmospheric pressure measurement. It varies with airspeed, altitude, and configuration, and may be a plus or minus value.

Density error—Changes in altitude and temperature are not compensated for by the instrument.

Compressibility error—Caused by the packing of air into the pitot tube at high airspeeds, resulting in higher than normal indications. It is usually not a factor at slower speeds.

8. What are the different types of aircraft speeds?
(FAA-H-8083-25)

Indicated airspeed (IAS)—The speed of the airplane as observed on the airspeed indicator. It is the airspeed without correction for indicator, position (or installation), or compressibility errors.

Calibrated airspeed (CAS)—The airspeed indicator reading corrected for position (or installation), and instrument errors. CAS is equal to TAS at sea level in standard atmosphere. The color-coding for various design speeds marked on airspeed indicators may be IAS or CAS.

Equivalent airspeed (EAS)—The airspeed indicator reading corrected for position (or installation), or instrument error, and for adiabatic compressible flow for the particular altitude. EAS is equal to CAS at sea level in standard atmosphere.

True airspeed (TAS)—CAS corrected for altitude and nonstandard temperature; the speed of the airplane in relation to the air mass in which it is flying.

9. **Name several important airspeed limitations not marked on the face of the airspeed indicator.** (FAA-H-8083-25)

Design maneuvering speed (V_A)—The maximum speed at which the structural design's limit load can be imposed (either by gusts or full deflection of the control surfaces) without causing structural damage. *Note:* Operating at or below V_A does not provide structural protection against multiple full control inputs in one axis or full control inputs in more than one axis at the same time.

Landing gear operating speed (V_{LO})—The maximum speed for extending or retracting the landing gear if using aircraft equipped with retractable landing gear.

Best angle-of-climb speed (V_X)—Important when a short-field takeoff to clear an obstacle is required.

Best rate-of-climb speed (V_Y)—The airspeed that will give the pilot the most altitude in a given period of time.

10. **What airspeed limitations apply to the color-coded marking system of the airspeed indicator?** (FAA-H-8083-25)

Marking	Meaning
White Arc	Flap operating range
Lower A/S limit white arc	V_{S0} (stall speed landing configuration)
Upper A/S limit white arc	V_{FE} (maximum flap extension speed)
Green arc	Normal operating range
Lower A/S limit green arc	V_{S1} (stall speed clean or specified configuration)
Upper A/S limit green arc	V_{NO} (normal operations speed or maximum structural cruise speed)
Yellow arc	Caution range (operations in smooth air only)
Red line	V_{NE} (never exceed speed; above this speed, structural failure may occur.)

11. How does the vertical speed indicator work?
(FAA-H-8083-15)

The vertical speed indicator is a pressure differential instrument. Inside the instrument case is an aneroid very much like the one in an airspeed indicator. Both the inside of this aneroid and the inside of the instrument case are vented to the static system, but the case is vented through a calibrated orifice that causes the pressure inside the case to change more slowly than the pressure inside the aneroid. As the aircraft ascends, the static pressure becomes lower and the pressure inside the case compresses the aneroid, moving the pointer upward, showing a climb and indicating the number of feet per minute the aircraft is ascending.

12. What are the limitations of the vertical speed indicator?
(FAA-H-8083-25)

The VSI is not accurate until the aircraft is stabilized. Because of the restriction in airflow to the static line, a 6 to 9 second lag is required to equalize or stabilize the pressures. Sudden or abrupt changes in aircraft attitude will cause erroneous instrument readings as airflow fluctuates over the static port. Both rough control technique and turbulent air result in unreliable needle indications.

D. Gyroscopic Flight Instruments

1. What instruments contain gyroscopes? (FAA-H-8083-25)

a. The turn coordinator
b. The heading indicator (directional gyro)
c. The attitude indicator (artificial horizon)

2. What are the two fundamental properties of a gyroscope? (FAA-H-8083-25)

Rigidity in space—A gyroscope remains in a fixed position in the plane in which it is spinning.

Precession—The tilting or turning of a gyro in response to a deflective force. The reaction to this force does not occur at the point where it was applied; rather, it occurs at a point that is 90° later in the direction of rotation. The rate at which the gyro precesses is inversely proportional to the speed of the rotor and proportional to the deflective force.

3. **What are the various power sources that may be used to power the gyroscopic instruments in an airplane?** (FAA-H-8083-25)

   In some airplanes, all the gyros are vacuum, pressure, or electrically operated; in others, vacuum or pressure systems provide the power for the heading and attitude indicators, while the electrical system provides the power for the turn coordinator. Most airplanes have at least two sources of power to ensure at least one source of bank information if one power source fails.

4. **How does the vacuum system operate?** (FAA-H-8083-25)

   An engine-driven vacuum pump provides suction which pulls air from the instrument case. Normal pressure entering the case is directed against rotor vanes to turn the rotor (gyro) at high speed, much like a water wheel or turbine operates. Air is drawn into the instrument through a filter from the cockpit and eventually vented outside. Vacuum values vary between manufacturers (usually between 4.5 and 5.5 inHg) but provide rotor speeds from 8,000 to 18,000 RPM.

5. **How does the attitude indicator operate?** (FAA-H-8083-25)

   The gyro in the attitude indicator is mounted on a horizontal plane and depends upon rigidity in space for its operation. The horizon bar represents the true horizon. This bar is fixed to the gyro and remains in a horizontal plane as the airplane is pitched or banked about its lateral or longitudinal axis, indicating the attitude of the airplane relative to the true horizon.

6. **What are the limitations of an attitude indicator?** (FAA-H-8083-25)

   The pitch and bank limits depend upon the make and model of the instrument. Limits in the banking plane are usually from 100° to 110°, and the pitch limits are usually from 60° to 70°. If either limit is exceeded, the instrument will tumble or spill and will give incorrect indications until reset. A number of modern attitude indicators will not tumble.

7. What are the errors of the attitude indicator?
(FAA-H-8083-15)

Attitude indicators are free from most errors, but depending upon the speed with which the erection system functions, there may be a slight nose-up indication during a rapid acceleration and a nose-down indication during a rapid deceleration. There is also a possibility of a small bank angle and pitch error after a 180° turn. These inherent errors are small and correct themselves within a minute or so after returning to straight-and-level flight.

8. How does the heading indicator operate?
(FAA-H-8083-25)

The operation of the heading indicator uses the principle of rigidity in space. The rotor turns in a vertical plane, and the compass card is fixed to the rotor. Since the rotor remains rigid in space, the points on the card hold the same position in space relative to the vertical plane. As the instrument case and the airplane revolve around the vertical axis, the card provides clear and accurate heading information.

9. What are the limitations of the heading indicator?
(FAA-H-8083-25)

The bank and pitch limits of the heading indicator vary with the particular design and make of instrument. On some heading indicators found in light airplanes, the limits are approximately 55° of pitch and 55° of bank. When either of these attitude limits is exceeded, the instrument tumbles or spills and no longer gives the correct indication until reset. After spilling, it may be reset with the caging knob. Many of the modern instruments used are designed in such a manner that they will not tumble.

10. What error is the heading indicator subject to?
(FAA-H-8083-25)

Because of precession, caused chiefly by friction, the heading indicator will creep or drift from a heading to which it is set. Among other factors, the amount of drift depends largely upon the condition of the instrument. The heading indicator may indicate as much as 15° error per every hour of operation.

11. How does the turn coordinator operate? (FAA-H-8083-15)

The turn part of the instrument uses precession to indicate direction and approximate rate of turn. A gyro reacts by trying to move in reaction to the force applied thus moving the needle or miniature aircraft in proportion to the rate of turn. The slip/skid indicator is a liquid-filled tube with a ball that reacts to centrifugal force and gravity.

12. What information does the turn coordinator provide? (FAA-H-8083-25)

The turn coordinator shows the yaw and roll of the aircraft around the vertical and longitudinal axes.

The miniature airplane will indicate direction of the turn as well as rate of turn. When aligned with the turn index, it represents a standard rate of turn of 3° per second. The inclinometer of the turn coordinator indicates the coordination of aileron and rudder. The ball indicates whether the airplane is in coordinated flight or is in a slip or skid.

13. What will the turn indicator indicate when the aircraft is in a skidding or a slipping turn? (FAA-H-8083-25)

Slip—The ball in the tube will be on the inside of the turn; not enough rate of turn for the amount of bank.

Skid—The ball in the tube will be to the outside of the turn; too much rate of turn for the amount of bank.

E. Magnetic Compass

1. How does the magnetic compass operate? (FAA-H-8083-25)

Magnetized needles fastened to a float assembly, around which is mounted a compass card, align themselves parallel to the Earth's lines of magnetic force. The float assembly is housed in a bowl filled with acid-free white kerosene.

2. What limitations does the magnetic compass have? (FAA-H-8083-15)

The jewel-and-pivot type mounting allows the float freedom to rotate and tilt up to approximately 18° angle of bank. At steeper bank angles, the compass indications are erratic and unpredictable.

3. What are the various compass errors? (FAA-H-8083-15)

Oscillation error—Erratic movement of the compass card caused by turbulence or rough control technique.

Deviation error—Due to electrical and magnetic disturbances in the aircraft.

Variation error—Angular difference between true and magnetic north; reference isogonic lines of variation.

Dip errors include:

Acceleration error—On east or west headings, while accelerating, the magnetic compass shows a turn to the north, and when decelerating, it shows a turn to the south.

Remember: ANDS

Accelerate

North

Decelerate

South

Northerly turning error—The compass leads in the south half of a turn, and lags in the north half of a turn.

Remember: UNOS

Undershoot

North

Overshoot

South

F. Advanced Avionics

1. Describe the function of the following avionics equipment acronyms: AHRS, ADC, PFD, MFD, FD, FMS, INS. (FAA-H-8083-25, DAT)

AHRS—Attitude and heading reference system. Composed of three-axis sensors that provide heading, attitude, and yaw information for aircraft. AHRS are designed to replace traditional mechanical gyroscopic flight instruments and provide superior reliability and accuracy.

ADC—Air data computer. An aircraft computer that receives and processes pitot pressure, static pressure, and temperature to calculate precise altitude, indicated airspeed, true airspeed, vertical speed, and air temperature.

PFD—Primary flight display. A display that provides increased situational awareness to the pilot by replacing the traditional six instruments with an easy-to-scan display that shows the horizon, airspeed, altitude, vertical speed, trend, trim, rate of turn, and more.

MFD—Multi-function display. A cockpit display capable of presenting information (navigation data, moving maps, terrain awareness, etc.) to the pilot in configurable ways; often used in concert with the PFD.

FD—Flight director. An electronic flight computer that analyzes the navigation selections, signals, and aircraft parameters. It presents steering instructions on the flight display as command bars or crossbars for the pilot to position the nose of the aircraft over or follow.

FMS—Flight management system. A computer system containing a database for programming of routes, approaches, and departures that can supply navigation data to the flight director/autopilot from various sources, and can calculate flight data such as fuel consumption, time remaining, possible range, and other values.

INS—Inertial navigation system. A computer-based navigation system that tracks the movement of an aircraft via signals produced by onboard accelerometers. The initial location of the aircraft is entered into the computer and all subsequent movement is then sensed and used to keep the aircraft's position updated.

2. What is the function of a magnetometer?
(FAA-H-8083-25)

A magnetometer is a device that measures the strength of the Earth's magnetic field to determine aircraft heading; it provides this information digitally to the AHRS, which then sends it to the PFD.

3. When powering up an aircraft with an FMS/RNAV unit installed, how will you verify the effective dates of the navigation database? (POH/AFM)

The effective dates for the navigation database are typically shown on a start-up screen that is displayed as the system cycles through its startup self-test.

4. Does an aircraft have to remain stationary during AHRS system initialization? (POH/AFM)

Some AHRSs must be initialized on the ground prior to departure. The initialization procedure allows the system to establish a reference attitude used as a benchmark for all future attitude changes. Other systems are capable of initialization while taxiing as well as in flight.

5. Which standby flight instruments are normally provided in an advanced avionics aircraft? (POH/AFM)

Every aircraft equipped with electronic flight instruments must also contain a minimal set of backup/standby instruments. Usually conventional round dial instruments, they typically include an attitude indicator, an airspeed indicator, and an altimeter.

6. If one display fails (PFD or MFD), what information will be presented on the remaining display? (POH/AFM)

In the event of a display failure, some systems offer a reversion capability to display the primary flight instruments and engine instruments on the remaining operative display.

7. When a display failure occurs, what other system components will be affected? (POH/AFM)

In some systems, failure of a display will also result in partial loss of navigation, communication, and GPS capability. Reference your specific POH/AFM.

8. What display information will be affected when an ADC failure occurs? (POH/AFM)

Inoperative airspeed, altitude, and vertical speed indicators, shown with red Xs on the PFD, indicate the failure of the air data computer.

9. What display information will be lost when an AHRS failure occurs? (POH/AFM)

An inoperative attitude indicator, shown with a red X on the PFD, indicates failure of the AHRS.

10. **How will loss of a magnetometer affect the AHRS operation?** (POH/AFM)

Heading information will be lost.

Exam Tip: Be prepared to answer questions about any and all equipment installed in the aircraft. For example, if your aircraft has an autopilot, have in-depth knowledge of its operation, even if you rarely use it.

11. **For aircraft with electronic flight instrumentation, what is the function of the standby battery?** (FAA-H-8083-15)

The standby battery is held in reserve and kept charged in case of a failure of the charging system and a subsequent exhaustion of the main battery. The standby battery is brought online when the main battery voltage is depleted to a specific value, approximately 19 volts. Generally, the standby battery switch must be in the ARM position for this to occur, but pilots should refer to the aircraft flight manual (POH/AFM) for specifics on an aircraft's electrical system.

12. **What are the two types of ADS-B equipment?** (AC 90-114)

Automatic Dependent Surveillance–Broadcast Out (ADS-B Out)— Automatically broadcasts aircraft's GPS position, altitude, velocity, and other information out to ATC ground-based surveillance stations as well as directly to other aircraft. It is required in all airspace where transponders are required.

*Automatic Dependent Surveillance–Broadcast In (ADS-B In)—*The receipt, processing, and display of ADS-B transmissions. ADS-B In capability is necessary to receive ADS-B traffic and broadcast services (e.g., FIS-B and TIS-B).

13. **Briefly describe Traffic Information Services–Broadcast (TIS-B).** (AIM 4-5-6, 4-5-8, AC 90-114)

TIS-B is the broadcast of ATC derived traffic information to ADS-B equipped (1090ES or UAT) aircraft from ground radio stations. The source of this traffic information is derived from ground-based air traffic surveillance sensors. TIS-B service is available throughout the NAS where there is both adequate surveillance coverage from ground sensors and adequate broadcast coverage from ADS-B ground radio stations.

Note: TIS-B is not related to Traffic Information Service (TIS). TIS is only available at specific terminal Mode S radar sites. Though similar in some ways, TIS is not related to TIS-B. (See AIM 4-5-6.)

14. **Explain the limitations pilots should be aware of when using TIS-B for situational awareness.** (AIM 4-5-8, AC 90-114)

   a. TIS-B is not intended to be used as a collision avoidance system and does not relieve the pilot's responsibility to see and avoid other aircraft, in accordance with §91.113b.

   b. A pilot may receive an intermittent TIS-B target of themselves, typically when maneuvering (e.g., climbing turns) due to the radar not tracking the aircraft as quickly as ADS-B.

   c. The ADS-B-to-radar association process within the ground system may at times have difficulty correlating an ADS-B report with corresponding radar returns from the same aircraft. When this happens, the pilot may see duplicate traffic symbols (e.g., TIS-B shadows) on the cockpit display.

   d. Updates of TIS-B traffic reports will occur less often than ADS-B traffic updates. TIS-B position updates will occur approximately once every 3 to 13 seconds depending on the type of radar system in use within the coverage area. In comparison, the update rate for ADS-B is nominally once per second.

   e. The TIS-B system only uplinks data pertaining to transponder-equipped aircraft. Aircraft without a transponder will not be displayed as TIS-B traffic.

Additional Study Questions

1. **Does the nose wheel turn when the rudder is depressed in flight?** (POH/AFM)

2. **If the braking system is not functioning, will the parking brake function?** (POH/AFM)

3. If the brakes on the left side (pilot) are not functioning, will the brakes on the right side also be inoperative? (POH/AFM)

4. Explain the procedure for starting your airplane with external power. (POH/AFM)

5. You cannot start your airplane due to a low battery, so you request an external start via a ground power cart. What problems might still occur after the engine has started? (POH/AFM)

6. What are sustainable aviation fuels (SAF)? (FAA Sustainability)

7. In the event of an electrical system failure, what time duration can you reasonably expect electrical power from the battery? (POH/AFM)

8. What effect would positioning the master switch to the Off position have on aircraft systems while in flight? (FAA-H-8083-25)

9. What instruments are affected when the pitot tube freezes? Static port freezes? (FAA-H-8083-25)

10. What is the purpose of the alternate static source? (FAA-H-8083-25)

11. If you set the altimeter from 29.15 to 29.85, what change occurs? (FAA-H-8083-25)

12. During the before takeoff magneto check, you notice that the right magneto is extremely rough. Explain what the problem could be and what actions you will take next. (POH/AFM)

13. **Automation in the cockpit has made aviation safer. Does total risk increase or decrease when passively monitoring an automated system for faults or abnormalities? How can you mitigate that risk?** (FAA-H-8083-2)

Human Factors   **8**

A. Flight Physiology

1. What is hypoxia? (AIM 8-1-2)

Hypoxia is a state of oxygen deficiency in the body sufficient to impair functions of the brain and other organs.

2. Give a brief explanation of the four forms of hypoxia. (FAA-H-8083-25)

Hypoxic—Any condition that interrupts the flow of O_2 into the lungs. This is the type of hypoxia encountered at altitude due to the reduction of the partial pressure of O_2.

Hypemic—Any condition that interferes with the ability of the blood to carry oxygen, such as anemia, bleeding, carbon monoxide poisoning, smoking, certain prescription drugs.

Stagnant—Any situation that interferes with the normal circulation of the blood arriving to the cells. Heart failure, shock, and positive G-forces will bring about this condition.

Histotoxic—Any condition that interferes with the normal utilization of O_2 in the cell. Alcohol, narcotics, and cyanide all can interfere with the cell's ability to use the oxygen in support of metabolism.

3. Where does hypoxia usually occur, and what symptoms should one expect? (AIM 8-1-2)

Although a deterioration in night vision occurs at a cabin pressure altitude as low as 5,000 feet, other significant effects of altitude hypoxia usually do not occur in the normal healthy pilot below 12,000 feet. From 12,000 feet to 15,000 feet of altitude, judgment, memory, alertness, coordination, and ability to make calculations are impaired, and headache, drowsiness, dizziness and either a sense of well-being or belligerence occur. Effects are worse above 15,000 feet.

4. What factors can make a pilot more susceptible to hypoxia? (AIM 8-1-2)

The altitude at which significant effects of hypoxia occur can be lowered by a number of factors. Carbon monoxide inhaled in smoking or from exhaust fumes, lowered hemoglobin (anemia), and certain medications can reduce the oxygen-carrying capacity of the blood. Small amounts of alcohol and low doses of certain drugs, such as antihistamines, tranquilizers, sedatives, and analgesics can, through their depressant action, render the brain much more susceptible to hypoxia. Extreme heat and cold, fever, and anxiety increase the body's demand for oxygen, and hence its susceptibility to hypoxia.

5. How can hypoxia be avoided? (AIM 8-1-2)

Hypoxia is prevented by heeding factors that reduce tolerance to altitude, by enriching the inspired air with oxygen from an appropriate oxygen system, and by maintaining a comfortable, safe cabin pressure altitude. For optimum protection, pilots are encouraged to use supplemental oxygen above 10,000 feet during the day, and above 5,000 feet at night.

6. What is hyperventilation? (AIM 8-1-3)

Hyperventilation, or an abnormal increase in the volume of air breathed in and out of the lungs, can occur subconsciously when a stressful situation is encountered in flight. This results in a significant decrease in the carbon dioxide content of the blood. Carbon dioxide is needed to automatically regulate the breathing process.

7. What symptoms can a pilot expect from hyperventilation? (AIM 8-1-3)

As hyperventilation blows off excessive carbon dioxide from the body, a pilot can experience symptoms of light-headedness, suffocation, drowsiness, tingling in the extremities, and coolness, and react to them with even greater hyperventilation. Incapacitation can eventually result from uncoordination, disorientation, and painful muscle spasms. Finally, unconsciousness can occur.

8. How can a hyperventilating condition be reversed? (AIM 8-1-3)

The symptoms of hyperventilation subside within a few minutes after the rate and depth of breathing are consciously brought back to normal. The buildup of carbon dioxide in the body can be hastened by controlled breathing in and out of a paper bag held over the nose and mouth.

9. What is ear block? (AIM 8-1-2)

As the aircraft cabin pressure decreases during ascent, the expanding air in the middle ear pushes the Eustachian tube open. The air then escapes down to the nasal passages and equalizes in pressure with the cabin pressure. But during descent, the pilot must periodically open the Eustachian tube to equalize pressure. Either an upper respiratory infection, such as a cold or sore throat, or a nasal allergic condition can produce enough congestion around the Eustachian tube to make equalization difficult. Consequently, the difference in pressure between the middle ear and aircraft cabin can build to a level that will hold the Eustachian tube closed, making equalization difficult if not impossible. An ear block produces severe pain and loss of hearing that can last from several hours to several days.

10. How is ear block normally prevented from occurring? (AIM 8-1-2)

Normally this can be accomplished by swallowing, yawning, tensing muscles in the throat or, if these do not work, by the combination of closing the mouth, pinching the nose closed and attempting to blow through the nostrils (Valsalva maneuver). It is also prevented by not flying with an upper respiratory infection or nasal allergic condition.

11. What is spatial disorientation? (FAA-H-8083-15)

Orientation is the awareness of the position of the aircraft and of oneself in relation to a specific reference point. Spatial disorientation specifically refers to the lack of orientation with regard to position in space and to other objects.

12. What causes spatial disorientation? (FAA-H-8083-15)

Orientation is maintained through the body's sensory organs in three areas:

a. Visual: the eyes maintain visual orientation.

b. Vestibular: the motion sensing system in the inner ear maintains vestibular orientation.

c. Postural: the nerves in the skin, joints, and muscles of the body maintain postural orientation.

When human beings are in their natural environment, these three systems work well. However, when the human body is subjected to the forces of flight, these senses can provide misleading information resulting in disorientation.

13. **What is the cause of motion sickness, and what are its symptoms?** (FAA-H-8083-25)

Motion sickness is caused by continued stimulation of the inner ear, which controls the sense of balance. The symptoms are progressive and include loss of appetite, saliva collecting in the mouth, perspiration, nausea, disorientation, headaches, and possible vomiting. The pilot may become incapacitated if it becomes severe enough.

14. **What action should be taken if a pilot or his passenger suffers from motion sickness?** (FAA-H-8083-25)

If suffering from airsickness while piloting an aircraft, open up the air vents, loosen the clothing, use supplemental oxygen, and keep the eyes on a point outside the airplane. Avoid unnecessary head movements. Terminate the flight and land as soon as possible.

15. **What is carbon monoxide poisoning?** (AIM 8-1-4)

Carbon monoxide is a colorless, odorless and tasteless gas contained in exhaust fumes. When inhaled, even in minute quantities over a period of time, it can significantly reduce the ability of the blood to carry oxygen. Consequently, effects of hypoxia occur.

16. **How does carbon monoxide poisoning occur, and what symptoms should a pilot be alert for?** (AIM 8-1-4)

Most heaters in light aircraft work by air flowing over the manifold. The use of these heaters while exhaust fumes are escaping through manifold cracks and seals is responsible every year for several nonfatal and fatal aircraft accidents from carbon monoxide poisoning. A pilot who detects the odor of exhaust or experiences symptoms of headache, drowsiness, or dizziness while using the heater should suspect carbon monoxide poisoning.

17. **What action should be taken if a pilot suspects carbon monoxide poisoning?** (AIM 8-1-4)

A pilot who suspects this condition to exist should immediately shut off the heater and open all air vents. If symptoms are severe, or continue after landing, medical treatment should be sought.

18. **Define the term *stress* and explain what the two main categories of stress are.** (FAA-H-8083-25)

    Stress is the body's response to physical and psychological demands placed upon it. The two main categories are:

    Acute stress (short term)—involves an immediate threat that is perceived as danger. This is the type of stress that triggers a "fight or flight" response in an individual, whether the threat is real or imagined.

    Chronic stress (long term)—defined as a level of stress that presents an intolerable burden, exceeds the ability of an individual to cope, and causes individual performance to fall sharply.

19. **The term *stressor* is used to describe an element that causes an individual to experience stress. What are the three types of stressors?** (FAA-H-8083-25)

    Physical stressors—Include conditions associated with the environment, such as temperature and humidity extremes, noise, vibration, and lack of oxygen.

    Physiological stressors—Include fatigue, lack of physical fitness, sleep loss, missed meals (leading to low blood sugar levels), and illness.

    Psychological stressors—Are related to social or emotional factors such as a death in the family, a divorce, a sick child, a demotion, etc. They may also be related to mental workload such as analyzing a problem, navigating an aircraft, or making decisions.

20. **What is the definition of *fatigue*?** (AC 117-3)

    Fatigue is a physiological state of reduced mental or physical performance capability resulting from lack of sleep or increased physical activity. It can reduce a crewmember's alertness and ability to safely operate an aircraft or perform safety-related duties.

21. **What are the two types of fatigue and when are they likely to occur?** (FAA-H-8083-25)

    Acute (short-term) fatigue—Occurs after a period of strenuous effort, excitement, or lack of sleep. Rest after exertion and eight hours of sound sleep ordinarily cures this condition. A proper diet is also helpful.

Chronic (long-term) fatigue—Has psychological roots and occurs over an extended period of time. Continuous high stress levels as well as underlying disease can produce chronic fatigue. It is not relieved by proper diet and adequate rest and sleep, and usually requires treatment by a physician.

22. How will a pilot's performance be affected by fatigue or prolonged stress? (FAA-H-8083-25)

Degradation of attention and concentration, impaired coordination, and decreased ability to communicate seriously influence the pilot's ability to make effective decisions.

23. Describe the common symptoms of fatigue. (AC 117-3)

a. Measurable reduction in speed and accuracy of performance.

b. Lapses of attention and vigilance.

c. Delayed reactions.

d. Impaired logical reasoning and decision-making, including a reduced ability to assess risk or appreciate consequences of actions.

e. Reduced situational awareness.

f. Low motivation to perform optional activities.

24. Define the term *dehydration* and describe the effect it has on a pilot. (FAA-H-8083-25)

Dehydration is the term given to a critical loss of water from the body. The first noticeable effect of dehydration is fatigue, which in turn makes top physical and mental performance difficult, if not impossible. If the fluid lost is not replaced, the symptoms will progress to dizziness, weakness, nausea, tingling of hands and feet, abdominal cramps, and extreme thirst.

25. What are several causal factors that increase a pilot's susceptibility to dehydration? (FAA-H-8083-25)

Causes of dehydration are hot flight decks and flight lines, wind, humidity, and diuretic drinks (coffee, tea, caffeinated soft drinks). Flying for long periods in hot summer temperatures or at high altitudes increases susceptibility to dehydration since dry air at high altitudes tends to increase the rate of water loss from the body.

26. What is the definition of *hypothermia*? (CAMI OK-06-033)

The average body temperature for the human body is 98.6°F. Any deviation from this normal temperature, even as little as one to two degrees, will reduce efficiency. Hypothermia, or exposure, is defined as body core temperature less than 95°F. As the body core temperature drops, so does mental and physical efficiency.

27. Explain how heat can be lost from the body. (CAMI OK-06-033)

a. *Conduction*—The primary cause of heat loss. A transfer of heat occurs when the body comes in contact with something colder than itself.

b. *Radiation*—The body will continually radiate heat from exposed areas. 50% of body heat is lost from the head.

c. *Convection*—Air current blows heat away from the body faster than it is produced.

d. *Evaporation*—Sweat (or other moisture) can moisten clothing and accelerate conduction.

e. *Respiration*—In a cold environment, cold air enters the body and leaves as warm air. The body loses heat by warming the colder air.

28. What are the symptoms of hypothermia? (CAMI OK-06-033)

Body Temperature	Symptoms
99°–96°F	Intense shivering and impaired ability to perform complex tasks.
95°–91°F	Violent shivering, difficulty in speaking, sluggish thinking, amnesia.
90°–86°F	Shivering is replaced by muscular rigidity. Exposed skin is blue or puffy. Movements are jerky.

29. What is the first line of defense against hypothermia? (CAMI OK-06-033)

The first line of defense against hypothermia is shelter. The most readily available shelter at a pilot's disposal is the aircraft fuselage. Clothing is considered shelter, in the sense that it is your first immediate measure to retain body heat. An important fact to keep in mind is that when clothing becomes wet, it will lose its insulative quality. Wet clothing in wind will draw off body heat 200 times faster than wind alone.

30. What are several examples of optical illusions that may lead to landing errors? (AIM 8-1-5)

Runway width illusion—A narrower-than-usual runway can create the illusion that the aircraft is at a higher altitude than it actually is. The pilot who does not recognize this illusion will fly a lower approach, with the risk of striking objects along the approach path or landing short. A wider-than-usual runway can have the opposite effect, with the risk of leveling out high and landing hard or overshooting the runway.

Runway and terrain slopes illusion—An upsloping runway, upsloping terrain, or both, can create the illusion that the aircraft is at a higher altitude than it actually is. The pilot who does not recognize this illusion will fly a lower approach. A downsloping runway, downsloping approach terrain, or both, can have the opposite effect.

Featureless terrain illusion—An absence of ground features, as when landing over water, darkened areas, and terrain made featureless by snow, can create the illusion that the aircraft is at a higher altitude than it actually is. The pilot who does not recognize this illusion will fly a lower approach.

31. Explain how rain on the windscreen (water refraction), haze, and fog can create optical illusions. (FAA-S-8083-25)

Water Refraction—Rain on the windscreen can create an illusion of being at a higher altitude due to the horizon appearing lower than it is. This can result in the pilot flying a lower approach.

(continued)

Haze—Atmospheric haze can create an illusion of being at a greater distance and height from the runway. As a result, the pilot will have a tendency to be low on the approach.

Fog—Flying into fog can create an illusion of pitching up. Pilots who do not recognize this illusion will often steepen the approach quite abruptly.

32. Discuss the effects of nitrogen excesses during scuba diving upon a pilot or passenger in flight. (AIM 8-1-2)

A pilot or passenger who intends to fly after scuba diving should allow the body sufficient time to rid itself of excess nitrogen absorbed during diving. If not, decompression sickness due to evolved gas can occur during exposure to low altitude and create a serious inflight emergency. The recommended waiting times before flight are as follows:

Flight altitudes up to 8,000 feet:
- Wait at least 12 hours after diving which has not required a controlled ascent.
- Wait at least 24 hours after diving which has required controlled ascent.

Flight altitudes above 8,000 feet:
- Wait at least 24 hours after any scuba dive.

Note: The recommended altitudes are actual flight altitudes above mean sea level and not pressurized cabin altitudes. This takes into consideration the risk of decompression of the aircraft during flight.

33. What restrictions apply to pilots concerning the use of drugs and alcohol? (14 CFR 91.17)

No person may act or attempt to act as a crewmember of a civil aircraft:

a. within 8 hours after the consumption of any alcoholic beverage;

b. while under the influence of alcohol;

c. while using any drug that affects the person's faculties in any way contrary to safety; or

d. while having an alcohol concentration of .04 percent or more in a blood or breath specimen.

34. What regulations apply and what common sense should prevail concerning the use of alcohol? (14 CFR 91.17, AIM 8-1-1)

The regulations prohibit pilots from performing crewmember duties within 8 hours after drinking any alcoholic beverage, while under the influence of alcohol, or having a blood alcohol concentration of .04 percent or more. Due to the slow destruction of alcohol in the bloodstream, a pilot may still be under influence, or over the .04 percent mark, 8 hours after drinking a moderate amount of alcohol. Therefore, an excellent rule is to allow at least 12 to 24 hours from "bottle to throttle," depending on the amount of alcoholic beverage consumed.

35. Is it permissible for a pilot to allow a person who is obviously under the influence of intoxicating liquors or drugs to be carried aboard an aircraft? (14 CFR 91.17)

No. Except in an emergency, no pilot of a civil aircraft may allow a person who appears to be intoxicated or who demonstrates by manner or physical indications that the individual is under the influence of drugs (except a medical patient under proper care) to be carried in that aircraft.

36. For a pilot who has been taking an over-the-counter (OTC) cold medication, how do the various environmental factors the pilot is exposed to inflight affect the drug's physiological impact on the pilot? (FAA-H-8083-25)

Drugs that cause no apparent side effects on the ground can create serious problems at relatively low altitudes. Even at typical general aviation altitudes, the changes in concentrations of atmospheric gases in the blood can enhance the effects of seemingly innocuous drugs and result in impaired judgment, decision-making, and performance.

37. What regulations apply and what common sense should prevail concerning the use of drugs and medication? (AIM 8-1-1)

Pilot performance can be seriously degraded by both prescribed and OTC medications, as well as by the medical conditions for which they are taken. The regulations prohibit pilots from performing crewmember duties while using any medication that affects the faculties in any way contrary to safety. The safest rule is not to fly as a crewmember while taking any medication, unless approved to do so by the FAA.

38. You recently experienced a bad cold and were treated by your personal physician. You continue to take the medications your physician prescribed, but feel much better. Can you resume flying on your current medical or must you first see an FAA Aviation Medical Examiner (AME)? (14 CFR 61.53)

Anytime you experience an illness or an injury that you feel may affect your ability to safely fly an aircraft, you must self-ground until you feel better. 14 CFR §61.53 requires that all pilots voluntarily self-ground if one of the following is true:

a. They know or have reason to know of any medical condition that would make them unable to meet the requirements for the medical certificate necessary for the pilot operation.

b. They are taking medication or receiving other treatment for a medical condition that results in them being unable to meet the requirements for the medical certificate necessary for the pilot operation.

If in doubt about your condition or the medications you are taking, consult with an AME before resuming your flying activities.

39. Can you operate an aircraft while taking an OTC medication for an on-going condition (allergies, hay fever, etc.)? (FAA-P-8740-41)

Self-medication or taking medication in any form while you are flying can be extremely hazardous. Even simple home or over-the-counter remedies such as aspirin, laxatives, tranquilizers, and appetite suppressants may seriously impair the judgment and coordination needed while flying. The safest rule is to take no medicine while flying, except with the advice of your AME.

B. Single-Pilot Resource Management

1. Define the term *single-pilot resource management*. (FAA-H-8083-9)

Single-pilot resource management (SRM) is the art and science of managing all the resources (both on-board the aircraft and from outside sources) available to a single pilot (prior to and during flight) to ensure that the successful outcome of the flight is never in doubt. SRM helps pilots learn to execute methods of gathering information, analyzing it, and making decisions.

2. What are examples of the skills necessary for effective SRM? (FAA-H-8083-25)

SRM includes the concepts of aeronautical decision making (ADM), risk management (RM), task management (TM), automation management (AM), controlled flight into terrain (CFIT) awareness, and situational awareness (SA).

3. What practical application provides a pilot with an effective method to practice SRM? (FAA-H-8083-9)

The **5P** checklist consists of the **P**lan, the **P**lane, the **P**ilot, the **P**assengers, and the **P**rogramming. It is based on the idea that the pilot has essentially five variables that impact his or her environment and that can cause the pilot to make a single critical decision, or several less critical decisions, that when added together can create a critical outcome.

4. Explain the use of the 5P model to assess risk associated with each of the five factors. (FAA-H-8083-2)

At key decision points, application of the **5P** checklist should be performed by reviewing each of the critical variables:

Plan—Weather, route, publications, ATC reroutes/delays, fuel onboard/remaining.

Plane—Mechanical status, automation status, database currency, backup systems.

Pilot—Illness, medication, stress, alcohol, fatigue, eating (IMSAFE).

Passengers—Pilots/non-pilots, nervous or quiet, experienced or new, business or pleasure.

Programming—Autopilot, GPS, MFD/PFD; anticipate likely reroutes/clearances. Questions to ask: What is it doing? Why is it doing it? Did I do it?

5. When is the use of the 5P checklist recommended? (FAA-H-8083-9)

The 5P concept relies on the pilot to adopt a scheduled review of the critical variables at points in the flight where decisions are most likely to be effective. These key decision points include preflight, pre-takeoff, hourly or at the midpoint of the flight, pre-descent, and just prior to the final approach fix (or, for VFR operations, just prior to entering the traffic pattern). They also should be used anytime an emergency situation arises.

C. Aeronautical Decision Making

1. Define the term *aeronautical decision making* (ADM). (FAA-H-8083-9)

ADM is a systematic approach to the mental process used by aircraft pilots to consistently determine the best course of action in response to a given set of circumstances.

2. Explain the basic steps in the decision-making process. (FAA-H-8083-9)

a. Define the problem.
b. Choose a course of action.
c. Implement the decision.
d. Evaluate the outcome.

3. What two models are commonly used when practicing aeronautical decision making? (FAA-H-8083-9)

The DECIDE model and the 3P model.

4. The DECIDE model of decision making involves which elements? (FAA-H-8083-2)

Remember: DECIDE

Detect a change needing attention.

Estimate the need to counter or react to a change.

Choose the most desirable outcome for the flight.

Identify actions to successfully control the change.

Do something to adapt to the change.

Evaluate the effect of the action countering the change.

5. How is the 3P model different from the DECIDE model of ADM? (FAA-H-8083-2)

The 3P process (discussed in the "Risk Management" section) is a continuous loop of the pilot's handling of hazards. The DECIDE model and naturalistic decision making focus on particular problems requiring resolution. Therefore, pilots exercise the 3P process continuously, while the DECIDE model and naturalistic decision making result from the 3P process.

6. Name five hazardous attitudes that can affect a pilot's ability to make sound decisions and properly exercise authority. (FAA-H-8083-9)

Attitude	Antidote
Anti-authority	Follow the rules—they are usually right.
Impulsivity	Think first—not so fast.
Invulnerability	It could happen to me.
Macho	Taking chances is foolish.
Resignation	I can make a difference, I am not helpless.

7. What is the first step towards neutralizing a hazardous attitude? (FAA-H-8083-25)

Recognition of hazardous thoughts is the first step toward neutralizing them. After recognizing a thought as hazardous, the pilot should label it as hazardous, and then state the corresponding antidote. Antidotes should be memorized for each of the hazardous attitudes so they automatically come to mind when needed.

D. Risk Management

1. Define the term *risk management*. (FAA-H-8083-9)

Risk management is a decision-making process designed to systematically identify hazards, assess the degree of risk, and determine the best course of action. It is a logical process of weighing the potential costs of risks against the possible benefits of allowing those risks to stand uncontrolled.

2. What is the definition of a *hazard*? (FAA-H-8083-2)

A hazard is a present condition, event, object, or circumstance that could lead to or contribute to an unplanned or undesired event such as an accident.

3. What are several examples of aviation hazards? (FAA-H-8083-2)

a. A nick in the propeller blade
b. Improper refueling of an aircraft
c. Pilot fatigue
d. Use of unapproved hardware on aircraft
e. Weather

4. What is the definition of *risk*? (FAA-H-8083-2)

Risk is the future impact of a hazard that is not controlled or eliminated.

5. How can the use of the "PAVE" checklist during flight planning help you to assess risk? (FAA-H-8083-9)

Use of the **PAVE** checklist provides pilots with a simple way to remember each category to examine for risk during flight planning. The pilot divides the risks of flight into four categories:

Pilot-In-Command—General health, physical/mental/emotional state, proficiency, currency.

Aircraft—Airworthiness, equipment, performance capability.

enVironment—Weather hazards, terrain, airports/runways to be used, conditions.

External pressures—Meetings, people waiting at destination, desire to impress someone, etc.

6. Explain the use of a personal minimums checklist and how it can help a pilot control risk. (FAA-H-8083-9)

One of the most important concepts that safe pilots understand is the difference between what is legal in terms of the regulations, and what is smart or safe in terms of pilot experience and proficiency. One way a pilot can control the risks is to set personal minimums for items in each risk category. These are limits unique to that individual pilot's current level of experience and proficiency.

7. **What is one method you can use to control and manage risk?** (FAA-H-8083-2)

One way a pilot can limit exposure to risks is to set personal minimums for items in each risk category, again using PAVE. These are limits unique to that individual pilot's current level of experience and proficiency:

Pilot—Experience/recency (takeoffs/landings, hours make/model), physical/mental condition (IMSAFE).

Aircraft—Fuel reserves VFR day/night, aircraft performance (weight and balance, density altitude, etc.), aircraft equipment (avionics familiarity, charts, survival gear).

enVironment—Airport conditions (runway condition/length), weather (winds, ceilings, visibilities).

External pressures—Allowance for delays, diversion, cancelation, alternate plans, personal equipment available for alternate plans (phone numbers, credit cards, medications).

8. **Explain the use of a personal checklist such as "I'M SAFE" to determine personal risks.** (FAA-H-8083-9)

Personal, self-assessment checklists assist pilots in conducting preflight checks on themselves, reviewing their physical and emotional states that could have an effect on their performance. The "I'M SAFE" checklist reminds pilots to consider the following:

Illness—Do I have any symptoms?

Medication—Have I been taking prescription or over-the-counter drugs?

Stress—Am I under psychological pressure from my job? Do I have money, family, or health problems?

Alcohol—Have I been drinking within 8 hours? Within 24 hours?

Fatigue—Am I tired and not adequately rested?

Emotions—Am I fully recovered from any extremely upsetting events?

9. **Describe how the 3P model can be used for practical risk management.** (FAA-H-8083-2)

The Perceive, Process, Perform (3P) model for risk management offers a simple, practical, and systematic approach that can be used during all phases of flight. To use it, pilots will:

Perceive—The hazards for a flight, which are present events, objects, or circumstances that could contribute to an undesired future event, given set of circumstances for a flight; think through circumstances related to the PAVE risk categories. The fundamental question to ask is, "What could hurt me, my passengers, or my aircraft?"

Process—The hazards by evaluating their impact on flight safety. Think through the Consequences of each hazard, Alternatives available, Reality of the situation, and External pressures (CARE) that might influence their analysis.

Perform—By implementing the best course of action. Remember the TEAM method: Transfer (Can the risk decision be transferred to someone else? Can you consult someone?); Eliminate (Is there a way to eliminate the hazard?); Accept (Do the benefits of accepting risk outweigh the costs?); Mitigate (What can you do to reduce the risk?).

10. **Explain how often a pilot should use the 3P model of ADM throughout a flight.** (FAA-H-8083-9)

Once a pilot has completed the 3P decision process and selected a course of action, the process begins again because the circumstances brought about by the course of action require analysis. The decision-making process is a continuous loop of perceiving, processing, and performing.

11. **What is a risk assessment matrix?** (FAA-H-8083-25, FAA-H-8083-2)

A risk assessment matrix is a tool used to assess the likelihood of an event occurring and the severity or consequences of that event. The matrix assists a pilot in differentiating between low, medium, and high-risk flights.

12. What is a flight risk assessment tool (FRAT)?
(FAA InFO 07015)

A FRAT is a preflight planning tool that uses a series of questions in each of the major risk categories (PAVE) to help a pilot identify and quantify risk for a flight. The tool enables proactive hazard identification, is easy to use, and can visually depict risk. It is an invaluable tool in helping pilots make better go/no-go decisions and should be a part of every flight. A FRAT fact sheet is available at www.faa.gov/news/safety_briefing/2016/media/SE_Topic_16 -12.pdf.

E. Task Management

1. Define the term *task management*. (FAA-H-8083-9)

Task management is the process by which pilots manage the many, concurrent tasks that must be performed to safely and efficiently operate an aircraft.

2. What are several factors that can reduce a pilot's ability to manage workload effectively? (FAA-H-8083-25)

Environmental conditions—Temperature and humidity extremes, noise, vibration, and lack of oxygen.

Physiological stress—Fatigue, lack of physical fitness, sleep loss, missed meals (leading to low blood sugar levels), and illness.

Psychological stress—Social or emotional factors, such as a death in the family, a divorce, a sick child, or a demotion at work. This type of stress may also be related to mental workload, such as analyzing a problem, navigating an aircraft, or making decisions.

3. What are several options that a pilot can employ to decrease workload and avoid becoming overloaded?
(FAA-H-8083-25)

Stop, think, slow down, and prioritize. Tasks such as locating an item on a chart or setting a radio frequency may be delegated to another pilot or passenger; an autopilot, if available, may be used; or ATC may be enlisted to provide assistance.

4. **What is one method of prioritizing tasks to avoid an overload situation?** (FAA-H-8083-25)

During any situation, and especially in an emergency, remember the phrase, "Aviate, navigate, and communicate."

5. **How can tasks be completed in a timely manner without causing a distraction from flying?** (FAA-H-8083-9)

By planning, prioritizing, and sequencing tasks, a potential work overload situation can be avoided. As experience is gained, a pilot learns to recognize future workload requirements and can prepare for high workload periods during times of low workload.

6. **Why are pilots encouraged to use checklists?** (FAA-H-8083-3)

The checklist is an aid to the memory and helps to ensure that critical items necessary for the safe operation of aircraft are not overlooked or forgotten. They provide a standardized method for verifying aircraft configuration and a logical sequence for accomplishing tasks inside and outside the cockpit.

7. **What are two common methods of checklist usage?** (AC 120-71B)

a. *Do-Verify (DV) method*—Consists of the checklist being accomplished in a variable sequence without a preliminary challenge. After all of the action items on the checklist have been completed, the checklist is then read again while each item is verified. The DV method allows the pilot/flightcrew to use flow patterns from memory to accomplish a series of actions quickly and efficiently.

b. *Challenge-Do-Verify (CDV) method*—Consists of a pilot/ crewmember making a challenge before an action is initiated, taking the action, and then verifying that the action item has been accomplished. The CDV method is most effective in two-pilot crews where one crewmember issues the challenge and the second crewmember takes the action and responds to the first crewmember, verifying that the action was taken.

8. **What are several examples of common errors that can occur when using a checklist?** (FAA-H-8083-3)

   a. Checklist items are missed because of distraction or interruption (by passengers, ATC, etc.).

   b. Checklist items are incorrectly performed (hurrying checklist; reading item but not verifying or setting).

   c. Failure to use the appropriate checklist for a specific phase of flight.

   d. Too much time spent with head down, reading the checklist and compromising safety.

   e. Checklist is not readily accessible in cockpit.

   f. Emergency/abnormal procedures checklist is not readily available.

   g. Memory items accomplished but not confirmed with checklist.

9. **In what phases of flight should a prepared checklist be used?** (FAA-H-8083-3)

   a. Preflight inspection.
   b. Before engine start.
   c. Engine starting.
   d. Before taxiing.
   e. Before takeoff.
   f. After takeoff.
   g. Cruise.
   h. Descent.
   i. Before landing.
   j. After landing.
   k. Engine shutdown and securing.

10. **What are several recommended methods for managing checklist accomplishment?** (AC 120-71B)

   a. The pilot should touch/point at each control, display or switch.

   b. Verbally state the desired status of the checklist item.

   c. When complete, announce that "___ checklist is complete."

11. What are immediate action items? (AC 120-71B)

An immediate action item is an action that must be accomplished so expeditiously (in order to avoid or stabilize a hazardous situation) that time is not available for the pilot/crewmember to refer to a manual or checklist. Once the emergency has been brought under control, the pilot refers to the actual checklist to verify that all action items were accomplished. Only after this is done should the remainder of the checklist be completed.

F. Situational Awareness

1. Define the term *situational awareness* (SA). (FAA-H-8083-25)

SA is the accurate perception and understanding of all the factors and conditions within the five fundamental risk elements (flight, pilot, aircraft, environment, external pressures) that affect safety before, during, and after the flight.

2. What are some of the elements inside and outside the aircraft that a pilot must consider to maintain situational awareness? (FAA-H-8083-9)

Inside the aircraft—The status of aircraft systems, pilot, and passengers.

Outside the aircraft—Awareness of where the aircraft is in relation to terrain, traffic, weather, and airspace.

3. What are several factors that reduce situational awareness? (FAA-H-8083-15)

Factors that reduce SA include fatigue, distractions, unusual or unexpected events, complacency, high workload, unfamiliar situations, and inoperative equipment.

4. When flying a technically advanced aircraft (TAA), what are several procedures that help ensure that situational awareness is enhanced, not diminished, by the automation? (FAA-H-8083-25)

Two basic procedures are to always double-check the system and to use verbal callouts. At a minimum, ensure the presentation makes sense. Was the correct destination entered into the navigation system? Callouts, even for single-pilot operations, are an excellent way to maintain situational awareness as well as manage information.

5. What additional procedures can be used for maintaining situational awareness in technically advanced aircraft? (FAA-H-8083-25)

a. Perform verification checks of all programming prior to departure.

b. Check the flight routing; ensure all routing matches the planned route of flight.

c. Always verify waypoints.

d. Make use of all onboard navigation equipment; use VOR to backup GPS, and vice versa.

e. Match the use of the automated system with pilot proficiency; stay within personal limitations.

f. Plan a realistic flight route to maintain situational awareness; ATC doesn't always give you direct routing.

g. Be ready to verify computer data entries; incorrect keystrokes can lead to loss of situational awareness.

G. CFIT Awareness

1. A majority of controlled flight into terrain (CFIT) accidents have been attributed to what factors? (AC 61-134)

a. Lack of pilot currency.

b. Loss of situational awareness.

c. Pilot distractions and breakdown of SRM.

d. Failure to comply with minimum safe altitudes.

e. Breakdown in effective ADM.

f. Insufficient planning, especially for the descent and arrival segments.

2. **A pilot can decrease the likelihood of a CFIT accident at the destination by identifying what risk factors prior to flight?** (AC 61-134)

Factors such as airport location, runway lighting, weather/daylight conditions, approach specifications, ATC capabilities and limitations, type of operation, departure procedures, controller/pilot phraseology, and crew configuration should all be considered prior to flight.

3. **Describe several operational techniques that will help you avoid a CFIT accident.** (AC 61-134)

a. Maintain situational awareness at all times.

b. Adhere to safe takeoff and departure procedures.

c. Familiarize yourself with surrounding terrain features and obstacles.

d. Adhere to published routes and minimum altitudes.

e. Fly a stabilized approach.

f. Understand ATC clearances and instructions.

g. Don't become complacent.

H. Automation Management

1. **What does the term *automation management* refer to?** (FAA-H-8083-9)

Automation management is the demonstrated ability to control and navigate an aircraft by means of the automated systems installed in the aircraft.

2. **In what three areas must a pilot be proficient when using advanced avionics or any automated system?** (FAA-H-8083-25)

The pilot must know what to expect, how to monitor the system for proper operation, and be prepared to promptly take appropriate action if the system does not perform as expected.

3. **What is the most important aspect of managing an autopilot/FMS?** (FAA-H-8083-9)

Knowing at all times the modes that are engaged or armed to engage, and being capable of verifying that armed functions (e.g., navigation tracking or altitude capture) engage at the appropriate time.

4. **At a minimum, the pilot flying with advanced avionics must know how to manage which three primary items?** (FAA-H-8083-25)

The course deviation indicator (CDI), the navigation source, and the autopilot.

5. **Automation management is a good place to practice the standard callout technique. What are standard callouts?** (FAA-H-8083-16)

To assist in maintaining situational awareness, professional flight crews often use standard callouts. For example, the non-flying pilot may call 2,000 and 1,000 feet prior to reaching an assigned altitude. The callout may be, "two to go" and "one to go." Single pilot operations can also benefit from this practice by adopting standard set callouts that can be used in the different segments of a flight. Examples of standard callouts are: "Power Set," "Airspeed Alive," "Rotate," "Positive Rate—Gear Up," "Localizer Alive," "Glideslope Alive," "Nav Source Verified," "Approach Mode Armed," "Approach Mode Active," and "Final Approach Fix."

Additional Study Questions

1. **What are several factors that may contribute to a pilot's impaired performance?** (AIM 8-1-1)

2. **What are several examples of illusions that can lead to spatial disorientation?** (AIM 8-1-5)

3. **Optical or visual illusions can increase the risk of an incident or accident occurring, even to the most experienced pilots. What can pilots do to mitigate that risk?** (FAA-H-8083-2)

4. **When should a pilot be particularly alert for the possibility of carbon monoxide poisoning?** (AIM 8-1-4)

5. **What is sinus block and what are the symptoms? How can it be prevented?** (AIM 8-1-2)

6. **Most pilots are goal-oriented, which can sometimes result in a tendency to ignore established personal limitations in favor of completing a flight. How can a pilot mitigate the risk of this occurring to them?** (FAA-H-8083-2)

7. **When planning a cross-country flight, how can a pilot mitigate the risk of inadvertent flight into IMC?** (FAA-H-8083-25)

8. **You have the proper charts, you have planned your route of flight, and you have a detailed navigation log. Once airborne, you decide that it's much easier to let the automation fly the airplane and manage the navigation. You will handle the communications and monitor the automation. Explain what the hazards are in this scenario.** (FAA-H-8083-2)

9. **How can a pilot mitigate the risk of the potentially dangerous distractions that can occur when flying with advanced avionics?** (FAA-H-8083-2)

Preflight
Procedures

9

A. Preflight Assessment

1. Explain how a pilot can perform an effective self-assessment before flight. (FAA-H-8083-25)

Prior to each and every flight, all pilots must do a proper physical self-assessment to ensure safety. One of the best ways to accomplish this is to use the IMSAFE checklist to determine physical and mental readiness for flying:

a. **Illness**—Am I sick? Illness is an obvious pilot risk.

b. **Medication**—Am I taking any medicines that might affect my judgment or make me drowsy?

c. **Stress**—Am I under excessive stress or psychological pressure?

d. **Alcohol**—Have I been drinking within 8 hours? Within 24 hours?

e. **Fatigue**—Am I tired and not adequately rested?

g. **Emotion**—Am I emotionally upset?

2. What is the purpose of performing a preflight inspection on the airplane? (FAA-H-8083-3)

The purpose of the preflight inspection is to ensure that the airplane meets regulatory airworthiness standards and is in a safe mechanical condition prior to flight.

3. Who is responsible for ensuring that an aircraft is "maintained" in an airworthy condition? (14 CFR 91.403)

The owner or operator of an aircraft is primarily responsible for maintaining an aircraft in an airworthy condition.

4. Who is responsible for determining that an aircraft is airworthy and in a condition for safe flight? (14 CFR 91.7)

The pilot-in-command of a civil aircraft is responsible for determining whether that aircraft is in condition for safe flight. The pilot-in-command shall discontinue the flight when unairworthy mechanical, electrical, or structural conditions occur.

5. **For an aircraft to be considered airworthy, what two conditions must be met?** (FAA-H-8083-19)

   a. The aircraft must conform to its type design (type certificate). This is attained when the required and proper components are installed consistent with the drawings, specifications, and other data that are part of the type certificate. Conformity includes applicable supplemental type certificate(s) (STC) and field-approval alterations.

   b. The aircraft must be in a condition for safe operation, referring to the condition of the aircraft in relation to wear and deterioration.

6. **Explain how a pilot determines if an aircraft conforms to its approved type design and is in a condition for safe operation.** (14 CFR Parts 21, 43, and 91)

   a. To determine that the aircraft conforms to its type design, a pilot must determine that the maintenance, preventive maintenance, and alterations have been performed in accordance with Parts 21, 43, and 91 and that the aircraft is registered in the United States. The pilot does this by ensuring that all required inspections, maintenance, preventive maintenance, repairs, and alterations have been appropriately documented in the aircraft's maintenance records.

   b. To determine that the aircraft is in condition for safe operation, the pilot conducts a thorough preflight inspection of the aircraft for wear and deterioration, structural damage, fluid leaks, tire wear, inoperative instruments, and equipment, etc. If an unsafe condition exists or inoperative instruments or equipment are found, the pilot uses the guidance in 14 CFR §91.213 for handling the inoperative equipment.

7. **When approaching the airplane on the ramp to begin the preflight inspection, what should a pilot be looking for?** (FAA-H-8083-3)

   The pilot should make note of the general appearance of the airplane, looking for discrepancies such as misalignment of the landing gear and airplane structure. The pilot should also take note of any distortions of the wings, fuselage, and tail, as well as skin damage and any staining, dripping, or puddles of fuel or oils.

8. **According to the POH/AFM, what is the recommended sequence when beginning the inspection of the outer wing surfaces and tail section of the airplane?** (FAA-H-8083-3)

   Generally, the POH/AFM specifies a sequence for the pilot to inspect the aircraft that begins from the cabin entry access opening and then continues, in a counterclockwise direction, until the aircraft has been completely inspected.

9. **Why is it important to inspect the airplane with reference to an appropriate checklist?** (FAA-H-8083-3)

   Checklists are guides for use in ensuring that all necessary items are not only checked but checked in a logical sequence. The pilot should never assume that the checklist is merely a crutch for poor memory, but instead should consider the checklist a necessary tool used to accomplish a complex task thoroughly and efficiently.

10. **In addition to items specified in the POH/AFM for inspection, what are other areas of concern to a pilot when inspecting the exterior structure of the aircraft?** (FAA-H-8083-3)

    a. A pilot should be aware of critical areas such as spar lines, wing, horizontal, and vertical attach points including wing struts and landing gear attachment areas. The airplane skin should be inspected in these areas as load-related stresses are concentrated along spar lines and attach points.

    b. Spar lines are lateral rivet lines that extend across the wing, horizontal stabilizer, or vertical stabilizer. Pilots should pay close attention to spar lines looking for distortion, ripples, bubbles, dents, creases, or waves as any structural deformity may be an indication of internal damage or failure.

    c. Inspect around rivet heads looking for cracked paint or a black-oxide film that forms when a rivet works free in its hole.

11. **Describe the additional inspections that may be required when conducting the preflight inspection of an airplane equipped with Integrated Flight Deck (IFD) glass-panel avionics.** (FAA-H-8083-3)

    Ground-based inspections may include verification that the flight deck reference guide is in the aircraft and accessible; checking of system driven removal of *X*s over engine indicators; checking pitot/static and attitude displays; testing of low-level alarms and annunciator panels; setting of fuel levels; and verification that the avionics cooling fans, if equipped, are functional. The POH/AFM specifies how these preflight inspections are to take place.

12. Explain the different types of airplane logbooks that should be available for inspection prior to flight. (FAA-H-8083-3)

Each airplane has a set of logbooks that include airframe and engine, and in some cases, propeller, and appliance logbooks, which are used to record maintenance, alteration, and inspections performed on a specific airframe, engine, propeller, or appliance.

13. Where are the airplane logbooks located and when should they be inspected? (FAA-H-8083-3)

It is important that the logbooks be kept accurate, secure, and available for inspection. Airplane logbooks are not normally kept in the airplane. It should be a matter of procedure by the pilot to inspect the airplane logbooks or a summary of the airworthy status prior to flight to ensure that the airplane records of maintenance, alteration, and inspections are current and correct.

14. How can the use of the "PAVE" checklist during preflight help a pilot to assess and mitigate risk? (FAA-H-8083-9)

Use of the PAVE checklist provides pilots with a simple way to remember each category to examine for risk during flight planning. The pilot divides the risks of flight into four categories:

Pilot—Illness, medication, stress, alcohol, fatigue, emotion (I'M SAFE), proficiency, currency.

Aircraft—Airworthiness, aircraft equipped for flight, proficiency in aircraft, performance capability.

enVironment—Weather hazards, type of terrain, airports/runways to be used, conditions.

External pressures—Meetings, people waiting at destination, desire to impress, desire to get there, etc.

B. Flight Deck Management

1. Do the regulations require pilots to provide a pre-takeoff safety briefing to their passengers? (14 CFR 91.107)

Yes. No pilot may take off an aircraft unless the PIC of that aircraft ensures that each person on board is *briefed* on how to fasten and unfasten that person's safety belt and, if installed, shoulder harness. Also, no pilot may cause to be moved on the surface, take off, or land an aircraft unless the pilot in command of that aircraft ensures that each person on board has been *notified* to fasten that person's safety belt and, if installed, a shoulder harness.

2. Which persons on board an aircraft are required to use seatbelts and when? (14 CFR 91.107)

Each person on board a U.S.-registered civil aircraft must occupy an approved seat or berth with a safety belt, and if installed, shoulder harness, properly secured during movement on the surface, takeoff, and landing. However, passengers who have not reached their second birthday and do not occupy or use any restraining device may be held by an adult who is occupying a seat or berth, and a person on board for the purpose of engaging in sport parachuting may use the floor of the aircraft as a seat.

3. Explain the items that should be included in a passenger preflight briefing. (FAA Safety Briefing)

Remember: SAFETY

Seat belts fastened for taxi, takeoff, landing. Shoulder harnesses fastened for takeoff, landing. Seat position adjusted and locked in place.

Air vents (location and operation). All environmental controls (discussed). Action in case of any passenger discomfort.

Fire extinguisher (location and operation).

Exit doors (how to secure; how to open). Emergency evacuation plan. Emergency/survival kit (location and contents).

Traffic (scanning, spotting, notifying pilot). Talking ("sterile cockpit" expectations).

Your questions? (Speak up!).

4. **When are flight crewmembers required to keep their seatbelts and shoulder harnesses fastened?** (14 CFR 91.105)

   During takeoff and landing and while en route, required flight crewmembers shall keep their seatbelt fastened while at their station. During takeoff and landing this includes shoulder harnesses, if installed, unless it interferes with other required duties.

5. **Why is the use of sterile cockpit procedures important when conducting taxi operations?** (AC 91-73)

   Pilots must be able to focus on their duties without being distracted by non–flight-related matters unrelated to the safe and proper operation of the aircraft. Refraining from nonessential activities during ground operations is essential. Passengers should be briefed on the importance of minimizing conversations and questions during taxi as well as on arrival, from the time landing preparations begin until the aircraft is safely parked.

6. **What are examples of hazards a pilot should consider when assessing flight deck management risk?** (FAA-S-ACS-6)

   a. Equipment, checklists, charts, etc., not readily available, or not secured.

   b. Not briefing crew and passengers.

   c. Poor ADM, SRM, CRM.

   d. Improper use of systems or equipment, to include automation and portable electronic devices.

   e. Flying with unresolved discrepancies.

7. **How can a pilot mitigate hazards and reduce the risk present when managing the flight deck?** (FAA-S-ACS-6)

   a. Secure all items in the aircraft.

   b. Conduct an appropriate passenger briefing, including identifying the pilot-in-command (PIC), use of safety belts, shoulder harnesses, doors, passenger conduct, sterile aircraft, propeller blade avoidance, and emergency procedures.

   c. Properly program and manage the aircraft's automation, as applicable.

   d. Appropriately manage risks by utilizing ADM, including SRM/CRM.

8. **May portable electronic devices be operated onboard an aircraft?** (14 CFR 91.21)

   Aircraft operated by a holder of an air carrier operating certificate or an aircraft operating under IFR may not allow operation of electronic devices onboard their aircraft. Exceptions are portable voice recorders, hearing aids, heart pacemakers, electric shavers, or any other device that the operator of the aircraft has determined will not cause interference with the navigation or communication system of the aircraft on which it is to be used.

9. **Are navigational databases required to be updated prior to a VFR flight? What about for an IFR flight?** (FAA-H-8083-15, AIM 1-1-17, AC 90-100)

   Databases must be updated for IFR operations and should be updated for all other operations. However, there is no requirement for databases to be updated for VFR navigation. It is not recommended to use a moving map with an outdated database in and around critical airspace. Databases are updated every 28 days and are available from various commercial vendors. For IFR operations, all approach procedures to be flown must be retrievable from the current airborne navigation database.

10. **Explain what the FAA policy is for carrying current charts.** (FAA AERONAV FAQ)

    The specific FAA regulation, FAR 91.103, "Preflight Actions," states that each pilot in command shall, before beginning a flight, become familiar with all available information concerning that flight. Although the regulation does not specifically require it, you should always carry current charts with you in flight. Expired charts may not show frequency changes or newly constructed obstructions both of which, when unknown, could be a hazard.

C. Engine Starting

1. **Explain why it is important to call, "Clear," prior to starting an aircraft engine.** (FAA-H-8083-3)

   The pilot needs to ensure that the ramp area surrounding the airplane is clear of persons, equipment, and other hazards that could come into contact with the airplane or the propeller. Just prior to starter engagement, the pilot should always call,

"CLEAR," out of the side window and wait for a response from anyone who may be nearby *before* engaging the starter.

2. **Describe several other precautions that can be taken to reduce risk prior to engine start.** (FAA-H-8083-3)

The pilot should always check the area behind the airplane prior to engine start as a standard practice. At all times before engine start, the anti-collision lights should be turned on. For night operations, the position (navigation) lights should also be on.

3. **Explain why an engine start procedure in the winter would be different from one in the summer.** (FAA-P-8740-24)

    a. Batteries can lose a high percentage of their effectiveness in cold weather.

    b. Oil can become partially congealed and turning the engines is difficult for the starter or by hand.

    c. There is a tendency to over prime, which results in washed-down cylinder walls and possible scouring of the walls. This results in poor compression and, consequently, harder starting.

    d. Sometimes aircraft fires have been started by over prime when the engine fires while the exhaust system contains raw fuel. Other fires are caused by backfires through the carburetor.

4. **When starting the engine, are there any limitations on the amount of time the starter can be operated?** (FAA-H-8083-3, POH/AFM)

Starter motors are not designed for continuous duty. Their service life may be drastically shortened during a prolonged or difficult start as an excess buildup of heat can damage internal starter components. Avoid continuous starter operation for periods longer than 30 seconds without a cool down period of at least 30 seconds to 1 minute (some POH/AFMs specify longer cool down routines). Reference your POH/AFM.

5. **Explain how an airplane engine is started through the use of external power.** (FAA-H-8083-3, POH/AFM)

Some aircraft have receptacles to which an external ground power unit (GPU) may be connected to provide electrical energy for starting. These are very useful, especially during cold weather starting. Procedures for use of external power are not the same for all aircraft. Follow the manufacturer's recommendations in the POH/AFM.

6. In warm weather, how long should it take for the oil pressure to rise and provide an indication on the oil pressure gauge? (FAA-H-8083-3, POH/AFM)

In most conditions, oil pressure should rise to at least the lower limit within 30 seconds. To prevent damage, the engine should be shut down immediately if the oil pressure does not rise to the POH/AFM values within the required time.

7. Identify hazards that a pilot should consider prior to conducting an engine start procedure. (FAA-S-ACS-6)

a. Propeller safety.

b. Use of external power unit.

c. Engine limitations during starting.

d. Engine fire due to excessive priming.

e. Foreign Object Debris (FOD) around the airplane.

D. Taxiing

1. Describe several sources of information that a pilot can reference for current airport data and conditions. (FAA-H-8083-25)

a. Aeronautical Charts.

b. Chart Supplement U.S.

c. Notices to Air Missions (NOTAMs).

d. Automated Terminal Information Service (ATIS) broadcasts.

e. GPS navigation databases and charting apps.

2. Preflight planning for taxi operations should be an integral part of the pilot's flight planning process. What information should this include? (AC 91-73)

a. Review and understand airport signage, markings, and lighting.

b. Review the airport diagram, planned taxi route, and identify any hot spots.

c. Review the latest airfield NOTAMs and ATIS (if available) for taxiway/runway closures, construction activity, etc.

d. Conduct a pre-taxi/pre-landing briefing that includes the expected/assigned taxi route and any hold short lines and restrictions based on ATIS information or previous experience at the airport.

e. Plan for critical times and locations on the taxi route (complex intersections, crossing runways, etc.).

f. Plan to complete as many aircraft checklist items as possible prior to taxi.

3. What is the purpose of an airport diagram and where can they be found? (AIM 9-1-4)

Full page airport diagrams are designed to assist in the movement of ground traffic at locations with complex runway/taxiway configurations and provide information for updating geodetic position navigational systems aboard aircraft. Airport diagrams are available for download at www.faa.gov/airports/runway_safety/diagrams/. They can also be found in the Chart Supplement U.S., the U.S. Terminal Procedures Publication (TPP), GPS navigation databases, and many charting apps.

4. Explain why it is important to review NOTAMs prior to conducting taxi operations. (FAA-H-8083-25)

NOTAMS will include information on temporarily closed runways and taxiways. Depending on the reason for the closure, duration of closure, airfield configuration, and the existence and the hours of operation of an ATC tower, a visual indication may not always be present. Pilots should always check NOTAMs and ATIS prior to taxi for information on taxiway and runway closures, construction, and other airport changes that would affect their departure or arrival.

5. What is a runway incursion? (FAA-H-8083-25)

A runway incursion is "any occurrence in the airport runway environment involving an aircraft, vehicle, person, or object on the ground that creates a collision hazard or results in a loss of required separation with an aircraft taking off, intending to take off, landing, or intending to land."

6. Where are runway incursions most likely to occur?
(FAA-H-8083-25)

Runway incursions most likely to cause accidents generally occur at complex, high-volume airports characterized by parallel/intersecting runways, multiple taxiway/runway intersections, complex taxi patterns, and the need for traffic to cross active runways. Historical data also shows that a large number of runway incursions involve general aviation pilots and often result from misunderstood controller instructions, confusion, disorientation, and/or inattention. Nearly all runway incursions are caused by human error.

7. What is an airport hot spot? (CSUS)

A hot spot is a runway safety related problem area on an airport that presents increased risk during surface operations. Typically, it is a complex or confusing taxiway/taxiway or taxiway/runway intersection. The area of increased risk has either a history of or potential for runway incursions or surface incidents, due to a variety of causes, such as but not limited to airport layout, traffic flow, airport marking, signage and lighting, situational awareness, and training. Hot spots are depicted on airport diagrams as open circles or polygons designated as HS 1, HS 2, etc.

8. What are three major areas that contribute to runway incursions? (FAA-H-8083-3)

a. *Communications*—Misunderstanding the given clearance; failure to communicate effectively.

b. *Airport knowledge*—Failure to navigate the airport correctly; unable to interpret airport signage.

c. *Cockpit procedures for maintaining orientation*—Failure to maintain situational awareness.

9. Identify hazards that should be considered when conducting taxi operations at a controlled airport.
(FAA-S-ACS-6, AC 91-73)

a. Activities and distractions in the flight deck; pilot/passenger communications.

b. Confirmation or expectation bias as related to taxi instructions.

c. A taxi route or departure runway change.

    d. ATC/pilot communications; not using standard phraseology, misunderstanding.

    e. Loss of situational awareness.

    f. Runway incursion.

10. Explain the terms *confirmation bias* and *expectation bias*. (FAA Safety, FAA-H-8083-2)

Confirmation bias—The human tendency to look for information to confirm a decision already made. This occurs when we only look for, listen to, or acknowledge information that confirms our own preconceptions. We tend not to seek out or pay attention to evidence that could disconfirm the belief.

Expectation bias—When we have a strong belief or mindset towards something we expect to see or hear, and act according to those beliefs. This often occurs on the ground while taxiing where a pilot expects a particular taxi route and perceives the clearance as expected rather than as given by ATC.

Note: The result of either, if uncorrected, may lead to an error. Either case results in the pilot continuing with a plan despite clues indicating the situation is not as perceived. Fatigue tends to stop pilots from taking extra steps to verify perceived reality and contributes to expectation and confirmation bias susceptibility.

11. What can a pilot do to mitigate confirmation and expectation biases? (FAA Safety)

Understand that expectation bias often affects the verbal transmission of information. When issued instructions by ATC, focus on listening and repeat to yourself exactly what is said in your head, and then apply that information actively. Does the clearance make sense? If something doesn't make sense (incorrect call sign, runway assignment, altitude, etc.), then query the controller about it.

12. Explain the recommended practices that can help prevent runway incursions and assist a pilot in maintaining situational awareness during taxi operations. (AC 91-73)

a. A current airport diagram should be available for immediate reference during taxi.

b. Monitor ATC instructions/clearances issued to other aircraft for the big picture.

c. Focus attention outside the cockpit while taxiing.

d. Use all available resources (airport diagrams, airport signs, markings, lighting, and ATC) to keep the aircraft on its assigned taxi route.

e. Cross-reference heading indicator to ensure turns are being made in the correct direction and that you're on the assigned taxi route.

f. Prior to crossing any hold short line, visually check for conflicting traffic - verbalize "clear left, clear right."

g. Be alert for other aircraft with similar call signs on the frequency.

h. Understand and follow all ATC instructions and if in doubt—Ask!

13. What information should a pilot always read back when receiving taxi instructions from a controller? (AIM 4-3-18)

a. The runway assignment.

b. Any clearance to enter a specific runway.

c. Any instruction to hold short of a specific runway or line up and wait.

Note: Good operating practice dictates that pilots read back *all* ATC taxi instructions to ensure that the pilot has received and clearly understands the instruction.

14. When issued taxi instructions to an assigned takeoff runway, are you automatically authorized to cross any runway that intersects your taxi route? (AIM 4-3-18)

No. Aircraft must receive a runway crossing clearance for each runway that their taxi route crosses. When assigned a takeoff runway, ATC will first specify the runway, issue taxi instructions, and state any hold short instructions or runway crossing clearances if the taxi route will cross a runway. When issuing taxi instructions to any point other than an assigned takeoff runway, ATC will specify the point to which to taxi, issue taxi instructions, and state any hold short instructions or runway crossing clearances if the taxi route will cross a runway. ATC is required to obtain a read back from the pilot of all runway hold short instructions.

15. When should a pilot request progressive taxi instructions? (AIM 4-3-18)

If the pilot is unfamiliar with the airport or for any reason confusion exists as to the correct taxi routing, a request may be made for progressive taxi instructions, which include step-by-step routing directions.

16. What are several good reasons to write down taxi instructions, especially at larger or unfamiliar airports? (AC 91-73)

Writing down taxi instructions, especially complex instructions, can reduce a pilot's vulnerability to forgetting part of the instructions and provides a reference for read-back of instructions to ATC. It can also be used as a means of reconfirming the taxi route and any restrictions at any time during taxi operations.

17. Why is use of sterile cockpit procedures important when conducting taxi operations? (AC 91-73)

Pilots must be able to focus on their duties without being distracted by non-flight-related matters unrelated to the safe and proper operation of the aircraft. Refraining from nonessential activities during ground operations is essential. Passengers should be briefed on the importance of minimizing conversations and questions during taxi as well as on arrival, from the time landing preparations begin until the aircraft is safely parked.

18. Describe the various types of taxiway markings.
(AIM 2-3-4)

Markings for taxiways are yellow and consist of the following types:

a. *Taxiway centerline*—Single continuous yellow line; aircraft should be kept centered over this line during taxi; however, being centered on the centerline does not guarantee wingtip clearance with other aircraft or objects.

b. *Taxiway edge*—Used to define the edge of taxiway; two types, continuous and dashed.

c. *Taxiway shoulder*—Usually defined by taxiway edge markings; denotes pavement unusable for aircraft.

d. *Surface painted taxiway direction*—Yellow background with black inscription; supplements direction signs or when not possible to provide taxiway sign.

e. *Surface painted location signs*—Black background with yellow inscription; supplements location signs.

f. *Geographic position markings*—Located at points along low visibility taxi routes; used to identify aircraft during low visibility operations.

19. What are the three types of runway holding position markings? (AIM 2-3-5)

a. *Runway holding position markings on taxiways*—These markings identify the locations on taxiways where aircraft MUST STOP when a clearance has not been issued to proceed on to the runway.

b. *Runway holding position markings on runways*—These markings identify the locations on runways where aircraft MUST STOP. These markings are located on runways used by ATC for LAHSO and taxiing operations.

c. *Holding position markings on taxiways located in runway approach areas*—These markings are used at some airports where it is necessary to hold an aircraft on a taxiway located in the approach or departure area of a runway so that the aircraft does not interfere with the operations on that runway.

20. You're taxiing up to your departure runway and have been instructed to hold short of that runway. On which side of the runway holding position markings (four yellow lines, two solid and two dashed) does ATC expect you to hold? (AIM 2-3-5)

Hold prior to the two solid yellow lines. When instructed by ATC, "Hold short of Runway XX," the pilot MUST STOP so that no part of the aircraft extends beyond the runway holding position marking. An aircraft exiting a runway is not clear of the runway until all parts of the aircraft have crossed the applicable holding position marking.

21. Describe the various types of runway markings (precision instrument runway). (AIM 2-3-3)

Markings for runways are white and consist of the following types:

a. *Runway designators*—Runway number is the whole number nearest one-tenth the magnetic azimuth of the centerline of the runway, measured clockwise from the magnetic north.

b. *Runway centerline marking*—Identifies the center of the runway and provides alignment guidance during takeoff and landings; consists of a line of uniformly spaced stripes and gaps.

c. *Runway aiming point marking*—Serves as a visual aiming point for a landing aircraft; two rectangular markings consist of a broad white stripe located on each side of the runway centerline and approximately 1,000 feet from the landing threshold.

d. *Runway touchdown zone markers*—Identifies the touchdown zone for landing operations and are coded to provide distance information in 500 feet increments; groups of one, two, and three rectangular bars symmetrically arranged in pairs about the runway centerline.

e. *Runway side stripe markings*—Delineate the edges of the runway and provide a visual contrast between runway and the abutting terrain or shoulders; continuous white stripes located on each side of the runway.

f. *Runway shoulder markings*—May be used to supplement runway side stripes to identify pavement areas contiguous to the runway sides that are not intended for use by aircraft; painted yellow.

g. *Runway threshold markings*—Used to help identify the beginning of the runway that is available for landing. Two configurations: either eight longitudinal stripes of uniform dimensions disposed symmetrically about the runway centerline, or the number of stripes is related to the runway width.

22. Describe the six types of signs installed at airports. (AIM 2-3-7 through 2-3-13)

a. *Mandatory instruction sign*—Red background/white inscription; denotes an entrance to a runway, a critical area, or a prohibited area.

b. *Location sign*—Black background/yellow inscription/yellow border; do not have arrows; used to identify a taxiway or runway location, the boundary of the runway, or identify an ILS critical area.

c. *Direction sign*—Yellow background/black inscription; identifies the designation of the intersecting taxiway(s) leading out of an intersection that a pilot would expect to turn onto or hold short of.

d. *Destination sign*—Yellow background/black inscription and also contain arrows; provides information on locating runways, terminals, cargo areas, and civil aviation areas, etc.

e. *Information sign*—Yellow background/black inscription; used to provide the pilot with information on areas that can't be seen from the control tower, applicable radio frequencies, and noise abatement procedures, etc.

f. *Runway distance remaining sign*—Black background/white numeral inscription; indicates the distance of the remaining runway in thousands of feet.

23. Describe the following types of airport taxiway and runway lighting. (AIM 2-1-4, 2-1-10)

a. *Runway edge lights*—Are white. On instrument runways, yellow replaces white on the last 2,000 feet or half the runway length (whichever is less), to form a caution zone for landings.

b. *Lights marking the ends of the runway*—Emit red light toward the runway to indicate the end of the runway to a departing aircraft, and green light outward from the runway end to indicate the threshold to landing aircraft.

c. *Runway end identifier lights (REIL)*—Provide rapid and positive identification of the approach end of a particular runway. The system consists of a pair of synchronized flashing lights located laterally on each side of the runway threshold. REIL may be either omnidirectional or unidirectional facing the approach area.

d. *Taxiway edge lights*—Emit blue light and are used to outline the edges of taxiways during periods of darkness or restricted visibility conditions.

e. *Taxiway centerline lights*—Taxiway centerline lights are steady-burning, green light.

24. Describe the different visual wind direction indicators at airports without operating control towers. (AIM 4-3-4)

a. *The segmented circle*—Located in a position affording maximum visibility to pilots in the air and on the ground and providing a centralized location for other elements of the system.

b. *The wind direction indicator*—A wind cone, windsock, or wind tee installed near the operational runway to indicate wind direction.

c. *The landing direction indicator*—a tetrahedron indicates the direction of landings and takeoffs. It may be located at the center of a segmented circle and may be lit for night operations. The small end of the tetrahedron points in the direction of landing.

d. *Landing strip indicators*—Installed in pairs as shown in the segmented circle diagram and used to show the alignment of landing strips.

e. *Traffic pattern indicators*—Arranged in pairs in conjunction with landing strip indicators and used to indicate the direction of turns when there is a variation from the normal left traffic pattern.

25. During calm or nearly calm wind conditions, at an airport without an operating control tower, a pilot should be aware of what potentially hazardous situations? (AC 91-73)

Aircraft may be landing and/or taking off on more than one runway at the airport. Also, aircraft may be using an instrument approach procedure to runways other than the runway in use for VFR operations. The instrument approach runway may intersect the VFR runway. It is also possible that an instrument arrival may be made to the opposite end of the runway from which takeoff is being made.

26. When taxiing, describe several precautionary measures a pilot should take prior to entering or crossing a runway. (AC 91-73)

Towered airport—Prior to entering or crossing any runway, the pilot must be positive that ATC has cleared them to enter or cross that runway. Pilots should scan the full length of the runway and also scan for aircraft on final approach. If there is any confusion about the scan results, the pilot should stop and ask ATC to clarify the situation.

Non-towered airport—Listen on the appropriate frequency (CTAF) for inbound aircraft information and always scan the full length of the runway, including the final approach and departure paths, before entering or crossing the runway. Self-announce your position and intentions and remember that not all aircraft are radio-equipped.

27. How can a pilot use aircraft exterior lighting to enhance situational awareness and safety during airport surface operations? (AC 91-73; SAFO)

To the extent possible and consistent with aircraft equipment, operating limitations, and pilot procedures, pilots should illuminate exterior lights as follows:

a. *Engines running*—Turn on the rotating beacon whenever an engine is running.

b. *Taxiing*—Prior to commencing taxi, turn on navigation/position lights and anti-collision lights.*

c. *Crossing a runway*—All exterior lights should be illuminated when crossing a runway.

d. *Entering the departure runway for takeoff*—All exterior lights (except landing lights) should be on to make your aircraft more conspicuous to aircraft on final and ATC.

e. *Cleared for takeoff*—All exterior lights, including takeoff/ landing lights should be on.

  * Strobe lights should not be illuminated during taxi if they will adversely affect the vision of other pilots or ground personnel.

28. Explain how a pilot can mitigate the risk of a runway incursion if it becomes necessary to taxi in low visibility conditions. (AC 91-73)

During low visibility conditions, all resources available should be used during taxi. Resources include the airport diagram, the heading indicators, and airport signs, markings, and lighting. These resources help keep the aircraft on its assigned taxi route, and not crossing any runway hold lines without clearance.

E. Before Takeoff Check

1. Explain the purpose of performing a before takeoff checklist. (FAA-H-8083-3)

The before-takeoff check is the systematic POH/AFM procedure for checking the engine, controls, systems, instruments, and avionics prior to flight. Its purpose is to verify the airplane is ready and safe for flight.

2. Why do aircraft checklists call for the engine run-up/ magneto checks be performed just before takeoff instead of prior to taxi? (FAA-H-8083-3)

Several reasons:

a. Taxiing to the run-up position usually allows sufficient time for the engine to warm up to at least minimum operating temperature. Most engines require that oil temperature reach a minimum value before takeoff power is applied.

b. Taxiing to a run-up position near the takeoff end of a runway provides a suitable location that is free of debris. Otherwise, the propeller may pick up pebbles, dirt, mud, sand, or other loose objects that could damage the propeller and also damage the tail of the airplane.

3. **When checking the carburetor heat (if equipped), during the before takeoff check, explain why a drop in RPM occurs.** (FAA-H-8083-25)

The use of carburetor heat causes a decrease in engine power, sometimes up to 15 percent, because the heated air is less dense than the outside air that had been entering the engine. This enriches the mixture. A mixture that is too rich or too lean will result in the engine losing power which is indicated by a loss of RPM (on fixed pitch propellers).

4. **Explain how a pilot should properly position the airplane in the run-up area prior to performing the before takeoff check.** (FAA-H-8083-3)

   a. To minimize overheating, the airplane should be headed as nearly as possible into the wind.

   b. The airplane should be positioned clear of other aircraft and the taxiway.

   c. There should not be anything behind the airplane that might be damaged by the propeller airflow blasting rearward.

   d. The airplane should be allowed to roll forward slightly to ensure that the nosewheel or tailwheel is in alignment with the longitudinal axis of the airplane.

5. **If the engine stops running when switched to one magneto or if the RPM drop exceeds the allowable limit, what does this indicate about the ignition system?** (FAA-H-8083-25)

The cause could be fouled plugs, broken or shorted wires between the magneto and the plugs, or improperly timed firing of the plugs. It should be noted that no drop in RPM is not normal and, in that instance, the aircraft should not be flown.

6. **Identify the hazards that can exist while performing a before takeoff checklist.** (FAA-S-ACS-6)

   a. Not dividing attention while conducting the before takeoff checks.

   b. Unexpected runway changes by ATC.

   c. Takeoff emergency procedures; failure to brief.

   d. Wake turbulence.

   e. Failure to brief potential for powerplant failure and other malfunctions during takeoff.

7. **Explain what a pilot can do to minimize the possibility of overheating the engine during the engine run-up prior to takeoff.** (FAA-H-8083-3)

   To minimize overheating during engine run-up, it is recommended that the airplane be headed as nearly as possible into the wind and, if equipped, engine instruments that indicate cylinder head temperatures should be monitored. Cowl flaps, if available, should be set according to the POH/AFM.

Additional Study Questions

1. **Explain how you would determine if a fuel sample obtained during your preflight inspection contained the incorrect grade of fuel or had signs of water contamination.** (AC 20-125, FAA-H-8083-25)

2. **When taxiing an airplane, what is considered a safe taxi speed?** (FAA-H-8083-3)

3. **You suspect a placard is missing on the flight deck. How will you determine that all required placards are present?** (POH/AFM, TCDS)

4. **When performing the magneto check before takeoff, explain why there is a small decrease in RPM when the ignition switch is first moved from BOTH to RIGHT, and then from BOTH to LEFT.** (FAA-H-8083-25)

5. Prior to taxiing onto a runway or landing area in preparation for takeoff, how will you scan the approach area for possible landing traffic? (FAA-H-8083-25)

6. What basic precaution should be taken when taxiing over grass or loose gravel? (FAA-H-8083-3)

7. Do you perform a pre-takeoff emergency briefing prior to departure and if so, provide an example? (FAA-H-8083-3)

Airport
Operations

10

A. Communications, Light Signals, and Runway Lighting Systems

1. **Explain where a pilot would look for radio communication frequencies and other airport data.** (FAA-H-8083-25)

   Communication frequencies and airport data may be found in the following:

   a. Aeronautical charts (on the chart tab).

   b. The Chart Supplement U.S.

   c. Notices to Air Missions (NOTAMs).

   d. Automated Terminal Information Service (ATIS) broadcasts.

   e. GPS navigation databases and charting apps.

2. **Explain the phraseology a pilot should use on initial contact with an ATC facility.** (AIM 4-2-3)

   Use the following format:

   a. Name of the facility being called.

   b. Your full aircraft identification.

   c. If on the ground, your position, if in the air, your location.

   d. Your request if it is short.

   Example: "Columbia Ground, Cessna Three One Six Zero Foxtrot, south ramp, ready to taxi, with information Bravo."

3. **When used to acknowledge time-critical ATC instructions, explain the meaning of the following words: Wilco, Roger, Affirmative, Negative.** (FAA-P-8740-47)

   Wilco, which means, "I will comply."

   Roger, which means, "I have received and understood your last transmission."

   Affirmative, which means, "Yes."

   Negative, which means, "No."

4. Is it acceptable to abbreviate your call sign on an initial contact with an ATC facility? (FAA-P-8740-47)

It is very important to ensure use of correct call signs. Aircraft with similar call signs may be on the same frequency, and improper use of call signs can result in one pilot executing a clearance intended for another aircraft. To avoid this problem, never abbreviate your call sign on an initial contact, or at any time when other aircraft call signs you hear on the frequency have similar numbers/sounds or identical letters/numbers to those of your own aircraft (e.g., Cessna 6132F, Cessna 1622F, Baron 123F, Cherokee 7732F, etc.).

5. What is the most common type of communication radio equipment installed in general aviation aircraft? How many channels are available? (FAA-H-8083-25)

In general aviation, the most common types of radios are VHF. A VHF radio operates on frequencies between 118.0 and 136.975 MHz and is classified as 720 or 760 depending on the number of channels it can accommodate. The 720 and 760 uses .025 spacing (118.025, 118.050, etc.) with the 720 having a frequency range up to 135.975 and the 760 going up to 136.975.

6. What frequencies are used for ground control?
(AIM 4-3-14)

The majority of ground control frequencies are 121.6 to 121.9 MHz

7. What is a Common Traffic Advisory Frequency (CTAF)?
(AIM 4-1-9)

A CTAF is a frequency designated for the purpose of carrying out airport advisory practices while operating to or from an airport without an operating control tower. The CTAF may be a UNICOM, MULTICOM, FSS or TOWER frequency and is identified in appropriate aeronautical publications.

8. What is UNICOM, and what frequencies are designated for its use? (AIM 4-1-9 and 4-1-11)

UNICOM is a nongovernment communication facility which may provide airport information at certain airports. Airports other than those with a control tower/FSS on airport will normally use 122.700, 122.725, 122.800, 122.975, 123.000, 123.050, and 123.075 MHz. Airports with a control tower or an FSS on airport will normally use 122.950 MHz.

9. What does ATIS mean? (AIM 4-1-13)

Automatic Terminal Information Service (ATIS) is the continuous broadcast of recorded noncontrol information in selected high-activity terminal areas. Its purpose is to improve controller effectiveness and to relieve frequency congestion by automating the repetitive transmission of essential but routine information.

10. What is an RCO? (P/CG)

A remote communications outlet (RCO) is an unmanned communications facility remotely controlled by ATC personnel, established for the purpose of providing ground-to-ground communications between ATC and pilots located at satellite airports. ATC may use the RCO to deliver en route clearances and departure authorizations, and to acknowledge IFR cancellations or departure/landing times. As a secondary function, RCOs may be used for advisory purposes whenever the aircraft is below the coverage of the primary air/ground frequency.

11. If operating into an airport without an operating control tower, FSS or UNICOM, what procedure should be followed? (AIM 4-1-9, P/CG)

Where there is no tower, FSS, or UNICOM station on the airport, use MULTICOM frequency 122.9 for self-announce procedures. MULTICOM is a mobile service not open to public use, used to provide communications essential to conduct the activities being performed by or directed from private aircraft.

12. What would be an indication that a microphone/PTT switch is stuck in the transmit position in your airplane? What would you do? (AIM 4-2-2)

One indication would be a lack of sounds from the receiver. Some aircraft transmitters will indicate that they're transmitting by displaying a "T" on the display. Check your volume, recheck your frequency, and make sure that your microphone/Push-To-Talk (PTT) button is not stuck in the transmit position. Depending on the airplane, other possible actions would be unplugging the microphone/PTT, unplugging a headset, etc.

13. **If operating into an airport *without* an operating control tower which is located within the Class D airspace of an airport with an operating control tower, is it always necessary to communicate with the tower?** (14 CFR 91.129)

    Yes, operations to or from an airport in Class D airspace (airport traffic area) require communication with the tower even when operating to/from a satellite airport.

14. **When conducting flight operations into an airport with an operating control tower, when should initial contact be established?** (AIM 4-3-2)

    When operating at an airport where traffic control is being exercised by a control tower, pilots are required to maintain two-way radio contact with the tower while operating within Class B, Class C, and Class D surface areas, unless the tower authorizes otherwise. Initial call-up should be made about 15 miles from the airport. Also, not all airports with an operating control tower will have Class D airspace. These airports do not have weather reporting, which is a requirement for surface-based controlled airspace. Pilots are expected to use good operating practices and communicate with the control tower.

15. **When departing a Class D surface area, what communications procedures are recommended?** (AIM 4-3-2)

    Unless there is good reason to leave the tower frequency before exiting the Class B, Class C, and Class D surface areas, it is good operating practice to remain on the tower frequency for the purpose of receiving traffic information. In the interest of reducing tower frequency congestion, pilots are reminded that it is not necessary to request permission to leave the tower frequency once outside of Class B, Class C, and Class D surface areas.

16. **Arrange the radio facilities listed below in the order they would be used when operating into or out of a tower controlled airport within Class B, C, or D airspace.**

    Approach Control, ATIS, Ground Control, Control Tower, Clearance Delivery, Departure Control

    Arriving Aircraft: ATIS, Approach Control, Control Tower, Ground Control

    Departing Aircraft: ATIS, Clearance Delivery (if required for the surrounding airspace, i.e., Class B, C or D airspace), Ground Control, Control Tower, Departure Control.

17. **What does the operation of an airport rotating beacon during the hours of daylight indicate?** (AIM 2-1-9)

    In Class B, Class C, Class D, and Class E surface areas, operation of the airport beacon during the hours of daylight often indicates that the ground visibility is less than 3 miles and/or the ceiling is less than 1,000 feet. ATC clearance in accordance with Part 91 is required for landing, takeoff and flight in the traffic pattern. Pilots should not rely solely on the operation of the airport beacon to indicate if weather conditions are IFR or VFR. There is no regulatory requirement for daylight operation, and it is the pilot's responsibility to comply with proper preflight planning as required by Part 91.

18. **When may a pilot intentionally deviate from an ATC clearance or instruction?** (14 CFR 91.123)

    No pilot may deviate from an ATC clearance unless:

    a. An amended clearance has been obtained;

    b. An emergency exists; or

    c. In response to a traffic and collision avoidance system resolution advisory.

19. As pilot-in-command, what action, if any, is required of you if you deviate from an ATC instruction and priority is given? (14 CFR 91.123)

Two actions are required of you as PIC:

a. Each pilot-in-command who, in an emergency or in response to a traffic alert and collision avoidance system resolution advisory, deviates from an ATC clearance or instruction must notify ATC of that deviation as soon as possible.

b. Each pilot-in-command who is given priority by ATC in an emergency shall submit a detailed report of that emergency within 48 hours to the manager of that ATC facility, if requested by ATC (on-the-ground responsibility).

20. In the event of radio failure while operating an aircraft to, from, through or on an airport having an operational tower, what are the different types and meanings of light gun signals you might receive from an ATC tower? (14 CFR 91.125)

Type	Color	Meaning On Ground	Meaning In Flight
Steady	Green	Cleared for takeoff	Cleared to land
Steady	Red	Stop	Give way/circle
Flashing	Green	Cleared to taxi	Return for landing
Flashing	Red	Taxi clear of landing area	Airport unsafe; Do not land
Flashing	White	Return to starting point	Not applicable
Alternating	Red/green	Use extreme caution	Use extreme caution

21. Explain when transponder and ADS-B Out equipment should be operated while on the ground. (AIM 4-1-20)

Civil and military aircraft should operate with the transponder in the altitude reporting mode and ADS-B Out transmissions enabled at all airports, any time the aircraft is positioned on any portion of the airport movement area. This includes all defined taxiways and runways. Pilots must pay particular attention to ATIS and airport diagram notations, General Notes (included on airport charts), and comply with directions pertaining to transponder and ADS-B usage.

22. If the aircraft radio fails in flight under VFR while operating into a tower controlled airport, what conditions must be met before a landing may be made at that airport? (14 CFR 91.126, 91.127, 91.129)

a. Weather conditions must be at or above basic VFR weather minimums;

b. Visual contact with the tower is maintained; and

c. A clearance to land is received.

23. What procedures should be used when attempting communications with a tower when the aircraft transmitter or receiver or both are inoperative? (AIM 4-2-13, 6-4-2)

Arriving aircraft receiver inoperative:

a. Remain outside or above Class D surface area.

b. Determine direction and flow of traffic.

c. Advise tower of aircraft type, position, altitude, and intention to land. Request to be controlled by light signals.

d. At 3 to 5 miles, advise tower of position and join traffic pattern.

e. Watch tower for light gun signals.

Arriving aircraft transmitter inoperative:

a. Remain outside or above Class D surface area.

b. Determine direction and flow of traffic.

c. Monitor frequency for landing or traffic information.

d. Join the traffic pattern and watch for light gun signals.

e. Daytime, acknowledge by rocking wings. Nighttime, acknowledge by flashing landing light or navigation lights.

Arriving aircraft transmitter and receiver inoperative:

a. Remain outside or above Class D surface area.

b. Determine direction and flow of traffic.

c. Join the traffic pattern and watch for light gun signals.

d. Acknowledge light signals as noted above.

Note: When an aircraft with a coded radar beacon transponder experiences a loss of two-way radio capability, the pilot should adjust the transponder to reply on Mode A/3, Code 7600. The pilot should understand that the aircraft may not be in an area of radar coverage.

24. Describe the type of information provided when receiving VFR radar assistance from ATC. (FAA-H-8083-25, AIM 4-1-17)

Radar equipped ATC facilities provide radar assistance to aircraft on instrument flight plans and VFR aircraft, provided the aircraft can communicate with the facility and are within radar coverage. This basic service includes safety alerts, traffic advisories, limited vectoring when requested, and sequencing at locations where this procedure has been established. ATC issues traffic advisories based on observed radar targets. This service is not intended to relieve the pilot of the responsibility to see and avoid other aircraft

25. Describe the various types of terminal radar services available for VFR aircraft. (AIM 4-1-18)

Basic radar service—Safety alerts, traffic advisories, limited radar vectoring (on a workload-permitting basis) and sequencing at locations where procedures have been established for this purpose and/or when covered by a letter of agreement.

TRSA service—Radar sequencing and separation service for participating VFR aircraft in a TRSA.

Class C service—This service provides, in addition to basic radar service, approved separation between IFR, and VFR aircraft, and sequencing of VFR arrivals to the primary airport.

Class B service—Provides, in addition to basic radar service, approved separation of aircraft based on IFR, VFR, and/or weight, and sequencing of VFR arrivals to the primary airport(s).

26. When is immediate notification to the NTSB required? (NTSB Part 830.5)

The operator of an aircraft shall immediately, and by the most expeditious means available, notify the nearest National Transportation Safety Board (NTSB) office when an aircraft accident or any of the following listed serious incidents occur:

a. Flight control system malfunction.

b. Crewmember unable to perform normal duties.

(continued)

   c. Inflight fire.

   d. Aircraft collision inflight.

   e. Property damage, other than aircraft, estimated to exceed $25,000.

   f. Overdue aircraft (believed to be in accident).

   g. Release of all or a portion of a propeller blade from an aircraft.

   h. Complete loss of information (excluding flickering), from more than 50 percent of an aircraft's EFIS cockpit displays.

27. Explain the difference between an aircraft incident and an aircraft accident. (NTSB Part 830.2)

Aircraft incident—Means an occurrence other than an accident associated with the operation of an aircraft, which affects or could affect the safety of operations.

Aircraft accident—Means an occurrence associated with the operation of an aircraft which takes place between the time any person boards the aircraft with the intention of flight and all such persons have disembarked, and in which any person suffers death or serious injury, or in which the aircraft receives substantial damage.

28. Define the term *serious injury*. (NTSB Part 830.2)

Serious injury means any injury that:

   a. Requires hospitalization for more than 48 hours, commencing within 7 days from the date the injury was received;

   b. Results in a fracture of any bone (except simple fractures of fingers, toes or nose);

   c. Causes severe hemorrhages, nerve, muscle, or tendon damage;

   d. Involves any internal organ; or

   e. Involves second- or third-degree burns affecting more than 5% of the body surface.

29. Define the term *substantial damage*. (NTSB Part 830.2)

Substantial damage means damage or failure which adversely affects the structural strength, performance or flight characteristics of the aircraft and which would normally require major repair or replacement of the affected component. Engine failure or damage limited to an engine if only one engine fails or is damaged; bent fairings or cowling; dented skin; small punctured holes in the skin or fabric; ground damage to rotor or propeller blades; and damage to landing gear, wheels, tires, flaps, engine accessories, brakes, or wing tips are not considered substantial damage for the purpose of this part.

30. Will notification to the NTSB always be necessary in any aircraft accident even if there were no injuries? (NTSB Part 830)

Refer to the definition of accident. An aircraft accident can involve substantial damage and/or injuries, and the NTSB always requires a report if this is the case.

31. Where are accident or incident reports filed? (NTSB Part 830)

The operator of an aircraft shall file any report with the field office of the Board nearest the accident or incident.

32. After an accident or incident has occurred, how soon must a report be filed with the NTSB? (NTSB Part 830)

The operator shall file a report on NTSB Form 6120.1/2, available from NTSB field offices, the NTSB in Washington D.C., or the FAA Flight Standards District Office:

a. Within 10 days after an accident.

b. When, after 7 days, an overdue aircraft is still missing.

Note: A report on an incident for which notification is required as described shall be filed only as requested by an authorized representative of the NTSB.

33. An airport diagram indicates the letters "RWSL." Explain what these letters indicate. (AIM 2-1-6, P/CG)

Runway Status Lights system—The RWSL is a system of runway and taxiway lighting to provide pilots increased situational awareness by illuminating runway entry lights (REL) when the runway is unsafe for entry or crossing, and take-off hold lights (THL) when the runway is unsafe for departure. The lights automatically turn red when other traffic makes it dangerous to enter, cross, or begin takeoff.

B. Traffic Patterns

1. What are the two main categories of airports?
(FAA-H-8083-25)

Towered airport—Pilots are required to maintain two-way radio communication with ATC and to acknowledge and comply with their instructions.

Non-towered airport—Two-way radio communications are not required, although it is a good operating practice for pilots to transmit their intentions on the specified frequency for the benefit of other traffic in the area.

Note: These two types of airports can be further subdivided into civil airports, military/federal government airports, and private airports.

2. Explain the purpose of an airport traffic pattern.
(FAA-H-8083-3)

An airport traffic pattern is the traffic flow or pattern that is prescribed for aircraft landing at, taxiing on, or taking off from the airport. To assure that air traffic flows into and out of an airport in an orderly manner, a traffic pattern is established based on the local conditions, to include the direction and altitude of the pattern and the procedures for entering and leaving the pattern.

3. What are the basic components of an airport traffic pattern? (FAA-H-8083-3)

a. *Upwind leg*—A flight path parallel to the landing runway in the direction of landing.

b. *Crosswind leg*—A flight path at right angles to the landing runway off its upwind end.

c. *Downwind leg*—A flight path parallel to the landing runway in the direction opposite to landing. The downwind leg normally extends between the crosswind leg and the base leg.

d. *Base leg*—A flight path at right angles to the landing runway off its approach end. The base leg normally extends from the downwind leg to the intersection of the extended runway centerline.

e. *Final approach*—A flight path in the direction of landing along the extended runway centerline. The final approach normally extends from the base leg to the runway. An aircraft making a straight-in approach VFR is also considered to be on final approach.

4. **When approaching an airport with an operating control tower, when should initial contact be made with the ATC tower?** (AIM 4-3-2)

Initial call-up should be made about 15 miles from the airport.

5. **Explain the general rules that apply when conducting traffic pattern operations at a non-towered airport within Class E or G airspace.** (14 CFR 91.126, 91.127)

Each person operating an aircraft to or from an airport without an operating control tower shall:

a. in the case of an airplane approaching to land, make all turns of that airplane to the left unless the airport displays approved light signals or visual markings indicating that turns should be made to the right, in which case the pilot shall make all turns to the right.

b. in the case of an aircraft departing an airport, comply with any traffic patterns established for that airport in Part 93.

6. **When operating in Class D airspace, what procedure should be used when approaching to land on a runway with a Visual Approach Slope Indicator?** (14 CFR 91.129)

Aircraft approaching to land on a runway served by a Visual Approach Slope Indicator shall maintain an altitude at or above the glide slope until a lower altitude is necessary for a safe landing.

7. **Explain the recommended traffic pattern entry procedure at a non-towered airport.** (AC 90-66, AIM 4-3-3)

Arriving aircraft should be at traffic pattern altitude and allow for sufficient time to view the entire traffic pattern before entering. Entries into traffic patterns while descending may create collision hazards and should be avoided. Entry to the downwind leg should be at a 45 degree angle abeam the midpoint of the runway to be used for landing. The pilot may use discretion to choose an alternate type of entry, especially when intending to cross over midfield, based upon the traffic and communication at the time of arrival.

8. **Explain the recommended traffic pattern departure procedure at a non-towered airport.** (AC 90-66, AIM 4-3-3)

   When departing the traffic pattern, airplanes should continue straight out or exit with a 45-degree left turn (right turn for right traffic pattern) beyond the departure end of the runway after reaching pattern altitude. Pilots need to be aware of any traffic entering the traffic pattern prior to commencing a turn.

9. **What is considered standard for a traffic pattern altitude?** (AIM 4-3-3)

   Unless otherwise required by the applicable distance from cloud criteria (14 CFR §91.155):

   a. Propeller-driven aircraft enter the traffic pattern at 1,000 feet AGL.

   b. Large and turbine-powered aircraft enter the traffic pattern at an altitude of not less than 1,500 feet AGL or 500 feet above the established pattern altitude.

   c. Helicopters operating in the traffic pattern may fly a pattern similar to the fixed-wing aircraft pattern, but at a lower altitude (500 AGL) and closer to the runway. This pattern may be on the opposite side of the runway from fixed-wing traffic when airspeed requires or for practice power-off landings (autorotation) and if local policy permits. Landings not to the runway must avoid the flow of fixed wing traffic.

   Note: Specific airport traffic pattern altitude information and any additional remarks may be found in the Chart Supplement U.S.

10. **Explain the different methods a pilot may use to determine the proper runway and traffic pattern in use at an airport without an operating control tower.** (AIM 4-1-9, 4-3-4)

    a. At an airport with a full or part-time UNICOM station in operation, an advisory may be obtained which will usually include wind direction and velocity, favored or designated runway, right or left traffic, altimeter setting, known traffic, NOTAMs, etc.

    b. Many airports are now providing completely automated weather, radio check capability and airport advisory information on an automated UNICOM system. Availability of the automated UNICOM will be published in the *Chart Supplement U.S.* and approach charts.

c. At those airports where these services are not available, a segmented circle visual indicator system, if installed, is designated to provide traffic pattern information. The segmented circle system consists of the following components:

- The segmented circle.
- The wind direction indicator (wind sock, cone, or tee).
- The landing direction indicator (a tetrahedron).
- Landing strip indicators.
- Traffic pattern indicators.

11. State the required action for each of the aircraft confrontations (same category), below. (14 CFR 91.113)

Converging

Approaching head-on

Overtaking

Converging—Aircraft on right has the right-of-way.

Approaching head-on—Both aircraft shall alter course to right.

Overtaking—Aircraft being overtaken has the right-of-way; pilot of the overtaking aircraft shall alter course to the right.

12. Explain the right-of-way rules that apply when two or more aircraft are approaching an airport for the purpose of landing. (14 CFR 91.113)

Aircraft on final approach to land or while landing have the right-of-way over aircraft in flight or operating on the surface, except that they shall not take advantage of this rule to force an aircraft off the runway surface which has already landed and is attempting to make way for an aircraft on final approach. When two or more aircraft are approaching an airport for the purpose of landing, the aircraft at the lower altitude has the right-of-way, but it shall not take advantage of this rule to cut in front of another which is on final approach to land or to overtake that aircraft.

13. **What is the order of right-of-way as applied to the different categories of aircraft?** (14 CFR 91.113)

    Balloons

    Gliders

    Airships

    Airplanes

    Rotorcraft

    Aircraft towing or refueling other aircraft have the right-of-way over all other engine-driven aircraft.

    Remember: BGAAR (BIG "R")

14. **When would an aircraft have the right-of-way over all other air traffic?** (14 CFR 91.113)

    An aircraft in distress has the right-of-way over all other air traffic.

15. **Identify several hazards that a pilot should consider when operating in an airport traffic pattern.** (FAA-S-ACS-6)

    a. Collision hazards.

    b. Distractions, task prioritization, loss of situational awareness, or disorientation.

    c. Windshear and wake turbulence.

16. **Explain how a pilot can mitigate the risk of an in-flight collision when operating in the traffic pattern at a non-towered airport.** (FAA Safety)

    a. Be conspicuous. Use landing lights and strobes.

    b. Announce your positions and intentions on the CTAF.

    c. Be aware of possible no-radio aircraft.

    d. Don't assert right-of-way if it will result in a collision hazard.

    e. If there's an unresolved conflict, break off the approach and go around to the non-pattern side of the runway.

17. Define the term *wake turbulence*. (AIM 7-4-1)

Every aircraft generates wake turbulence while in flight. Wake turbulence is a function of an aircraft producing lift, resulting in the formation of two counter-rotating vortices trailing behind the aircraft.

18. Explain how wake vortices are created. (AIM 7-4-2)

The creation of a pressure differential over the wing surface generates lift. The lowest pressure occurs over the upper wing surface and the highest pressure under the wing. This pressure differential triggers the roll up of the airflow at the rear of the wing resulting in swirling air masses trailing downstream of the wing tips. After the roll up is completed, the wake consists of two counter-rotating cylindrical vortices.

19. What factors govern the strength of a vortex generated by an aircraft? (AIM 7-4-3)

Weight, speed, wingspan, and shape of the generating aircraft's wing all govern the strength of the vortex. The vortex characteristics of any given aircraft can also be changed by extension of flaps or other wing configuring devices. However, the vortex strength from an aircraft increases proportionately to an increase in operating weight or a decrease in aircraft speed. Since the turbulence from a "dirty" aircraft configuration hastens wake decay, the greatest vortex strength occurs when the generating aircraft is HEAVY, CLEAN, and SLOW.

20. Where is an encounter with wake turbulence likely to occur? (AIM 7-4-5)

Pilot should avoid the area below ad behind the wake generating aircraft, especially at low altitude where even a momentary wake encounter could be catastrophic. Pilots should also be particularly alert in calm wind conditions and situations where the vortices could:

a. Remain in the touchdown area.

b. Drift from aircraft operating on a nearby runway.

c. Sink into the takeoff or landing path from a crossing runway.

d. Sink into the traffic pattern from other airport operations.

e. Sink into the flight path of VFR aircraft operating on the hemispheric altitude 500 feet below.

21. Explain the operational procedures that should be followed when wake vortices are suspected to exist? (AIM 7-4-6)

a. *Landing behind a larger aircraft on the same runway*—Stay at or above the larger aircraft's final approach flight path. Note its touchdown point and land beyond it.

b. *Landing behind a larger aircraft, when parallel runway is closer than 2,500 feet*—Consider possible drift to your runway. Stay at or above the larger aircraft's final approach flight path, and note its touchdown point.

c. *Landing behind a larger aircraft, crossing runway*—Cross above the larger aircraft's flight path.

d. *Landing behind a departing larger aircraft on the same runway*—Note the larger aircraft's rotation point, and land well prior to rotation point.

e. *Landing behind a departing larger aircraft, crossing runway*—Note the larger aircraft's rotation point. If past the intersection, continue the approach, and land prior to the intersection. If larger aircraft rotates prior to the intersection, avoid flight below the larger aircraft's flightpath. Abandon the approach unless a landing is ensured well before reaching the intersection.

f. *Departing behind a large aircraft*—Note the larger aircraft's rotation point and rotate prior to the larger aircraft's rotation point. Continue climbing above the larger aircraft's climb path until turning clear of the larger aircraft's wake. Avoid subsequent headings that will cross below and behind a larger aircraft.

g. *Intersection takeoffs, same runway*—Be alert to adjacent larger aircraft operations, especially of your runway. If intersection takeoff clearance is received, avoid subsequent heading which will cross below a larger aircraft's path.

h. *Departing or landing after a larger aircraft executing a low approach, missed approach or touch-and-go landing*—Vortices settle and move laterally near the ground. Because of this, the vortex hazard may exist along the runway and in your flight path after a larger aircraft has executed a low approach, missed approach or a touch-and-go landing, particularly in light

quartering wind conditions. You should ensure that an interval
of at least 2 minutes has elapsed before your takeoff or landing.

i. *En route VFR (thousand-foot altitude plus 500 feet)*—Avoid
flight below and behind a large aircraft's path. If a larger
aircraft is observed above or on the same track (meeting or
overtaking) adjust your position laterally, preferably upwind.

Remember: Acceptance of instructions from ATC is an
acknowledgment that the pilot will ensure safe takeoff and
landing intervals and accept the responsibility for providing wake
turbulence separation.

22. What type of automated weather is provided at most controlled airports? (AIM 4-1-13)

The Automated Terminal Information Service (ATIS) is a recording
of the local weather conditions and other pertinent non-control
information broadcast on a local frequency in a looped format.
It is normally updated once per hour but is updated more often
when changing local conditions warrant. Important information is
broadcast on ATIS including weather, runways in use, specific ATC
procedures, and any airport construction activity that could affect
taxi planning.

23. What type of automated weather is available at uncontrolled airports? (AIM 4-3-26)

Many airports throughout the National Airspace System are
equipped with either ASOS or AWOS. At uncontrolled airports
that are equipped with ASOS/AWOS with ground-to-air broadcast
capability, the one-minute updated airport weather should be
available to you within approximately 25 NM of the airport below
10,000 feet. The frequency for the weather broadcast will be
published on sectional charts and in the Chart Supplement U.S.

Additional Study Questions

1. The acronym LAHSO refers to what specific air traffic control procedure? (AIM 4-3-11)

2. Where can available landing distance (ALD) data be found? (AIM 4-3-11)

3. **Discuss recommended collision avoidance procedures and considerations in the following situations: Before takeoff, climbs and descents, straight and level, traffic patterns, traffic at VOR sites, training operations.**
(AIM 4-4-15)

4. **Where are UAS (drones) allowed to operate?** (AIM 7-6-6, AC 107-2)

5. **What is the Aviation Safety Reporting System (ASRS)?**
(FAA-H-8083-19, AC 00-46)

6. **Can the FAA use ASRS reports submitted to NASA for enforcement purposes?** (14 CFR 91.25, AC 00-46)

7. **ATC has instructed you to line up and wait on the departure runway due to crossing traffic on an intersecting taxiway. What is considered a reasonable amount of time to wait for a takeoff clearance before calling ATC?** (AIM 5-2-5, SAFO 11004)

8. **Demonstrate the following hand signals utilized by a lineman when directing you to or from a ramp:**
(AIM 4-3-25)
   a. **All clear (OK)**
   b. **Start engine**
   c. **Pull chocks**
   d. **Come ahead**
   e. **Left turn**
   f. **Right turn**
   g. **Slow down**
   h. **Stop**
   i. **Insert chocks**
   j. **Cut engines**
   k. **Emergency stop**

Night Operations **11**

A. Night Vision

1. Name the two distinct types of light-sensitive cells located in the retina of the eye. (FAA-H-8083-3)

Rods and cones are the light-sensitive cells located in the retina.

2. Where are the cones located in the eye and what is their function? (FAA-H-8083-3)

The cones are located in higher concentrations than rods in the central area of the retina known as the macula. The exact center of the macula has a very small depression called the fovea, which contains cones only. The cones are used for day or high-intensity light vision. They are involved with central vision to detect detail, perceive color, and identify far-away objects.

3. What is the function of the rods and where are they located in the eye? (FAA-H-8083-3)

The rods are located mainly in the periphery of the retina—an area that is about 10,000 times more sensitive to light than the fovea. Rods are used for low light intensity or night vision and are involved with peripheral vision to detect position references, including objects (fixed and moving) in shades of gray, but cannot be used to detect detail or to perceive color. The rods make night vision possible.

4. What is the average time it takes for the rods and cones to become adapted to darkness? (FAA-H-8083-3)

The cones will take approximately 5 to 10 minutes to become adjusted to darkness. Much more time—about 30 minutes—is needed for the rods to become adjusted to darkness.

5. What should the pilot do to accommodate changing light conditions? (FAA-H-8083-3)

The pilot should allow enough time for the eyes to become adapted to the low light levels, and then should avoid exposure to bright light which could cause temporary blindness.

6. What is the night blind spot and how does it affect a pilot's visual field? (FAA-H-8083-3)

The night blind spot refers to the absence of rods in the fovea, affecting the central 5 to 10 degrees of the visual field under conditions of low ambient illumination. This can cause an object viewed directly at night to go undetected or fade away after initial detection.

7. **What is the false horizon illusion, and how can it affect pilots flying at night?** (FAA-H-8083-3)

Flying at night under clear skies with ground lights below can result in situations where it is difficult to distinguish the ground lights from the stars. A dark scene spread with ground lights and stars, and certain geometric patterns of ground lights can provide inaccurate visual information, making it difficult to align the aircraft correctly with the actual horizon.

8. **What is autokinesis, and how can it lead to spatial disorientation in pilots?** (FAA-H-8083-3)

In the dark, a stationary light will appear to move about when stared at for many seconds. The disoriented pilot could lose control of the aircraft in attempting to align it with the false movements of this light.

9. **What is the featureless terrain illusion, and how can it cause problems for pilots during landing?** (FAA-H-8083-3)

A black-hole approach occurs when the landing is made from over water or non-lighted terrain where the runway lights are the only source of light. Without peripheral visual cues to help, orientation is difficult. The runway can seem out of position (down-sloping or up-sloping) and in the worst case, results in landing short of the runway.

10. **How can bright runway and approach lighting systems create illusions for pilots, and what should pilots do to mitigate these illusions?** (FAA-H-8083-3)

Bright runway and approach lighting systems, especially where few lights illuminate the surrounding terrain, may create the illusion of being lower or having less distance to the runway. In this situation, the tendency is to fly a higher approach. Also, flying over terrain with only a few lights makes the runway recede or appear farther away. With this situation, the tendency is to fly a lower-than-normal approach.

11. What are ground lighting Illusions, and how can they be mistaken for runway and approach lights? (FAA-H-8083-3)

Lights along a straight path, such as a road or lights on moving trains, can be mistaken for runway and approach lights. Bright runway and approach lighting systems, especially where few lights illuminate the surrounding terrain, may create the illusion of less distance to the runway. The pilot who does not recognize this illusion will often fly a higher approach.

12. What can a pilot do to prevent the optical illusions that can occur at night and cause landing errors? (FAA-H-8083-3)

a. Anticipate the possibility of visual illusions during approaches to unfamiliar airports, particularly at night or in adverse weather conditions.

b. Use airport diagrams and the Chart Supplements for information on runway slope, terrain, and lighting.

c. Make frequent reference to the altimeter, especially during all approaches, day and night.

d. If possible, conduct aerial visual inspection of unfamiliar airports before landing.

e. Use VASI or PAPI systems for a visual reference or an electronic glideslope, when available.

f. Utilize the visual descent point (VDP) found on many non–precision instrument approach procedure charts.

g. Recognize that the chances of an approach accident increase when an emergency or other activity distracts from normal procedures.

h. Maintain optimum proficiency in night landing procedures.

13. What should the pilot do to maintain good eyesight? (FAA-H-8083-3)

Good eyesight depends upon physical condition. Fatigue, colds, vitamin deficiency, alcohol, stimulants, smoking, or medication can seriously impair vision.

14. What are some self-imposed stresses that can impair vision during flight at night? (FAA-H-8083-3)

Self-imposed stresses such as self-medication, alcohol consumption (including hangover effects), tobacco use (including withdrawal), hypoglycemia, sleep deprivation/fatigue, and extreme emotional upset can seriously impair vision.

15. How does hypoxia impair visual performance during night flight? (FAA-H-8083-25)

Unaided night vision depends on optimum function and sensitivity of the rods of the retina. Lack of oxygen to the rods (hypoxia) significantly reduces their sensitivity. Sharp clear vision (with the best being equal to 20–20 vision) requires significant oxygen especially at night. Without supplemental oxygen, an individual's night vision declines measurably at pressure altitudes above 4,000 feet.

B. Airport Lighting

1. Describe runway end identifier lights (REIL)? (AIM 2-1-3)

REILs are installed at many airfields to provide rapid and positive identification of the approach end of a particular runway. The system consists of a pair of synchronized flashing lights located laterally on each side of the runway threshold. REILs may be omnidirectional or unidirectional facing the approach area.

2. Describe a runway edge light system. (AIM 2-1-4)

Runway edge lights are used to outline the edges of runways during periods of darkness or restricted visibility conditions. They are white, except on instrument runways yellow replaces white on the last 2,000 feet or half the runway length, whichever is less, to form a caution zone for landings. The lights marking the ends of the runway emit red light toward the runway to indicate the end of runway to a departing aircraft and emit green outward from the runway end to indicate the threshold to landing aircraft. These light systems are classified according to the intensity or brightness they are capable of producing. Examples are high intensity runway lights (HIRL), medium intensity runway lights (MIRL), and the low intensity runway lights (LIRL).

3. Describe a Runway Centerline Lighting System (RCLS). (AIM 2-1-5)

Runway centerline lights—are installed on some precision approach runways to facilitate landing under adverse visibility conditions. They are located along the runway centerline and are spaced at 50-foot intervals. When viewed from the landing threshold, the runway centerline lights are white until the last 3,000 feet of the runway. The white lights begin to alternate with red for the next 2,000 feet, and for the last 1,000 feet of the runway, all centerline lights are red.

4. What are Touchdown Zone Lights (TDZLs)? (AIM 2-1-5)

TDZLs consist of two rows of transverse light bars disposed symmetrically about the runway centerline. The system consists of steady-burning white lights that start at 100 feet beyond the landing threshold and extend to 3,000 feet beyond the landing threshold or to the midpoint of the runway, whichever is less.

5. Describe several different types of taxiway lighting. (AIM 2-1-10)

a. *Taxiway edge lights*—outline the edges of taxiways; consist of blue lights.

b. *Taxiway centerline lights*—assists ground traffic in low visibility conditions; consists of steady-burning green lights.

c. *Clearance bar lights*—installed at holding positions on taxiways; consist of three in-pavement steady-burning yellow lights.

d. *Runway guard lights*—installed at taxiway/runway intersections; consists of either a pair of elevated flashing lights on either side of taxiway or in-pavement yellow lights installed across the taxiway.

e. *Stop bar lights*—used to confirm ATC clearance to enter or cross an active runway in low visibility conditions; consists of a row of red, unidirectional, steady-burning in-pavement lights installed across the taxiway and a pair of elevated steady burning red lights on each side.

6. What are the different types of rotating beacons used to identify airports? (AIM 2-1-9)

White and green—Lighted land airport

Green alone*—Lighted land airport

White and yellow—Lighted water airport

Yellow alone*—Lighted water airport

Green, yellow, and white—Lighted heliport

White (dual peaked and green)—Lighted military airport

*Green alone or yellow alone is used only in connection with a
white and green or white and yellow beacon display, respectively.

7. What type of aeronautical lighting is a visual approach slope indicator (VASI)? (AIM 2-1-2)

VASI is a system of lights arranged to provide visual descent
guidance information during the approach to a runway. The basic
principle of VASI is that of color differential between red and
white: each light projects a beam of light having a white segment
in the upper half and a red segment in the lower part of the beam.
The lights in a two-bar VASI will be as follows:

Red over red—Below glide path

Red over white—On glide path

White over white—Above glide path

8. What is a precision approach path indicator (PAPI)? (AIM 2-1-2)

PAPI uses light units similar to VASI but are installed in a single
row of either two- or four-light units. These systems have an
effective visual range of about 5 miles during the day and up to 20
miles at night. The row of light units is normally installed on the
left side of the runway.

Four white lights—High (More than 3.5 degrees)

Three white one red—Slightly high (3.2 degrees)

Two white two red—On glide path (3 degrees)

One white three red—Slightly low (2.8 degrees)

Four red lights—Low (Less than 2.5 degrees)

9. Describe several types of obstruction lighting.
(AIM 2-2-3)

a. *Aviation red obstruction lights*—flashing aviation red beacons and steady burning aviation red lights during nighttime operations.

b. *Medium and high intensity white obstruction lights*—may be used during daytime and twilight with reduced intensity for nighttime operation. Not normally installed on structures less than 200 feet.

c. *Dual lighting*—a combination of flashing aviation red beacons and steady-burning aviation red lights for nighttime operations and flashing high intensity white lights for daytime operation.

d. *Catenary lighting*—medium and high intensity flashing white markers for high voltage transmission lines and support structures.

10. How does a pilot determine the status of a light system at a particular airport? (FAA-H-8083-3)

The pilot needs to check the *Chart Supplement U.S.* and any Notices to Airmen (NOTAMs) to find out about available lighting systems, light intensities, and radio-controlled light system frequencies.

Exam Tip: Be prepared to determine and explain the type and status of airport and runway lighting at your departure and destination airports.

11. How does a pilot activate a radio-controlled runway light system while airborne? (AIM 2-1-8)

The pilot activates radio-controlled lights by keying the microphone on a specified frequency. The following sequence can be used for typical radio-controlled lighting systems:

a. On initial arrival, key the microphone seven times to turn the lights on and achieve maximum brightness.

b. If the runway lights are already on upon arrival repeat the above sequence to ensure a full 15 minutes of lighting.

c. The intensity of the lights can be adjusted by keying the microphone seven, five, or three times within 5 seconds.

C. Airplane Equipment

1. What instruments and equipment are required for VFR night flight? (14 CFR 91.205)

For VFR flight at night, all the instruments and equipment for VFR day flight are required, plus the following:

Fuses—One spare set or three fuses of each kind required accessible to the pilot in flight.

Landing light—If the aircraft is operated for hire.

Anticollision light system—Approved aviation red or white.

Position lights—Navigation lights.

Source of electrical energy—Adequate for all installed electrical and radio equipment.

Remember: FLAPS

2. Explain the arrangement and interpretation of the position lights on an aircraft. (FAA-H-8083-3)

A red light is positioned on the left wingtip, a green light on the right wingtip, and a white light on the tail. If both a red and green light of another aircraft are observed, and the red light is on the left and the green to the right, the airplane is flying in the same direction. Care must be taken not to overtake the other aircraft and to maintain clearance. If red were on the right and green to the left, the airplane could be on a collision course.

3. Position lights are required to be on during what period of time? (14 CFR 91.209)

From sunset to sunrise.

4. When an aircraft is operated in, or in close proximity to, a night operations area, what is required of an aircraft? (14 CFR 91.209)

The aircraft must:

a. Be clearly illuminated;

b. Have lighted position lights; or

c. Be in an area which is marked by obstruction lights.

5. **Explain how a pilot can mitigate the risk present when starting an engine at night on a dark ramp.** (FAA-H-8083-3)

   a. Before entering the airplane, clear the area around the airplane.

   b. Inform ramp personnel and others of the intention to start.

   c. Switch on the NAV lights and rotating beacon prior to start.

   d. Carefully scan the area around the aircraft.

   e. If all is clear, announce "clear prop," pause and listen, clear the area again, then start the engine.

   f. While on the ramp, remain alert for activity outside the aircraft.

   g. Always be ready for an immediate engine shutdown.

6. **Are aircraft anticollision lights required to be on during night flight operations?** (14 CFR 91.209)

   Yes, however, the anticollision lights need not be lit when the pilot-in-command determines that, because of operating conditions, it would be in the interest of safety to turn the lights off.

7. **What are the three definitions of *night*?** (14 CFR 1.1, 61.57, 91.209)

   14 CFR §1.1—the time between the end of evening civil twilight and the beginning of morning civil twilight, as published in the Air Almanac, converted to local time. Use this definition when logging night flight time.

   14 CFR §61.57—the period beginning one hour after sunset and ending one hour before sunrise. Use this definition when determining currency to act as pilot in command of an aircraft carrying passengers.

   14 CFR §91.209—the period from sunset to sunrise. Use this definition to determine when you are required to have position and anti-collision lights on.

D. Pilot Equipment

1. What standard equipment should a pilot have for all night flight operations? (FAA-H-8083-3)

At least one reliable flashlight is recommended as standard equipment on all night flights. A reliable incandescent or LED dimmable flashlight able to produce white/red light is preferable. The flashlight should be large enough to be easily located in the event it is needed. It is also recommended to have a spare set of batteries for the flashlight readily available. Some pilots prefer two flashlights, one with a white light for preflight and the other a penlight type with a red light.

2. What color of light is recommended for preflight inspection, general flight deck activities and chart reading at night? (FAA-H-8083-3)

The white light is used while performing the preflight visual inspection of the airplane, the red light is used when performing flight deck operations, and the dim white light may be used for chart reading.

3. What is the effect of red-light illumination on aeronautical charts? (FAA-H-8083-3)

Red light illumination distorts colors (magenta and yellow pigments both appear as red, and cyan pigment appears black) on aeronautical charts.

4. What other items should the pilot have on board for night flights? (FAA-H-8083-3)

Aeronautical charts are essential for night cross-country flight and, if the intended course is near the edge of the chart, the adjacent chart should also be available. It is also recommended to have a spare set of batteries for the flashlight readily available. Organize equipment and charts and place them within easy reach prior to taxiing.

5. **Explain how use of an EFB for chart reference can increase risk during night operations?** (FAA-H-8083-3)

Use of an EFB that hasn't been adjusted for night operations can significantly reduce night vision. When using an EFB on the flight deck at night, ensure that the device brightness has been set so as not to seriously impair night vision.

6. **Describe the equipment checks a pilot should prioritize prior to a night flight.** (FAA-H-8083-3)

a. Personal equipment such as flashlights, EFBs and portable transceivers.

b. Spare batteries charged and available.

c. The aircraft's position lights, landing light, and rotating beacon.

E. Night Flight

1. **What is the first indication of flying into restricted visibility conditions at night?** (FAA-H-8083-3)

The first indication of flying into restricted visibility conditions is the gradual disappearance of lights on the ground. If the lights begin to appear surrounded by a halo or glow, continued flight in the same direction calls for caution. Such a halo or glow around lights on the ground is indicative of ground fog.

2. **What are the hazards of crossing large bodies of water at night in single-engine airplanes?** (FAA-H-8083-3)

a. In the event of an engine failure, the pilot may be forced to land (ditch) the airplane in the water.

b. Due to limited or no lighting the horizon blends with the water.

c. During poor visibility conditions over water, the horizon becomes obscure and may result in a loss of orientation.

d. Even on clear nights, the stars may be reflected on the water surface, which could appear as a continuous array of lights, thus making the horizon difficult to identify.

3. **What should a pilot pay particular attention to when reviewing weather reports and forecasts for a planned night flight?** (FAA-H-8083-3)

Particular attention should be directed towards temperature/dewpoint spreads to detect the possibility of fog formation.

4. **Explain why it is important to determine wind directions and speeds along the proposed route of flight at night.** (FAA-H-8083-3)

Perception of drift at night is generally inaccurate so accurate drift calculations are necessary to prevent drifting off course.

5. **Explain how a pilot should prepare aeronautical charts before a flight at night.** (FAA-H-8083-3)

a. Study the planned route of flight thoroughly.

b. Mark lighted checkpoints clearly.

c. Obtain charts for the proposed route, as well as any adjacent charts, if the intended course is near the edge of the chart.

d. Taxi operations are more challenging at night. Have an airport diagram available.

6. **Prior to a night flight, what steps should a pilot take if they are planning on using radio navigational aids or GPS for navigation?** (FAA-H-8083-3)

a. Review all radio navigational aids for correct frequencies and availability.

b. If a GPS is being used for navigation, ensure that it is working properly before the flight. All necessary waypoints should be loaded properly before the flight and the database should be checked for accuracy prior to taking off, and then checked again once in flight.

7. **You notice an aircraft's green position light at your 10 o'clock, same altitude. In what direction is the aircraft moving?**

Green position lights are installed on the right wing (or starboard side of an aircraft) therefore the airplane is moving from your left to right.

8. **Describe several hazards related to the pilot, aircraft, environment, and external pressures when conducting night flight operations.** (FAA-H-8083-3)

   Remember: PAVE

   Pilot—Fatigue, night flying currency and proficiency, deficiencies in night vision, optical illusions.

   Aircraft—Airworthiness, inoperative lighting, lack of proper equipment (flashlights, batteries etc.).

   EnVironment—Weather, situational awareness, terrain, obstacles, CFIT, airport lighting familiarity.

   External pressures—Need to get there, pressure from passengers, someone waiting.

Additional Study Questions

1. **What is good operating practice concerning the use of aircraft lighting (taxi, landing, strobes) while on the ground at night?** (FAA-H-8083-3)

2. **Are there any differences in minimum cloud clearance and visibility requirements at night?** (14 CFR 91.155)

3. **What is the first action to take when an airplane engine fails at night?** (FAA-H-8083-3)

4. **When flying VFR at night, what are examples of IFR practices a pilot can use to minimize risk?** (AIM 5-1-2)

5. **Explain the various types of cockpit and exterior lighting equipment installed in your airplane.** (POH/AFM)

6. **Describe the difference between aircraft position lights and anti-collision lights.** (FAA-H-8083-3)

7. **Discuss your method of route and checkpoint selection, when planning a night VFR cross-country flight.** (FAA-H-8083-3)

8. **The weather has dropped below VFR minimums at your destination airport (tower-controlled). Can you obtain a Special VFR clearance into that airport at night?** (AIM 4-4-6, 14 CFR 91.157)

9. **Using a VFR sectional chart only, how can a pilot determine if an ATC tower is open all night?** (USRGD)

Postflight Procedures

12

A. After Landing, Parking and Securing

1. After landing, when is it considered safe to begin performing the after-landing checklist items? (FAA-H-8083-3)

The after-landing checks should be performed only after the airplane is brought to a complete stop beyond the runway holding position markings. There have many cases of a pilot mistakenly grasping the wrong handle and retracting the landing gear instead of the flaps due to improper division of attention while the airplane was moving.

2. After landing at an airport with an operating control tower, when is an airplane considered clear of the runway? (AIM 4-3-20)

A pilot or controller may consider an aircraft, which is exiting or crossing a runway, to be clear of the runway when all parts of the aircraft are beyond the runway edge and there are no restrictions to its continued movement beyond the applicable runway holding position marking.

3. While taxiing to parking, what are several examples of collision avoidance procedures a pilot might employ to mitigate risk and avoid an accident? (FAA-H-8083-3)

a. Be familiar with the parking, ramp, and taxi environment. Have an airport diagram, if available, out and in view at all times.

b. The pilot's eyes should be looking outside the airplane scanning from side to side while looking both near and far to assess routing and potential conflicts.

c. Be vigilant of the entire area around the airplane to ensure that the airplane clears all obstructions. If there is any doubt about a safe clearance from an object, the pilot should stop the airplane and check the clearance.

d. A safe taxiing speed should be maintained. The speed should be slow enough so when the throttle is closed, the airplane can be stopped promptly.

e. When yellow taxiway centerline stripes are present, the pilot should visually place the centerline stripe so it is under the center of the airplane fuselage.

4. **When approaching the ramp for parking and maneuvering with power into or near the parking spot, what precautions should be taken?** (FAA-H-8083-3)

Maneuver the airplane so that the tail is not pointed at an open hangar door, toward a parked automobile, or towards a group of bystanders in the area. Blowing dirt, small rocks, and debris is not only discourteous and thoughtless, but could result in personal injury and serious damage to the property of others.

5. **On an unfamiliar ramp, why would a pilot want to inspect their tie-down spot prior to parking and shutdown?**

Foreign object debris (FOD) and other unknown objects can be a significant hazard that could cause damage to the aircraft and subject other aircraft and/or people nearby to the flying FOD.

6. **After parking and shutdown, what are several considerations a pilot should have when securing the aircraft?** (FAA-H-8083-3)

   a. Unless parking in a designated, supervised area, the pilot should select a location and heading that will prevent the propeller or jet blast of another aircraft from striking the aircraft broadside.

   b. Consider the existing (or forecast) wind when parking the airplane. Whenever possible, the aircraft should be parked headed into the existing wind.

   c. Consider allowing the airplane to roll straight ahead enough to straighten the nosewheel or tailwheel.

   d. Consider whether the tiedown method actually secures the aircraft. Check rope, chain, and hook integrity.

   e. If using ropes as tiedowns, consider whether the knot used will be effective.

7. **After the aircraft is safely hangered or tied down, what other actions can a pilot take to further enhance safety and security of the airplane?** (FAA-H-8083-3)

Flight controls should be secured and any security locks in place. Also consider utilizing pitot tube covers, cowling inlet covers, rudder gust locks, window sunscreens, and propeller security locks to enhance safety.

8. **Describe inspections and procedures a pilot should perform when conducting a post-flight inspection of an aircraft.** (FAA-H-8083-3)

A pilot should always use the recommended procedures in the airplane's POH/AFM. A postflight inspection is similar to a preflight inspection and should include -

a. Inspection near and around the cowling for signs of oil or fuel streaks and around the oil breather for excessive oil discharge.

b. Inspect under wings and other fuel tank locations for fuel stains.

c. Inspect landing gear and tires for damage and the brakes for any leaking hydraulic fluid.

d. Inspect cowling inlets for obstructions.

e. Oil levels should be checked, and quantities brought to POH/AFM levels.

f. Fuel should be added based on the immediate use of the airplane.

g. If the airplane is going to be inactive, it is a good operating practice to fill the fuel tanks to prevent water condensation from forming inside the tank.

9. **If a possible mechanical problem is detected during a post-flight inspection, what procedure should be followed?**

Document the problem and notify maintenance personnel. A maintenance problem detected during a post flight inspection and appropriately documented will allow maintenance personnel more time to make appropriate repairs and prepare the aircraft for subsequent flights. If the airplane is a rental or belongs to a flying club or flight school, there is usually a "squawk" sheet or book for the airplane where the pilot can document the discrepancy.

10. **When boarding or deplaning passengers, what is the safest, most effective procedure to follow to reduce the possibility of an accident?**

The engine of a fixed wing aircraft or of a helicopter should always be shut down prior to boarding or deplaning passengers. The pilot can be most effective in ensuring that his or her passengers arrive and depart the vicinity of the airplane safely by stopping the engine completely at the time of loading and unloading, or by providing a definite means of keeping them clear of the propeller if it is left in motion.

B. Aviation Security

1. What are several actions you can take to enhance aircraft security? (TSA)

a. Always lock your aircraft.

b. Keep track of door/ignition keys and don't leave keys in unattended aircraft.

c. Use secondary locks (prop, tie down, throttle, and wheel locks) or aircraft disabler if available.

d. Lock hangar when unattended.

2. What is a SIDA? (AIM 2-3-15)

Security identification display areas (SIDAs) are limited access areas that require a badge issued in accordance with procedures in 49 CFR Part 1542. A SIDA can include the air operations area (AOA) (e.g., aircraft movement area or parking area) or a secured area, such as where commercial passengers enplane. The AOA is not required to be a SIDA, but a secured area is always a SIDA. Movement through or into a SIDA is prohibited without authorization and proper identification being displayed. If you are unsure of the location of a SIDA, contact the airport authority for additional information. Airports that have a SIDA will have a description and map detailing boundaries and pertinent features available.

3. What type of airport security procedures should you review regularly to prevent unauthorized access to aircraft at your airport? (FSSAT)

a. Limitations on ramp access to people other than instructors and students.

b. Standards for securing aircraft on the ramp.

c. Securing access to aircraft keys at all times.

d. New auxiliary security items for aircraft (prop locks, throttle locks, locking tie downs).

e. After-hours or weekend access procedures.

4. Give some examples of what you would consider suspicious activity at an airport. (TSA)

a. Aircraft with unusual modifications (such as modified N-numbers) or activity.

b. Unfamiliar persons loitering for extended periods in the vicinity of parked aircraft.

c. Anyone making threats.

d. Events or circumstances that do not fit the pattern of lawful, normal activity at an airport.

e. Pilots appearing to be under the control of others.

5. When witnessing suspicious or criminal activity, what are three basic ways for reporting the suspected activity? (TSA)

If you determine that it's safe, question the individual. If their response is unsatisfactory and they continue to act suspiciously:

a. Alert airport or FBO management.

b. Contact local law enforcement if the activity poses an immediate threat to persons or property.

c. Contact the 866-GA-SECURE hotline to document the reported event.

6. What is the purpose of the 866-GA-SECURE phone number? (TSA)

866-GA-SECURE is a toll-free hotline operated by the Transportation Security Administration (TSA) Security Operations Center. It is staffed 24/7 to take reports of suspicious or criminal activity occurring at general aviation airports. TSA personnel will document the reported activity, collect your personal contact numbers, and pass the information on to the appropriate regulatory office within the TSA.

Note: Calling 866-GA-SECURE will not dispatch local law enforcement. In the event of an immediate emergency, 911 or local law enforcement should be contacted first.

7. **What are several sources of information available to pilots interested in additional guidance on aviation security?** (TSA; FSSAT)

Security Guidelines for General Aviation Airports is a set of federally endorsed guidelines that offers an extensive list of options, ideas, and suggestions for the airport operator, sponsor, tenant and/or user to choose from when considering security enhancements for GA facilities.

Flight School Security Awareness Training for Aircraft and Simulators is an online training course designed to raise the general security awareness levels of employees working in the flight training industry.

Scenario-Based Training

13

by Arlynn McMahon

Introduction

Pilot examiners are encouraged by the FAA to develop a scenario as part of the "plan of action" used during the practical tests they conduct. Usually, the examiner will ask the applicant to pre-plan a cross-country. The assigned cross-country, then, is the beginning of the scenario and is the basis for this part of the oral exam.

The examiner is not required to follow the order of tasks as they appear in the ACS. Therefore, the questions in this chapter are presented as they might appear in an actual oral exam, rather than in the order given in the ACS. However, these questions alone do not make a complete oral exam. Usually, examiners will first ask a scenario-based question, and then, building from your response, construct additional questions as they go to further probe into your knowledge of an ACS Task.

Scenario questions are intentionally open-ended. Don't get frustrated. They are designed to allow you to go freely in any direction that you feel is pertinent in demonstrating your ability to apply aeronautical knowledge and to be a safe pilot.

Answers to scenario questions can be lengthy. Feel free to use scrap paper to organize your thoughts before answering. For example, "TOMATO FLAMES" by itself is not a suitable answer to a question, but writing this acronym on a piece of paper will help you organize a better answer as you begin reciting the required equipment. Draw a diagram if that helps you to discuss the fuel system or to more clearly describe a concept to the examiner.

Ideally, your responses to scenario-questions will demonstrate that you understand the underlying concepts of what's important and why. This is the *Practical Test*. To perform your best, you need to convey the practical application of *what* to do, *when* to do it, *why* do it, or *how* to do it.

ADM is a special emphasis area on the Practical Test. Feel free to think out loud, so the examiner can hear the reasoning in your answers. Discuss the plans you considered but discarded, and why you did so. By all means, include the elements that you feel make a good pilot, rather than one who just meets minimum standards. Show that you are prepared to be a responsible aviation-citizen.

The questions in this scenario-based training chapter are worded similarly to the way that the designated examiner might ask them during your exam, and your answers should reflect the specifics of the scenario presented to you. Scenario questions don't have one universal correct answer; your correct answers will depend on the presented scenario, the specific aircraft used for the practical exam and preparations you completed in planning the cross-country.

For this reason, the answers provided here indicate the concepts your answer should or could include, but for your exam you should revise them with your specific information, as necessary. Also included with many of the answers are tips, suggestions, or notes (in *italic* type), which draw attention to the specific areas you should address in your responses to the examiner's questions.

Scenario-Based Questions

1. **Your good friend has requested you to fly as safety pilot in his retractable gear Piper Arrow while he practices flight by reference to instruments. What do regulations require for you to be able to do this?**

   Your answer should include knowledge of safety pilot requirements, currency requirements to carry passengers, and the requirements for a complex endorsement.

   I must meet safety pilot requirements, currency requirements to carry passengers, and the requirements for a complex endorsement, including:

   - To be a safety pilot I must hold at least a private pilot certificate with single-engine land.
   - I must be endorsed to act as PIC in a complex airplane.
   - I must hold a valid medical certificate.
   - I must have satisfactorily met the requirements of a flight review, and
   - I must have logged at least three takeoffs and landings in the preceding 90 days to carry passengers.

2. **What personal items will you take with you to ensure that you are legal for this flight, carrying me as your passenger?**

   - Pilot certificate, photo ID and a current medical certificate (duration based on age). These must be available in the cockpit.
   - Verify in the logbook the following were completed:
     › A flight review (or equivalency) within the previous 24 months.
     › 3 takeoffs and landings within the previous 90 days (to a full stop if at night).

3. Tell me about the FAA Pilot Proficiency Program (WINGS).

A good pilot is always in training, even after passing the practical exam. The FAA Pilot Proficiency Program:

- Is an FAA and industry accident prevention initiative.
- Is based on the premise that pilots who maintain proficiency are safer pilots.
- Encourages on-going flight training and aviation education.
- Is accomplished in little bits, throughout the year, encouraging pilots to fly in different seasons and in different flight conditions.
- Satisfies the flight review recency requirement as prescribed in §61.56(e), as long as the requirements for at least the "basic WINGS" level are met within the preceding 24 months.
- Has its official home at faasafety.gov, where free online courses are available.
- Specifics of the program are outlined in Advisory Circular 61-91.

4. Let's talk about the plane: How do you know that it is airworthy?

An airplane's airworthiness involves three different levels of verification:

- The Airworthiness Certificate proves that the aircraft was manufactured in compliance with regulations.
- The maintenance technician having an Inspector Authorization (IA certificate) certifies the airworthiness at least annually by the "return to service" statement upon completion of the annual inspection.
- The pilot certifies airworthiness, and is the final authority, before each flight with a thorough preflight inspection and inspection status review.

5. Prove to me the airplane is airworthy for our flight today.

Include required inspections, documents, and instruments/ equipment, as well as your statement that the preflight inspection shows the aircraft to be satisfactory.

Here are my pertinent aircraft documents and papers:

- Airworthiness Certificate.
- Registration.
- Operating limitations *[which is probably in the AFM or POH]*—and here are the placards and markings on the instruments *[when appropriate]*.
- Weight and balance data.

Regarding the aircraft maintenance records for this airplane:

- The annual inspection was completed within the past 12 months and a mechanic with an Inspector Authorization stated that the aircraft was "returned to service."
- The 100-hour inspection was completed *[if appropriate]*.
- The transponder inspection was completed within the previous 24 months *[if appropriate]*.
- The ELT battery is current, and the system was inspected within the previous 12 months.
- ADs are complied with.
- Outstanding maintenance discrepancies have been checked and the status of inoperative equipment verified.

Also, the aircraft has the required instruments and equipment (i.e., day VFR versus night VFR); a thorough preflight inspection has been completed, the aircraft is properly serviced, and it is in airworthy condition—safe for this flight.

6. **You planned a cross-country. Show me your true course, and what items you considered when choosing this course.**

For extra credit and to demonstrate good ADM, experienced instructors suggest you discuss alternative courses that were considered but discarded, and why.

My chosen course considered:

- Terrain—and I considered circumnavigating extreme high terrain, or areas of dense forest with no possible emergency landing areas.
- Checkpoints that are easy to see and identify.
- Navigation and communication reception—I considered altering course and/or altitude for reliable reception.

(continued)

- Airspace—I considered altering course and/or altitude to avoid SUA and Class B airspace, etc.
- Weather avoidance.

7. Immediately after takeoff, you're at 100 feet AGL when your kneeboard falls onto the floor. You reach down to get it and suddenly become aware of a buffeting feeling. What should you be concerned about?

Demonstrate here that you recognize and understand stalls and spins and know how to recover from them.

My first concern is to immediately get the nose down—reduce the angle of attack.

- The buffeting means the aircraft is on the brink of an unintended stall without having sufficient altitude to recover.
- The distraction may also mean that the aircraft is not in coordinated flight.

8. Beginning with takeoff, and along your true course until landing, talk me through the different airspace we will fly through, and what implications each has on our flight.

Use the sectional chart and begin with the airspace surrounding your departure airport, then proceed along your route, describing each airspace area as you come to it and how it may impact your flight. Continue describing the airspace and special use airspace as you encounter it along your route, and mention how that airspace may impact your decisions and requirements to be there— or not be there!

- Class D airspace extends to the blue dashed line—while in this area I must maintain two-way communications with the control tower.
- Assuming a normal climb, by the time I clear the "D" airspace, I'll be above 700 feet AGL. At this point, I will be at the area depicted on the chart where the base of the Class E airspace is at 700 feet AGL. Therefore, I am required to maintain VFR cloud clearances and 3 SM visibility.
  › If I'm not above 700 feet AGL, then I'll be in Class G airspace where I'm required to remain clear of the clouds and at least 1 SM visibility.
- Further along the course, I'm now in an area where the base of Class E airspace is at 1,200 AGL.

9. Why did you choose this altitude?

Consider the following, as appropriate for your planned flight:

- Terrain clearances—high enough to exceed minimum safe altitudes. As a new pilot, I will fly at least 1,500 feet AGL.
- Cloud clearances—it meets the requirements (for example, 500 feet below the clouds).
- Direction of flight—complies with regulations.
- Airspace—stays clear of any airspace I'd rather not fly close to or into (such as TFRs, prohibited, or restricted areas).
- Favorable winds—a suitable altitude that allows the most favorable ground speed.
- Allows me to see visual checkpoints easily.
- Best for aircraft performance (true airspeed vs. economic fuel burn).
- Personal minimums—this is an altitude I feel comfortable flying and allows safety margins.

10. Looking at your Nav Log, how did you calculate fuel requirements?

Here, demonstrate your ability to use performance charts and graphs located in the POH/AFM. Calculate precisely, but add a safety margin at the end; also, remember to apply any and all pertinent notes included in the performance charts. Show and discuss your precise calculations (do not round-off, do not add "fudge factors").

Here are my precise calculations for:

- Fuel required for start, runup and taxi.
- Fuel for takeoff and climb.
- The chosen power setting and its associated fuel flow for the duration of cruise.
- Fuel required for descent and landing.
- +30 minutes for required fuel reserve.

In addition to the above, I added fuel as necessary to meet my personal safety minimums (for example, a new pilot should carry enough fuel to fly to a suitable alternate airport or +30 minutes cruise fuel after that—a total 1 hour reserve).

11. You are required to prepare a navigation log. Why is having a nav log important?

Demonstrate your own routine use of a nav log.

I use a nav log because:

- "All available information" is organized on one piece of paper—that's good cockpit management.
- It provides a mental rehearsal and preparation for each aspect of the flight—that's good situational awareness.
- During flight, it is used to monitor the plan by:
  - › Verifying ground speeds and fuel consumption.
  - › Verifying ETAs to checkpoints and final destination.
  - › Helping me in thinking and planning ahead.
  - › Helping to prevent me from getting lost.
  - › Reminding me of routine cockpit tasks (change fuel tanks, listen to ATIS, cancel flight plan, etc.).
  - › Assisting in diversion to an alternate, if it should become necessary.

12. When planning a cross-country that will require a fuel stop, what factors do you feel are important in selecting an airport for a stop?

Demonstrate here your understanding of aeronautical decision making.

In selecting an airport for a fuel stop, important factors to consider include:

- Airport airspace—airspace similar to my training and/or experience.
- Runways—length and relation to the wind.
- Size of the airport—not too small but not so big that the amount and type of traffic is intimidating.
- Pilot support facilities available (FSS access, weather station, hours of operation, etc.)
- Amenities (restrooms, service, loaner car, restaurant at the airport, etc.)
- Price of fuel or method for payment.

13. Considering your calculated takeoff distance for our flight, how would that change if the outside air temperature were 20° warmer or 20° cooler?

Your specific answer to this question will depend on the individual circumstances of your practical exam; but whatever your situation is, the answer should demonstrate your ability to accurately use the performance table and your understanding of the effects of atmospheric conditions on the airplane's performance. You should include the table or chart in your aircraft's POH, specifically:

- *How your calculations were carefully performed. Interpolate as necessary for accuracy and apply any "Notes" that may be applicable.*
- *Re-calculate performance using the 20° warmer and 20° cooler scenarios.*

Discuss the differences in performance and effects of density altitude on performance, not only for takeoff but through each of the phases of flight.

14. Are the runways you plan to use today suitable for us?

Demonstrate your ability to use the performance tables in your aircraft's POH and your understanding of the need to include a safety margin. Show your calculations.

Yes, using the takeoff and landing performance charts, I calculated the required distance to takeoff and to land. This shows what the aircraft is capable of; however, as a new pilot, I am not always able to achieve takeoffs or landings that precisely—so, I added 50% *[or whatever your safety margin is]* more to my calculations as my personal minimum when determining runway suitability.

15. During our flight today, with whom will you communicate?

Demonstrate your knowledge of available resources and your willingness to use them.

- Ground/Tower/Departure (if departing from a controlled airport), or
- Unicom or Multicom (if from an uncontrolled airport).
- Enroute: Flight Following to assist in knowing about pop-up TFRs and to assist with traffic avoidance.

(continued)

- FSS for update weather, altimeter settings and possible revisions to the filed flight plan.
- Destination airport communications *[as appropriate to the destination]*.

16. How did you obtain weather information for our flight?

- Beginning last night, I watched the weather channel on TV. The weather channel is not a specific aviation weather source, but it helps me to hear the meteorologist talk about the weather patterns.
- Then I logged online to Leidos Flight Service and received an outlook briefing.
- This morning I logged on to Leidos Flight Service for a standard weather briefing to complete my planning and nav log.
- I was confused about an abbreviation that I didn't know, so I called Flight Service and got their help.
- Then about 1 hour ago I called FSS again for an abbreviated weather briefing, just to make sure that nothing had changed since this morning's briefing.

17. Tell me about the weather along our flight.

Demonstrate your understanding of meteorology and what entails a complete weather briefing.

My standard weather briefing shows:
- Pressure areas affecting weather.
- Fronts affecting weather and their direction of movement.
- Ceilings, winds, and visibility at departure, at several points en route and at the destination.
- Wind direction and speed at cruise altitude.
- Significant or adverse weather near the route or during possible flight time, and how it may affect the flight; it includes a plan to escape a possible problem of this kind.
- NOTAMs.

18. **Tell me about two different weather charts that you used in preparing for our flight and how you used them.**

    It's easy to get confused when discussing these charts. To make answering this question easier, bring printouts to the exam of the charts you used and show them as you answer.

    - I used the **surface analysis chart** to see the pressure areas, fronts, wind, local weather, and visual obstructions. It is transmitted every 3 hours and covers the country.

    - I used the **weather depiction chart** to get an overview of the surface conditions as derived from METAR and other surface observations. It gives me an overall picture of the weather across the United States. It is transmitted every 3 hours.

    - I used the **significant weather prognostic chart** to see the forecast. The chart has four panels that include 12- and 24-hour forecasts. Charts are issued four times a day. The valid time is printed on each panel. The upper two panels show forecast significant weather, which may include turbulence, freezing levels, and IFR or MVFR weather.

19. **Tell me about two different weather forecasts that you used in preparing for our flight and how you used them.**

    Include, as appropriate for your flight planning purposes, details of weather forecasts such as:

    - I used the **GFA** to get the big picture about the general weather in the area, what is causing the weather, and how it may change during the upcoming 24 hours.

    - I used the **TAF** to get specific weather for certain weather reporting areas along my route, and for how conditions at those airports may change. This allows me to evaluate if the clouds and visibility will allow my flight to continue VFR. I could also find areas of VFR in case I run into unforecasted weather that I need to escape.

    - I used the **winds and temperatures aloft forecast**. With the wind direction and velocity, I found the most desirable altitude giving the best ground speeds. I also used the temperatures aloft to determine probable altitudes for clouds to form.

20. **How will you obtain updated weather information while enroute?**

Demonstrate your understanding of all resources available and how to choose the best resource to use in a given situation. For example:

- I will use technology. (As an example, the GNS530 or G1000 supplies weather information. Handheld units such as the GNS 396, 496, or 696 supply weather, etc.). But technology by itself shouldn't be used to make decisions—there are too many problems with updating and interpreting the information.

- If I only need recorded information (for instance, to update an altimeter setting), I could listen to a nearby AWOS/ASOS/ ATIS.

- If I need to ask questions (for example, if I guess that weather is unexpectedly changing), I would contact FSS on 122.2 or one of the remote transmitters associated with a VOR.

- If I'm in a pinch, or if the flight is becoming unsafe, ATC might be of assistance.

- For the best weather update, I would collect information from a variety of resources before making a decision.

21. **While enroute, we listen to the ATIS of a Class D airport near our course to update the altimeter setting and find that the ATIS is reporting visibility as 2 SM. What does that mean for us?**

Demonstrate your understating of VFR weather minimums in Class E and Class G airspace, and the special VFR clearance. Show your aeronautical decision-making ability by evaluating your options and choosing the best option based on the specifics of your flight.

We have two priorities: (1) to remain legal, and (2) as a new pilot, the prudent choice is an immediate diversion to an alternate airport to land.

- Option 1 is to fly in "G" airspace, where regulations allow us to remain clear of clouds with 1 SM visibility while enroute to an uncontrolled airport and land.

- Option 2 is to fly in "G" airspace while heading for the Class D airport and request a special VFR from ATC to land there.

22. **You have chosen to divert to an airport that you were not intending to visit. How will you obtain the needed information about your alternate airport?**

Demonstrate your understanding of all resources available and how to choose the best resource for a given situation. For extra credit, mention that you would turn on the autopilot to help relieve workload while researching information.

The most pressing information needed is airport airspace, runway length, airport elevation, and an airport communication frequency. I would:

- Use technology—most GPS databases include all of this information.
- Use the sectional chart—the needed information is on the airport legend.
- Use the *Chart Supplement U.S.*
- Use a combination of the above.

23. **What deice or anti-ice equipment is your airplane equipped with?**

Demonstrate that you know the specific equipment installed on your airplane, as well as when to use it.

- Defrost—used to keep the windshield clear. Turn it on in advance of a possible icing situation.
- Pitot heat—used to keep the pitot/static instruments operational. Turn it on in advance of a possible icing situation.
- Carburetor heat—used to keep fuel and air flowing to the engine. It's normally turned on after the first sign of possible carburetor icing.
- The most important piece of equipment is a thinking pilot who, when encountering dangerous icing conditions, can make a timely decision to turn around or land as soon as practical.

24. Tell me about the fuel system on your airplane.

Include the components of your airplane's fuel system, the normal operation of the system, and how you interact with it. Be specific, using the information contained in the POH for your airplane. The following answer, based on an example airplane, illustrates the type of details you might cover.

- Twenty-eight gallons are stored in each wing tank. Three gallons are unusable and a total of 53 gallons are usable. I would order and verify that 100LL is being serviced into the airplane.

- Fuel quantity is measured by float-type quantity indicators, but good pilots always verify the fuel visually. Annunciators show L and R "LOW FUEL" if the fuel quantity is below 5 gallons in a tank.

- The tank has a visual FUEL TAB, allowing verification that 17.5 gallons are on board when takeoffs are performed with less than full fuel.

- The tanks are vented, and I ensure the vents are not blocked during the preflight inspection.

- Also on the preflight inspection, I drain fuel from 13 fuel sumps to verify fuel grade and to remove any possible sediment. Ten of these sumps are on the wings, two are on the belly, and there is a fuel strainer in the cowling that is pulled to collect a fuel sample.

- Fuel flows by gravity from the wing tanks to the fuel selector value. I control fuel to the engine being fed from the L, R or BOTH tanks. I select "BOTH" for takeoff, climbs, landings, and maneuvers that involve slips or skids of more than 30 seconds.

- From the fuel selector, fuel flows to a reservoir tank, aux fuel pump, fuel shutoff valve, and into the engine.

- I activate the auxiliary fuel pump for start and during engine emergencies.

- The fuel shutoff valve shuts off fuel to the engine. I activate this to decrease the likelihood of fire upon ditching, and during an extended period of aircraft storage.

25. What method of navigation will you use today and what are the advantages and limitations of that method?

Demonstrate your understanding of navigation methods and resources available and how to choose the best resource to use in a given situation. For extra credit and to demonstrate ADM, point out that the best way to navigate is by using a combination of methods.

Dead Reckoning—Advantages are that it is simple. When everything else fails, it will bring us home. The limitations are that it requires accurate winds and performance calculations, and careful timekeeping.

Pilotage—Advantages: It builds confidence; you see it on the chart and see it on the ground. Limitations: It requires prominent checkpoints and enough visibility to see them.

VOR—Advantages: It's more reliable than dead reckoning or pilotage; an accurate form of navigation over an area where no prominent checkpoints exist. Limitations: Line-of-sight navigation, somewhat dependent on altitude, less accurate when far away from the station.

GPS—Advantages: It is not limited to line-of-sight; ground speed and other calculations are provided. Distance is not slant distance. Limitations: There are occasional outages, and the database must be current for reliable data. Ground speeds are instantaneous but not point-to-point, as is needed for calculating accurate ETAs and fuel remaining.

26. Let's talk about your passenger safety briefing. Assume that I am your good friend who has never been in a small plane. Give me your passenger safety briefing.

The items below (indicated as bold initials of the word "safety") are what you are required to include in a safety briefing. Demonstrate your knowledge of the elements of a complete safety briefing and your understanding that an effective briefing at the start of the flight can add to the safety and enjoyment of the flight for everyone.

S Seat belts—fastened for taxi, takeoff, and landing
Shoulder harness—fastened for takeoff and landing
Seat—adjusted and locked into place

A Air vents—location and operation; you can adjust

All environmental controls—what's available; you shouldn't adjust (ask me)

Action—in case of passenger discomfort

F Fire extinguisher—location and operation

E Exit doors (and windows)—how to secure, how to operate

Emergency evacuation plan

Emergency equipment—location and operation

T Traffic (scanning, spotting, and notifying pilot)

Talking (sterile cockpit expectations)

Y Your questions? There are no dumb questions. It's more fun when you ask.

27. Enroute you notice a discharge on the ammeter. What will you do?

Demonstrate your understanding of the electrical system, using specifics relevant to your airplane.

A discharge on the ammeter indicates the possibility of an electrical problem. If left unchecked, it might exhaust the battery, causing a partial or total loss of electrical equipment. I would:

- Turn off the avionics master switch (if appropriate) and the master switch to reset what may be an over-voltage relay.

- Turn the master back on and notice the indication on the ammeter. If it is still not showing a charge, then:

  › Turn off any unnecessary electrical equipment, and

  › Re-evaluate how this may affect the safety of continued flight.

  › Consider landing as soon as practical during the day or as soon as possible at night, for repairs.

28. As you approach the airport of intended landing with your battery now dead, are we in danger of the engine quitting? If not, what problems might we encounter while landing with a dead battery?

Demonstrate your understanding of the electrical system, using specifics relevant to your airplane.

- No, the engine will not quit; it derives its electrical ignition power from magnetos—not the electrical system.

- We may have to land without flaps—a slip might be needed to descend.
- We will not have engine gauges—the fuel gauges will show empty which is always uncomfortable to see.
- We will not have lights—if at night, a flashlight will be needed in the cockpit. The landing will be made without a landing light.
- We will not have a turn coordinator, but the pitot/static and gyro instruments will be operational.
- We will not have COM radios—if landing at a controlled airport, we should look for light gun signals. If landing at an uncontrolled airport at night, we might not be able to turn on the pilot-controlled lighting.

29. Are there specific techniques that you normally use for collision avoidance?

Demonstrate the need for good collision avoidance habits during each phase of flight.

- Ensure that the windshield is as clean as possible.
- Organize the cockpit to avoid a lot of "head down" time— pre-fold charts, pre-select frequencies, etc.
- Keep my head up and eyes outside during all ground maneuvering. On the ground, stop while copying ATC clearances.
- Perform clearing turns before performance maneuvers requiring rapid changes in heading or altitude.
- Scan for traffic often when in straight-and-level flight and during maneuvers.
- Don't practice maneuvers over VORs, airports, or other areas where traffic normally converges.
- Enter traffic patterns correctly and at proper traffic pattern altitude.
- Listen on frequencies, especially at uncontrolled airports, to hear possible traffic in the area.
- Visually verify that final approach is clear before taking the runway for takeoff.
- Use anti-collision lights and a landing light at night and during times of low visibility.

(continued)

- Comply with right of way rules (14 CFR §91.113).
- In the radar environment, if ATC issues traffic, I look to see it and maneuver to avoid it. If I lose sight of the traffic, I report that to ATC.
- Use flight following en route as another tool for traffic avoidance.

30. With our head in the cockpit reading the taxi diagram, we accidentally hit a large taxiway light. The prop is chewed up pretty bad and the lower nose cowling is banged up but nothing else seems to be damaged. Are you required to report this to the NTSB?

This does not require a report to the NTSB because the damage is limited to the prop and the damage to other people's property probably doesn't exceed $25,000. Therefore, I would:

- Have the airplane towed to the maintenance shop for repairs.
- Contact the airport manager to have possible foreign object debris cleaned from the taxiway.

31. Tell me about the emergency equipment and survival gear that is onboard for our flight today.

Show your awareness that the need for emergency equipment and survival gear is not limited to flights over extreme terrain or extreme temperature changes.

If the emergency originates in flight and there is time:

- The autopilot could be considered emergency equipment to help relieve workload.
- The communications radio can be used to send a "mayday."
- The GPS could be used for "NRST" and "DIRECT TO" navigation to an airport.
- The transponder could be used to signal "7700."

I have the following items onboard that could be useful after ditching:

- Fire extinguisher—It is charged, and I know how to use it.
- Cell phone.
- Water and snacks.
- Pocket knife/all-purpose tool.
- First aid kit.

- Emergency locator transmitter (ELT)—I can manually activate it.
- Other items that I routinely carry that would be of use in an emergency are _____ [if relevant].

32. What do you feel are the major differences between the PAVE checklist and the 5P checklist?

Show your awareness of the need to manage the risks of flight and the tools available to help pilots.

- Both checklists are tools recommended for pilots in managing the risks associated in flying.
- Both consider the risk elements, those are: the pilot, the airplane, the environment, and the external factors.
- The PAVE checklist encourages the pilot to react to a risk element that he finds unacceptable.
- The 5P checklist encourages the pilot to be proactive: to do surveillance, look ahead for changes in a risk element, and take early action to prevent a problem.

33. For a flight involving first time fliers as passengers, how would you manage the risks pertaining to their aeromedical factors?

Demonstrate your knowledge of aeromedical factors as well as your understanding of what causes them and how to address them.

- If possible, I would sit the passenger most likely to experience motion sickness in the front seat so I can keep his attention outside—far, far away on the horizon.
- I keep a Sic-Sac onboard in case of motion sickness or hyperventilation.
- If possible, I would sit the passenger most likely to experience ear or sinus problems in the front seat so I can watch for early signs of problems and possibly take corrective action, especially during climbs and descents.

34. Your friend owns a condo in Colorado ski country. It's a long trip from the East Coast. How would you manage the risks pertaining to the aeromedical factors?

Demonstrate your knowledge of relevant aeromedical factors as well as your understanding of what causes them and how to address them.

- I would consider each element of the "I'M SAFE" checklist before takeoff.

- Although the regulations require supplemental oxygen when flying over 12,500 feet for more than 30 minutes, if flying at an altitude of more than 10,000 feet MSL, I would carry supplemental oxygen, especially at night to aid my eyesight.

- Unless terrain (as an example) requires otherwise, I would plan to fly below 8,000 feet MSL to prevent possible hypoxia.

- I would carry a small bottle of water to ward off the possibility of dehydration (but not a big bottle because that might create another problem!).

- Rather than planning long legs (more than 4 hours), I'd plan shorter legs with a fuel/rest stop every 2 to 3 hours to prevent stress and fatigue.

35. You are considering the flight home after a scuba diving vacation during the week of Christmas. You want to enjoy every minute possible in the water and partying on the beach. How would you manage the risks pertaining to aeromedical factors on the flight home?

Demonstrate your knowledge of the relevant aeromedical factors as well as your understanding of what causes them and how to address them.

- I would consider each element of the "I'M SAFE" checklist before takeoff.

- Because it's Christmas week (winter), the cabin heat will probably be on. I would place the carbon monoxide detector near the heat outlet on the floor of the cabin for the earliest possible detection of carbon monoxide.

- Winter may involve snow showers. If flying in low visibility conditions, I scan instruments more often to prevent spatial disorientation. If an autopilot is available, it should be turned on to assist in better aircraft control and keeping the wings level, whenever spatial disorientation is a concern.

- I would wait 12 to 24 hours after scuba diving, depending on if it were a controlled descent or not, to ward off possible nitrogen oxide symptoms.
- I would wait at least 8 hours after drinking alcohol before takeoff.

36. Hazardous weather caused you to delay your return flight home by a few days. As a result, the annual inspection and transponder check are now both out of date. Do regulations permit you to fly home with these items out of date?

Yes, I can legally fly home without the transponder inspection, provided that:

- The transponder is not turned ON.
- An "INOP" sticker is placed near the ON/OFF switch (to indicate inoperative equipment).
- I avoid flight into Class C airspace, above Class C airspace, within 30 NM of Class B airspace, above Class B airspace, anywhere above 10,000 MSL; or
- If flying in airspace normally requiring a transponder, I have the authorization of the air traffic facility chief to operate in airspace without it. (I would call the facility chief on the phone before takeoff.)

Flight without an annual inspection can be initiated only with the issuance of a special flight permit issued by the FSDO. So, I can fly home provided I've been issued a permit and am in compliance with the conditions listed on the permit.

37. It's Saturday morning and you are ready for the flight home. During your preflight, you find that the landing light is inoperative. Will this affect your ability to fly home?

Demonstrate your awareness that all installed equipment must be operational on the airplane before takeoff, and the two legal ways to fly with inoperative equipment.

Regulations require that:

- All installed equipment be operational before takeoff, unless:
  - › The flight is in compliance with an approved minimum equipment list, or
  - › The inoperative equipment is not required by type design, regulations, or ADs.
- The pilot can safely operate the airplane without the equipment that has become inoperative.
- The pilot removes or deactivates any inoperative equipment.
- The pilot has placarded any inoperative equipment near the ON/OFF switch.

Because the landing light is not required, I feel that I can safely fly the airplane during the day without it. Simply pulling a circuit breaker and placarding it, may not be considered "deactivation" of the system, so I will consult with maintenance personnel first before departing on my flight.

Note: Deactivation means to make a piece of equipment or an instrument unusable to the pilot/crew by preventing its operation. Not tie wrapping or collaring a CB would allow for continued operation of that system. A pilot should consult maintenance personnel before deactivating or removing any item of equipment from an airplane.

38. **You have volunteered to fly a sick child to meet an ambulance at a Class B airport. It's a clear night when at 60 NM out you notice an ammeter discharge. You guess you have about 30 minutes of battery remaining. What will you do?**

    There is no right answer; this is simply your opportunity to demonstrate your ADM. You should show a willingness to declare an emergency and divert. Include a discussion of ways to manage the electrical system until landing. Include your thoughts out loud until you make a final decision. You could also mention whether you would you do anything differently if this was a Pilot-N-Paws flight with a sick animal rather than a sick child.

    - Within 30 minutes, I might make Big Controlled Airport, but may not be able to communicate with ATC when I get there.

    - I could declare an emergency (to obtain radar assistance and priority handling into Big Controlled Airport).

    - It might be safer to divert to the "NRST" airport, but then we would miss the ambulance pre-arranged for the patient. I would reduce the electrical load by turning off all unnecessary electrical system equipment. *[Specify the particular cockpit equipment you would turn off in your training airplane.]*

39. **After an exhausting three-day business meeting, you are loading up the rental airplane for the two-hour flight home when you discover you have lost your reading glasses. You can see in the distance but can't read instruments or a chart very easy. The weather is good and if you depart in the next 20 minutes you can be home before dark. What will you do?**

    There is no right answer; this is simply an opportunity to demonstrate your risk management and ADM. Voice your thought process out loud until you make a final decision.

    - I would ask passengers or others (if available) to assist me in searching for my lost glasses.

    - If possession of corrective lenses is required on my medical certificate, then takeoff is not permitted.

    - How familiar am I with the rental plane? Can I see "well enough" to fly a plane I don't often fly?

    - I could spend the night, buy a new pair of glasses, get some rest, and depart fresh in the morning.

Maneuvers
Table

Appendix 1

Private Pilot Airman Certification Standards (condensed)

Task	Objective Minimum acceptable standard of performance			
Takeoff				
Normal/Crosswind	V_Y +10 / -5			
Short/Soft	V_X +10 / -5, then V_Y +10 / -5			
Landing				
Normal/Crosswind	1.3 V_{S0} +10 / -5, touch at or within 400 feet beyond target			
Forward Slip	Min float, touch at or within 400 feet beyond target			
Short	1.3 V_{S0} +10 / -5, touch at or within 200 feet beyond target			
Soft	1.3 V_{S0} +10 / -5, touch at minimum speed and descent rate			
Go Around	Apply Power (Carb Heat Off), pitch for V_X or V_Y +10/-5 kts, then V_Y +10/-5 kts to safe altitude			
Emergency Operations				
Emergency Descent	Bank angle 30°–45°, airspeed +0/-10 kts, level off ±100 feet.			
Emergency Approach and Landing	Best glide airspeed, ±10 kts, recommended descent configuration			
		Heading or bank ±°	**Altitude ± ft**	**Speed ± kts**
Traffic Pattern	Accurate track and safe spacing		100	10
Pilotage/NAV/Diverting	Know position ±3 NM	15	200	ETA ±5min
Instrument Flying				
Straight and level		20	200	10
Constant airspeed climb and descend		20	200	10
Turns and rollouts on heading		10	200	10
Communications, Navigation, Radar Services		20	200	10
Recovery from unusual attitudes	Recover to stabilized flight w/o excesses			
Slow Flight and Stalls (no flight below 1,500 AGL)				
Power-off Stalls	S & L or max. 20° bank Full-stall then recover	10		
Power-on Stalls	S & L or max. 20° bank Full-stall then recover	10		
Maneuvering during Slow Flight Straight & level, turns, climbs, descents		10	100	No stall warning +10/-0 kts
Performance Maneuvers				
Steep turns 360° with 45° ±5° bank, coordinated		10	100	10
Ground Reference Maneuvers	Enter downwind 600–1,000 AGL		100	10

Exam Tip: Remember to always perform "clearing turns" prior to beginning any flight maneuver.

Applicant's Practical Test Checklist

Appendix 2

Applicant's Practical Test Checklist

Appointment with Examiner

Examiner's Name _____

Location _____

Date/Time _____

Acceptable Aircraft

Aircraft Documents

____ Airworthiness certificate

____ Registration certificate

____ Operating limitations

Aircraft Maintenance Records

____ Logbook record of airworthiness inspections and AD compliance

____ Pilot's Operating Handbook, FAA-approved Airplane Flight Manual

____ Current weight and balance data

Personal Equipment

____ View-limiting device

____ Current aeronautical charts (printed or electronic)

____ Computer and plotter

____ Flight plan form and flight logs (printed or electronic)

____ *Chart Supplement U.S.*, airport diagrams, and appropriate publications

____ Current FAR/AIM

Personal Records

____ Identification—photo/signature ID

____ Pilot certificate

____ Current medical certificate or BasicMed qualification (when applicable)

____ Completed FAA Form 8710-1, Airman Certificate and/or Rating Application, with instructor's signature (or IACRA equivalent with applicant's FTN and application ID)

___ Original Knowledge Test Report

___ Pilot logbook with appropriate instructor endorsements

___ FAA Form 8060-5, Notice of Disapproval of Application (if applicable)

___ Letter of Discontinuance (if applicable)

___ Approved school graduation certificate (if applicable)

___ Evaluator's fee (if applicable)

Operations of Aircraft Without/ With an MEL

Appendix 3

Operations of Aircraft *Without* a Minimum Equipment List (MEL)

(14 CFR 91.213, AC 91-67, AC 120-71B)

During the preflight inspection, the pilot discovers inoperative instruments or equipment.

DECISION SEQUENCE:

1. **Are the inoperative instruments or equipment part of the VFR-day type certification?** (14 CFR 91.213(d)(2)(i))

   These are the instruments and equipment prescribed in the applicable airworthiness regulations under which the aircraft was type-certificated (Part 23 for newer aircraft and CAR Part 3 for much older aircraft).

   Note: Referencing the aircraft certification regulations to determine if instruments and equipment are required can be a complex task. In general, the instruments and equipment required by the aircraft certification regulations can be found in the aircraft's Equipment List and Type Certificate Data Sheet (TCDS).

   If YES, the aircraft is not airworthy and maintenance is required before you can fly.

   If NO, go to next the step.

2. **Are the inoperative instruments or equipment listed as "Required" on the aircraft's equipment list, or "kinds of operations equipment list" (KOEL) for the kind of flight operation being conducted?** (14 CFR 91.213 (d)(2)(ii))

   Note: Many newer aircraft have a "Kinds of Operations" equipment list which refers to the kinds of operations (VFR Day, VFR Night, IFR Day, IFR Night, Icing) in which the aircraft can operate. The equipment list and KOEL are located in the AFM.

   If YES, the aircraft is not airworthy and maintenance is required before you can fly.

   If NO, go to next the step.

3. **Are the inoperative instruments or equipment required by 14 CFR §91.205, 91.207, or any other rule of Part 91 for the specific kind of flight operation being conducted?** (14 CFR 91.213(d)(2)(iii))

   Note: Other required equipment regulations include: §91.205 VFR Day, VFR Night, IFR; §91.207 – ELTs; §91.209 – Aircraft Lights; §91.215 – ATC Transponders.

   If YES, the aircraft is not airworthy and maintenance is required before you can fly.

   If NO, go to the next step.

4. **Are the inoperative instruments or equipment required to be operational by an Airworthiness Directive (AD)? Check the aircraft maintenance logs and/or consult with a maintenance technician to determine AD compliance.** (14 CFR 91.213(d)(2)(iv))

   If YES, the aircraft is not airworthy and maintenance is required before you can fly.

   If NO, go to the next step.

5. **At this point, the inoperative instruments or equipment must be:**

   REMOVED from the aircraft (14 CFR §91.213(d)(3)(i)), the cockpit control placarded, and the maintenance record (logbook) updated in accordance with 14 CFR §43.9.

   OR

   DEACTIVATED and PLACARDED "Inoperative"(14 CFR §91.213(d)(3)(ii). If deactivation of the inoperative instrument or equipment involves maintenance, it must be accomplished and recorded in accordance with Part 43.

6. **Finally, a determination is made by a certificated and appropriately rated pilot or mechanic that the inoperative instrument or equipment does not constitute a hazard to the aircraft for the anticipated conditions of the flight, e.g., day VFR, night VFR etc.**

Operations of Aircraft *With* a Minimum Equipment List (MEL)

(14 CFR 91.213, AC 91-67, AC 120-71B)

During the preflight inspection, the pilot discovers inoperative instruments or equipment.

DECISION SEQUENCE:

1. **Is the inoperative equipment not included in the MEL, but required by the type certification, AD or other special conditions?**

   If YES, the aircraft is not airworthy and maintenance is required before flight.

   If NO, go to next step.

2. **The pilot performs or has a qualified person perform the appropriate "O" or "M" deactivation or removal procedure.**

   Note: Two categories of maintenance procedures:

   "O" Operations procedures—can be performed by pilot; must be accomplished before or during operation with listed item of equipment inoperative.

   "M" Maintenance procedures—must be done by maintenance personnel and be accomplished before beginning operation with the listed item of equipment inoperative.

3. **The pilot or maintenance personnel placards the inoperative equipment and updates the maintenance record (logbook).**

4. **The pilot confirms that the inoperative equipment does not present hazards to the conditions of flight.**